— ॐ —

श्रीमद्भगवद्गीता
सप्तमोऽध्यायः – ज्ञानविज्ञानयोगः

śrīmadbhagavadgītā
saptamo'dhyāyaḥ - jñānavijñānayogaḥ

— ॐ —

Bhagavad-Gītā Chapter Seven
Sanskrit Text with Transliteration, Translation & Brief Commentary

— ॐ —

गीता-मूलम् ०७

gītā-mūlam 07

— ॐ —

गीता या मधुसूदनप्रभविणी युक्ता परं ब्रह्मणि
gītā yā madhusūdana-prabhaviṇī yuktā paraṁ brahmaṇi
या कृष्णेन कृताऽखिलं नयनवद् वक्षोऽतिगूढार्थिनी ।
yā kṛṣṇena kṛtā-'khilaṁ nayanavad vakṣo-'tigūḍhārthinī ,
या लोकत्रयस्य मार्गविधिनी धर्मस्य साक्षात्पथा
yā lokatrayasya marga-vidhinī dharmasya sākṣāt-pathā ,
सा श्रीकृष्णमुखारविन्दजनिता तस्याः मूलं प्रयच्छामि॥
sā śrī-kṛṣṇa-mukhāravinda-janitā tasyāḥ mūlaṁ prayacchāmi .

That Gītā—which's born from Madhusūdana -- who exists in Oneness with Braham;
that Gītā—which's uttered by Krishna -- of profound visions of deep mysteries concealed within;
that Gītā—which lights the Dharma-path across the threefold world;
that Gītā—that sprung from Shri Krishna's lotus-lips
—to Her sacred roots I proceed and take refuge.

— ॐ —

Belongs to ______________________

____

____

____

॥ यतो धर्मस्ततो जयः - एकं-सनातन-धर्म विजयः ॥
- yato dharmastato jayaḥ -- ekaṁ sanātana-dharma vijayaḥ -
- Where Dharma abides Victory abides -- Victory unto Ekam-Sanātana-Dharma -

Published by: only **RAMA** only

Title: **Gita-Mulam 07 – Bhagavad Gita Chapter Seven**
Sub-Title: **Sanskrit Text with Transliteration, Translation & Brief Commentary**
A No-Opinions Commentary. Only Facts. Bhagavad-Gita As It Truly Is.
An Excellent Resource for Sectless Gita-Study (With Wide Margin for Taking Notes)

गीता-मूलम् ०७
gītā-mūlam 07
श्रीमद्भगवद्गीता सप्तमोऽध्यायः – ज्ञानविज्ञानयोगः
śrīmadbhagavadgītā saptamo'dhyāyaḥ - jñānavijñānayogaḥ

Authors: Adarsh Saxena & Vijay Kumar

IDENTIFIERS

ISBN: 979-8-90060-747-4 (Paperback)
—o—

Books in the Gita-Mulam series: Gita-Mulam **01** (isbn: 979-8-90060-**741-2**). Gita-Mulam **02** (isbn: 979-8-90060-**742-9**). Gita-Mulam **03** (isbn: 979-8-90060-**743-6**). Gita-Mulam **04** (isbn: 979-8-90060-**744-3**). Gita-Mulam **05** (isbn: 979-8-90060-**745-0**). Gita-Mulam **06** (isbn: 979-8-90060-**746-7**). Gita-Mulam **07** (isbn: 979-8-90060-**747-4**). Gita-Mulam **08** (isbn: 979-8-90060-**748-1**). Gita-Mulam **09** (isbn: 979-8-90060-**749-8**). Gita-Mulam **10** (isbn: 979-8-90060-**750-4**). Gita-Mulam **11** (isbn: 979-8-90060-**751-1**). Gita-Mulam **12** (isbn: 979-8-90060-**752-8**). Gita-Mulam **13** (isbn: 979-8-90060-**753-5**). Gita-Mulam **14** (isbn: 979-8-90060-**754-2**). Gita-Mulam **15** (isbn: 979-8-90060-**755-9**). Gita-Mulam **16** (isbn: 979-8-90060-**756-6**). Gita-Mulam **17** (isbn: 979-8-90060-**757-3**). Gita-Mulam **18** (isbn: 979-8-90060-**758-0**). All books will be released by 2027. Some books might become available sooner, please check your bookstore/online.
[We have priced the books at the bare minimum. Yet, if the cost of the entire set appears too daunting, see if your library can get one; or try to form your own little library-circle of Gītā books. If any large non-profit foundation—aligned with the vision of Sanātana-Dharma—wishes to distribute our books free of cost, they may—so long as they do it as printed books, exactly-as-is, making absolutely no changes in interior or cover, and never in any digital form. Books are copyrighted. You must have our written permission.]

—o—

Our Bhagavad-Gītā Books:
Bhagavad Gita, The Holy Book of Hindus, with Sanskrit Text, English Translation & Transliteration, No Commentary.
  -ISBN: 978-1-945739-36-1 / 978-1-945739-37-8 (Paperback/Hardback. Book Size 6.14"x9.21"x190 pages)
  -ISBN: 978-1-945739-39-2 (For Gitā Journaling. 8"x8"x390 pages)
  -ISBN: 978-1-945739-43-9 (Convenient Pocket-Sized Edition. 4"x6"x180 pages)
  -ISBN: 978-1-945739-40-8 (Legacy Book. 7.5"x9.25"x246 pages)
  -ISBN: 978-1-945739-55-2 / 978-1-945739-56-9 (Paperback/Hardback. For Note-Taking. 7.5"x9.25"x190 pages)
Also Available:
- **Tulsi Ramayana—Hindu Holy Book:** Ramcharitmanas with English Translation (ISBNs: 978-1-945739-**60-6**, 978-1-945739-**61-3**)
- **Ramcharitmanas - Large/Medium/Small** (No Translation)
- **Sundarakanda:** The Fifth-Ascent of Tulsi Ramayana (ISBNs: 978-1-945739-**05-7**, 978-1-945739-**15-6**)
- **Rama Hymns:** Hanuman-Chalisa, Rāma-Raksha-Stotra, etc. (ISBNs: 978-1-945739-**25-5**, 978-1-945739-**09-5**)
- **Vivekachudamani, Fiery Crest-Jewel of Wisdom** (ISBNs: 978-1-945739-**44-6**, 978-1-945739-**45-3**, 978-1-945739-**41-5**)
- **Ashtavakra Gītā, the Fiery Octave** (ISBNs: 978-1-945739-**46-0**, 978-1-945739-**47-7**, 978-1-945739-**42-2**)
- **Legacy Books - Endowment of Devotion (several):** Journal Books of sacred Hindu Hymns around which the Holy-Name Rama Name can be written; available in Paperback and Hardcover for: **Hanuman Chalisa** (ISBN: 978-1-945739-**274**/ 978-1-945739-**940**) **Sundara-Kanda** (ISBN: 978-1-945739-**908**/ 978-1-945739-**916**) **Rama-Raksha-Stotra** (ISBN: 978-1-945739-**991**/ 978-1-945739-**967**) **Bhushundi-Ramayana** (ISBN: 978-1-945739-**983**/ 978-1-945739-**975**) **Nama-Ramayanam** (ISBN: 978-1-945739-**309**/ 978-1-945739-**958**)
- **Rama Jayam - Likhita Japam Rama-Nama Mala alongside Sacred Hindu Texts (several):** Books for writing the 'Rama' Name 100,000 Times. Rama Jayam - Likhita Japam:Rama-Nama Mala. Available in Book Size 8"x10" (Paperback) for: **Hanuman Chalisa** (ISBN: 978-1-945739-**169**) **Rama Raksha Stotra** (ISBN: 978-1-945739-**185**) **Nama-Ramayanam** (ISBN: 978-1-945739-**045**) **Ramashtakam** (ISBN: 978-1-945739-**177**) **Rama Shatanama Stotra** (ISBN: 978-1-945739-**266**) **Rama-Shatnamavalih** (ISBN: 978-1-945739-**134**) **Simple (I)** (ISBN: 978-1-945739-**142**)
- **Likhita Japam** - Paperback books for writing the 'Rama' Name in dotted grids: **One-Lettered Rama Mantra**, Book Size 8"x10" (ISBN: 978-1-945739-**312**) **Two-Lettered Rama Mantra**, Book Size 8"x10" (ISBN: 978-1-945739-**320**) **Three-Lettered Rama Mantra**, Book Size 8"x10" (ISBN: 978-1-945739-**339**) **Four-Lettered Rama Mantra**, Book Size 8"x10" (ISBN: 978-1-945739-**347**) **Simple (II)** Book Size 7.5"x9.25" (ISBN: 978-1-945739-**193**) **Simple (III)** Book Size 8"x8" (ISBN: 978-1-945739-**282**) **Simple (IV)** Book Size 8.5"x8.5" (ISBN: 978-1-945739-**878**) **Simple (V)** Book Size 8.5"x11" (ISBN: 978-1-945739-**924**)

CONTENTS

Bhagavad-Gītā Chapter Seven
गीता-मूलम् ०७
gītā-mūlam 07
श्रीमद्भगवद्गीता सप्तमोऽध्यायः – ज्ञानविज्ञानयोगः
śrīmadbhagavadgītā saptamo'dhyāyaḥ - jñānavijñānayogaḥ

श्रीमद्भगवद्गीता

प्रथमोऽध्यायः - अर्जुनविषादयोगः

द्वितीयोऽध्यायः - साङ्ख्ययोगः

तृतीयोऽध्यायः - कर्मयोगः

चतुर्थोऽध्यायः - ज्ञानकर्मसन्न्यासयोगः

पञ्चमोऽध्यायः - संन्यासयोगः

षष्ठोऽध्यायः - ध्यानयोगः

सप्तमोऽध्यायः - ज्ञानविज्ञानयोगः

अष्टमोऽध्यायः - अक्षरब्रह्मयोगः

नवमोऽध्यायः - राजविद्याराजगुह्ययोगः

दशमोऽध्यायः - विभूतियोगः

एकादशोऽध्यायः - विश्वरूपदर्शनयोगः

द्वादशोऽध्यायः - भक्तियोगः

त्रयोदशोऽध्यायः - क्षेत्रक्षेत्रज्ञविभागयोगः

चतुर्दशोऽध्यायः - गुणत्रयविभागयोगः

पञ्चदशोऽध्यायः - पुरुषोत्तमयोगः

षोडशोऽध्यायः - दैवासुरसम्पद्विभागयोगः

सप्तदशोऽध्यायः - श्रद्धात्रयविभागयोगः

अष्टादशोऽध्यायः - मोक्षसन्न्यासयोगः

—ॐ— ध्यानम् —ॐ— dhyānam —ॐ—

ॐ INVOCATIONS

ॐ श्री परमात्मने नमः
— om śrī paramātmane namaḥ —
[Om—I bow down to the Supreme-Energy, Supreme-Being]

त्वमेव माता च पिता त्वमेव । त्वमेव बंधुश्च सखा त्वमेव ।
tvameva mātā ca pitā tvameva , tvameva baṁdhuśca sakhā tvameva ,
त्वमेव विद्या द्रविणं त्वमेव । त्वमेव सर्वं मम देवदेव ॥
tvameva vidyā draviṇaṁ tvameva , tvameva sarvaṁ mama devadeva .

Thou art my mother and my father, Thou alone my kin, kith, friend; Thou alone my wisdom, knowledge, wealth; Thou alone—O God of gods—my all, and everything!

— ॐ —

शान्ताकारं भुजगशयनं पद्मनाभं सुरेशं । विश्वाधारं गगनसदृशं मेघवर्णं शुभाङ्गम् ।
sāntākāraṁ bhujagaśayanaṁ padmanābhaṁ sureśaṁ
viśvādhāraṁ gaganasadṛśaṁ meghavarṇaṁ śubhāṅgam ,
लक्ष्मीकान्तं कमलनयनं योगिभिर्ध्यानगम्यं । वन्दे विष्णुं भवभयहरं सर्वलोकैकनाथम् ॥
lakṣmīkāntaṁ kamalanayanaṁ yogibhirdhyānagamyaṁ
vande viṣṇuṁ bhavabhayaharaṁ sarvalokaikanātham .

I venerate Shri Vishnu—of a serene appearance who slumbers upon the serpent *Shesha-Nāga*, from whose navel has sprung the lotus of creation, who presides over as the God of gods, who is the substratum of the universe, boundless and infinite like the sky. Of a dark hue like the clouds, of a form radiating everlasting auspiciousness, with eyes beautiful like lotus petals, who is the beloved of Devī Lakshmī, who is reachable only through devotional meditation by Yogīs, who removes all fears of worldly existence—upon Him, Vishnu, the One Great Lord of all the worlds, I meditate.

— ॐ —

यं ब्रह्मा वरुणेन्द्ररुद्रमरुतः स्तुन्वन्ति दिव्यैः स्तवैः
yaṁ brahmā varuṇendrarudramarutaḥ stunvanti divyaiḥ stavaiḥ
वेदैः साङ्गपदक्रमोपनिषदैर्गायन्ति यं सामगाः ।
vedaiḥ sāṅgapadakramopaniṣadairgāyanti yaṁ sāmagāḥ ,
ध्यानावस्थिततद्गतेन मनसा पश्यन्ति यं योगिनो
dhyānāvasthitatadgatena manasā paśyanti yaṁ yogino
यस्यान्तं न विदुः सुरासुरगणा देवाय तस्मै नमः ॥
yasyāntaṁ na viduḥ surāsuragaṇā devāya tasmai namaḥ .

Unto That Supreme—whom Brahammā, Varuna, Indra, Rudra and the Mārutas praise with excellent holy hymns; who is versified throughout the Vedas and Upanishads by the chanters of Sāma; who—in perfect meditations deep—the

yogis see within their own minds while absorbed in "That-One"; whose beginning and end, even gods and demi-gods never know of—unto That Supreme-Being, I offer my many venerations.

— ॐ — स्तुतिः — ॐ — stutiḥ — ॐ —

— ॐ — ॐ — ॐ — ॐ — ॐ — ॐ —

VENERATIONS

— ॐ —

पार्थाय प्रतिबोधितां भगवता नारायणेन स्वयम्
pārthāya pratibodhitāṁ bhagavatā nārāyaṇena svayam
व्यासेनग्रथितां पुराणमुनिना मध्ये महाभारते ।
vyāsenagrathitāṁ purāṇamuninā madhye mahābhārate ,
अद्वैतामृतवर्षिणीं भगवतीमष्टादशाध्यायिनीम्
advaitāmṛtavarṣiṇīṁ bhagavatīmaṣṭadaśādhyāyinīm
अम्ब त्वामनुसन्दधामि भगवद्गीते भवेद्वेषिणीम् ॥
amba tvāmanusandadhāmi bhagavadgīte bhavedveṣiṇīm .

O Thou Bhagavad-Gītā—with whom Pārtha was enlightened by the Lord Nārāyaṇa himself; who was integrated into the Mahābhārata by the ancient sage Vyāsa; O Thou blessed Mother—who with her eighteen Cantos shower humanity with the nectar of Advaita; O Thou destroyer of rebirths, upon Thee—O Bhagavad-Gītā, O loving Mother—I meditate.

— ॐ —

नमोऽस्तु ते व्यास विशालबुद्धे फुल्लारविन्दायतपत्रनेत्र ।
namo'stu te vyāsa viśālabuddhe phullāravindāyatapatranetra ,
येन त्वया भारततैलपूर्णः प्रज्वालितो ज्ञानमयः प्रदीपः ॥
yena tvayā bhāratatailapūrṇaḥ prajvālito jñānamayaḥ pradīpaḥ .

Salutations to Thee O Vyāsa—of a mighty intellect and with eyes large like the petals of a full-blossomed lotus; by whom has been forever lit in this world the Lamp-of-Wisdom, filled with the oil in the form of the great epic: Mahābhārata.

— ॐ —

प्रपन्नपारिजाताय तोत्रवेत्रैकपाणये ।

prapannapārijātāya totravetraikapāṇaye ,

ज्ञानमुद्राय कृष्णाय गीतामृतदुहे नमः ॥

jñānamudrāya kṛṣṇāya gītāmṛtaduhe namaḥ .

He—who is the wish-granting tree of the suppliant—in whose one hand is held the rope for cow and with the other hand who holds the Yogic posture of *Jnana*—who is the milcher of the nectar known as Gītā—unto Him, Krishna, my repeated venerations.

— ॐ —

सर्वोपनिषदो गावो दोग्धा गोपालनन्दनः ।

sarvopaniṣado gāvo dogdhā gopālanandanaḥ ,

पार्थो वत्सः सुधीर्भोक्ता दुग्धं गीतामृतं महत् ॥

pārtho vatsaḥ sudhīrbhoktā dugdhaṁ gītāmṛtaṁ mahat .

All the Upanishads are the cows; the milcher is the joy of cowherds, Krishna; Pārtha is the calf; the man of purified understanding is the partaker; and the milk is verily the supreme nectar known as Gītā.

— ॐ —

वसुदेवसुतं देवं कंसचाणूरमर्दनम् ।

vasudevasutaṁ devaṁ kaṁsacāṇūramardanam ,

देवकीपरमानन्दं कृष्णं वन्दे जगद्गुरुम् ॥

devakīparamānandaṁ krishnaṁ vande jagadgurum .

I worship the charioteer, the Lord-God, the destroyer of Kamsa and Chānura, the supreme joy of Devakī, the son of Vāsudeva—Shri Krishna, the Universal Guru.

— ॐ —

भीष्मद्रोणतटा जयद्रथजला गान्धारनीलोत्पला

bhīṣmadroṇataṭā jayadrathajalā gāndhāranīlotpalā

शल्यग्राहवती कृपेण वहनी कर्णेन वेलाकुला ।

śalyagrāhavatī kṛpeṇa vahanī karṇena velākulā ,

अश्वत्थामविकर्णघोरमकरा दुर्योधनावर्तिनी

aśvatthāmavikarṇaghoramakarā duryodhanāvartinī

सोत्तीर्णा खलु पाण्डवैरणनदी कैवर्तकः केशवः ॥

sottīrṇā khalu pāṇḍavairaṇanadī kaivartakaḥ keśavaḥ .

That terrible battle-river—which had Bhīṣma and Droṇa as its two banks, and Jayadrathaja as its waters; which had the king of Gāndhāra as its blue lotus, and Śalya as its shark; whose currents and billows were Kṛipā and Karṇa; which had Aśvatthāmā and Vikarṇa as its terrible alligators; and of which Duryodhana was the deadly whirlpool—that ferocious river could be forded by the Pāṇḍavas only because they had Keśava as their helmsman.

— ॐ —

पाराशर्यवचः सरोजममलं गीतार्थगन्धोत्कटं
pārāśaryavacaḥ sarojamamalaṁ gītārthagandhotkaṭaṁ
नानाख्यानककेसरं हरिकथासम्बोधनाबोधितम् ।
nānākhyānakakesaraṁ harikathāsambodhanābodhitam |
लोके सज्जनषट्पदैरहरहः पेपीयमानं मुदा
loke sajjanaṣaṭpadairaharahaḥ pepīyamānaṁ mudā
भूयाद्भारतपङ्कजं कलिमलप्रध्वंसिनः श्रेयसे ॥
bhūyādbhāratapaṅkajaṁ kalimalapradhvaṁsinaḥ śreyase .

May this Lotus called Mahābhārata—which was born on the lake of the words of Vyāsa—which is perfumed with the fragrance of the Purport-of-Gītā—which has its innumerous stories as the pollen—which became fully bloomed through the discourses of Hari—which is the destroyer of the sins of the Kali-Yuga—which is everyday partaken joyously by the bees in the shape of good people of the world—may it bestow all goodness upon us.

— ॐ —

मूकं करोति वाचालं पङ्गुं लङ्घयते गिरिम् ।
mūkaṁ karoti vācālaṁ paṅguṁ laṅghayate girim ,
यत्कृपा तमहं वन्दे परमानन्दमाधवम् ॥
yatkṛpā tamahaṁ vande paramānandamādhavam .

I salute the Supreme-Being of the nature of supreme bliss, by whose very grace the dumb become eloquent and the cripples step across mountains.

— ॐ —

ॐ पूर्णमदः पूर्णमिदं पूर्णात् पूर्णमुदच्यते ।
om pūrṇamadaḥ pūrṇamidaṁ pūrṇāt pūrṇamudacyate ,
पूर्णस्य पूर्णमादाय पूर्णमेवावशिष्यते ।
pūrṇasya pūrṇamādāya pūrṇamevāvaśiṣyate ,
ॐ शान्तिः शान्तिः शान्तिः ॥
om śāntiḥ śāntiḥ śāntiḥ .

Om—That One (the unmanifest Brahma)—is infinite, complete, Entire; this (the manifest universe) is entire; And from That One fullness has emerged this entire universe here; And even when this entirety here is taken out of that One-Entire, It still abides complete in all Its entireness! Om, peace—let there be tranquility all around me!

— ॐ — ॐ — ॐ — ॐ — ॐ — ॐ — ॐ — ॐ — ॐ —

ॐ Our Gītā-Journey Thus Far

— ॐ तत् सत् ॐ —

The Bhagavad-Gītā: Supreme Divine Word

The Bhagavad-Gītā is not merely a scripture—it is a mirror to the soul. It is a fiery flame of wisdom most ancient that burns through the veils of illusion, and then, with the precision of a chisel, it shapes the rock until one day, looking into the mirror, man finds himself looking at a god.

The Gītā-Journey begins with Arjuna's cry of anguish in Chapter — and then gradually ascends, step by sacred step, into realms of unshakable serenity, sovereign wisdom, and divine intimacy. Each chapter is a rung on the ladder from despair to deliverance, from the ego's confusion to the soul's awakening. By the time we reach Chapter 7, the Gītā's tone has deepened much. The voice of the Lord shifts from one who instructs to one who reveals. Yogeshwara Shri Krishna, the Lord of Yoga, who has until now guided Arjuna through reason, through the balance of action and renunciation, now begins to unfold His own inner mystery—not as a distant deity, but as the very essence of all that exists in Creation!

Our Journey Thus Far: The Vessel Stands Prepared

Now let us take a quick look at our Gītā-journey thus far. Our journey began in Chapter 1, where Arjuna, overwhelmed at the prospect of fratricidal war, is shaken to the core. This is no ordinary sorrow—it is the collapse of worldly certainty; and Arjuna turns, not to his weapons, but to the eternal.

In Chapter 2, the foundation is laid. The Lord speaks of the immortal Self, untouched by time or circumstance. Here begins the true instruction—of steady wisdom, detached action, and the call to rise above fleeting dualities.

Through Chapters 3 to 5, Bhagwān Shri Krishna expounds the secret of karma-yoga: performing karmas ordained by one's varna-āshram—duty done without selfish desire, performed as an offering unto the Divine. The Lord declares that true renunciation is not withdrawal from life, but the abandonment of possessiveness and doership. The wise see all creation as pervaded by the Divine and thus remain untouched by the ups and downs in this fluxing ocean of consciousness.

Chapter 6 leads us further inward. The way of meditation is shown—solitude, self-discipline, quietude, and unwavering focus. But above even the silent yogin there stands the devotee who takes the sport up a notch—he whose heart, filled with devotion, ever stays resting in the Divine, ever unwavering.

Thus far, the Gītā has been preparing the ground—refining the intellect, steadying the mind, and purifying the heart. Now, in Chapter 7, the Lord begins to unveil His own Being, not as a concept, but as the very substratum of existence. Matter or mind, sentient or insentient, life or the supposed dead-matter—this is all satt-chitt-ānanda braham, the ocean of consciousness -- whose perfect manifest form is as the Avatār Bhagwān Shri Krishna.

CHAPTER-SEVEN: WHERE THE VEILS BEGIN TO LIFT

In this Chapter Jñāna-Vijñāna Yoga, the Lord offers more than **jñāna** (knowledge); He offers **vijñāna**—the **realized, living experience of that knowledge.** What has been hinted at earlier, now begins to shine clearly: "**I am the essence of all. I am the cause, the sustainer, and the end of the universe. Nothing exists apart from Me.**"

Shri Krishna reveals Himself as both the manifest and the unmanifest, the known and the unknowable. The five elements, the mind, the intellect, the ego, all arise from Him. He is the taste in water, the light in the sun, the life in all beings. Yet, due to māyā—His own inscrutable power—we humans of little intellect fail to recognize Him—even though we abide living and moving in Him.

Here begins the **para-vidyā**, higher knowledge. No longer does the teaching stay confined to duties and disciplines—it becomes a **direct disclosure of the Supreme Reality**. And yet, this knowledge is not for the casual seeker. It is for those who come to the Lord with a pure heart, freed from worldliness, moved not by fear or gain, but by longing for Truth alone.

A GLIMPSE OF THE PATH AHEAD

From this chapter onward, the Gītā enters its more exalted phase. In the chapters which follow the Lord speaks of His divine manifestations throughout the cosmos, of the greatness of devotion, and of the unity behind all forms. The teaching becomes ever more intimate, culminating in Chapter 11 with the wondrous vision of the Cosmic-Form—a glimpse that shatters all human pride, all limitation, and brings the soul to its knees in awe.

Further ahead—right up to Chapter 18—the Lord continues to guide us through the web of guṇas, of prakṛti and puruṣa, of faith, knowledge, and the fruits of action. But always, the core remains the same: to know Him, to love Him, and to surrender to Him is the highest path, for it leads to our emancipation: that state wherein "I", the little soul gains self-realization and directly realizes: I am one in Him.

FROM SEEKING TO SEEING: INTO THE HEART OF THE DIVINE

So then, with Chapter 7, the Gītā has turned from instruction to illumination. The Lord is no longer merely the charioteer—He is revealed as the very ground of existence, the source of all knowledge, the inner Self of all beings. And yet, He remains ever accessible to the one whose heart stays devoted to Him.

Now begins a journey not of ascent, but of unveiling. The seeker, purified through discipline and longing, is now ready to behold what was always near—**closer than breath, nearer than thought: the all-pervading, all-sustaining, all-loving Lord-God Bhagwān Shri Krishna.**

Come now O pilgrims, let our mind grow still, let the heart grow receptive to what Bhagwān Krishna has to tell; for what lies ahead cannot be taught—only received, by the direct grace of His.

— ॐ श्रीकृष्णाय नमः ॐ —

Eighteen Chapters of Inner Ascent
O Bhagavad-Gītā—You are not a single peak.
You are a range of revelations.
Each chapter—a new sky, fresh descents of bolts of light.

Sāṅkhya-Yoga decimates illusion upon the Self.
Karma-Yoga sets fire to attachments.
Bhakti-Yoga floods the soul in nectar.
Jñāna-Yoga strikes like the lightning—
Revealing, in one flash, the entire mountain of Existence!

O Bhagavad-Gītā, You guide us seekers—
From confusion to clarity, from false-identity to Infinity.

You teach not escapism—but engagement without bondage.
You command not submission, but surrender with full knowledge.

Gītā is not ordinary spiritual wisdom—it is liberation in motion.
It is **meditation** and **moksha**—but **with eyes wide open.**

ॐ Chapter-Seven, A Bird's-Eye View

— ॐ तत् सत् ॐ —

Jñāna-Vijñāna Yoga: The Lord Reveals Himself

In the sacred unfolding of the Bhagavad-Gītā, this chapter-seven marks a moment of profound inward turning. It is as though—after leading us through the disciplines of action, renunciation, and meditation—the Bhagavad-Gītā decides to begin lifting the veils—not just over our heart, but over **the face of the Divine** Himself.

Here begins a new phase in the Gītā's sacred dialogue. The voice of Shri Krishna now resounds with a quiet majesty—not just a **teacher** now, but the very Lord-God: the very **goal** of all human seeking.

Until now, the focus has been on right conduct, inner stillness, and the path toward the Self. But in Jñāna-Vijñāna Yoga, the Lord unveils **His own Self**—revealing the sublime truths of His immanence and transcendence: that it is He, who is the **very Manifest Form, the very Divine Will of the formless ocean of consciousness: satt-chitt-ānanda braham.**

— ॐ —

Bhagwān Shri Krishna speaks not only of the principles of knowledge (**jñāna**) but also of its living realization (**vijñāna**)—knowledge that is not merely grasped by the intellect, but touched, felt, and seen with the purified heart. It is not merely the knowledge of Braham as abstract reality, but directly of Bhagwān—the all-pervading, all-sustaining Lord who is both beyond the world and fully pervaded in it.

This is the beginning of the path of bhakti in its highest form—not as sentiment or ritual, but as the very **recognition of the Divine: within all beings and things; and of all beings and things: within the Divine.**

Let us now sail through the luminous verses of this chapter, tracing the arc of revelation—to prepare ourselves for what is ahead.

A Verse-by-Verse Overview of Jñāna-Vijñāna Yoga, Chapter 7

Verse 1

Krishna invites Arjuna—and through him, all earnest seekers—to hear Him with mind and heart absorbed. Only with devotion and unwavering attention, one can come to know Him completely—not just in parts, not as in theory, but as **He is**, truly.

Verses 2–3

Krishna declares that He will now reveal the highest knowledge and its direct experience (jñāna and vijñāna), knowing which, nothing more remains to be known. Yet few among thousands strive for this, and even fewer attain full realization of His true nature.

Verses 4–5

Krishna speaks of His twofold nature: the lower—comprised of the five elements, mind, intellect, and ego; and the higher—His conscious nature (jīva-bhūta), which sustains the world. The entire universe is upheld by this dual aspect of the Divine.

Verse 6

From these two principles arise all beings. He is the origin and dissolution of the entire cosmos.

Verse 7

There is nothing higher than Krishna. **All things rest in Him as pearls strung on a thread.** He is the unseen essence that supports all existence.

Verses 8–11

The Lord reveals Himself as the subtle essence within all things: the taste in water, the radiance in the moon and sun, the praṇava in the Vedas, the sound in space, the strength in the strong, and even the desire which remains harmonized with Dharma. He is the life of all.

Verses 12–13

Though the three guṇas—sattva, rajas, and tamas—arise from Him, He remains beyond them. Deluded by these guṇas, the world fails to recognize His divine nature.

Verses 14–15

This delusion, born of māyā, is hard to cross. Only those who surrender to God Krishna can pass beyond it. As to the deluded, enslaved by ego and false views, they do not even seek Him.

Verses 16–19

Four kinds of people turn to God: the distressed, the seeker of knowledge, the seeker of wealth, and the wise. Of these, the wise— who seek Him for His own sake—are dearest to Krishna. After many births, the sage comes to know that all Existence is just He Vāsudeva, and surrenders to Him fully. Such a soul is rare indeed.

Verses 20–23

Others, driven by worldly desires, worship various deities according to their nature. The Lord, dwelling in all hearts, establishes their faith and grants their prayers—but such rewards are finite. Those who worship lesser manifestations go to the gods they worship, but His devotees attain to Krishna alone: the God of gods.

Verse 24

The deluded think of God as limited or embodied, not knowing His supreme, immutable nature. They fail to recognize Him as the One who is beyond time and form.

Verse 25

Veiled by yoga-māyā, Krishna remains unseen by the world. The ignorant know Him not to be the unborn eternal.

Verse 26

Krishna knows all beings—past, present, and future. But none know Him fully, bound as they are in Ignorance.

Verses 27–28

Born of desire and aversion, all beings are subject to delusion from birth. But those of virtuous deeds, whose sins are cleansed, worship Krishna with firm resolve.

Verse 29

Those who strive for liberation, taking refuge in Bhagwān Shri Krishna, get to know both Braham, the Self, and the entire field of karmic law.

Verse 30

Such souls, even at the time of death, know Him as the Lord of all worlds, of all gods and yajnas—and thus attain to that Supreme.

CLOSING REFLECTIONS

Jñāna-Vijñāna Yoga is a chapter of divine intimacy. It speaks not of distant heavens or abstract theories, but of the Lord who dwells in every atom, who is the life in all lives, the joy behind joy, the light within all forms. The world, which once appeared as fragmented and veiled, is now seen as a manifestation of the-One.

Mind it: this vision is not granted through intellect alone. It comes to those who surrender in love, whose devotion is without condition, whose seeking is no longer driven by fear, gain, rewards, but by the longing to know and be with Him—as He truly is.

Beyond Chapter-seven, our Gītā-Journey enters even deeper sanctuaries. In the chapters to come, Shri Krishna will reveal more of His divine opulences, the secret workings of His presence in the world, the supremacy of bhakti, and the cosmic-form that silences all doubt and dissolves man's ego.

But for now in Chapter-seven, our path opens with the sacred whisper of Bhagwān Shri Krishna: "**Know Me—not only as the origin of the cosmos but as the very essence of your own Self.**"

— ॐ श्रीकृष्णाय नमः ॐ —

With Canto-Seven—Jnâna made radiant and personal—
The Bhagavad-Gītā, starts removing the veils.

O Seventh Revelation—the hidden Sun of Gītā—we bow to Thee,
For here Bhagwân Krishna tears the veils from the Cosmo's face—
And He names Himself its origin, source, substance—
Not as a convenient symbol. Not as myth—but as Reality itself.

Krishna Declares:
"I am the origin of all. From Me, all have arisen—like waves in a Sea."
Not mere whisper. Not some conjecture—but Reality of Existence.

Krishna Unveils Two Natures:
· Lower—earth, water, fire, wind, mind.
· Higher—the living soul, the conscious spark.
And He declares—both are from Him. Both are He: the Sea.

Even those who forget Him, or know not of Bhagwân Krishna—
In fact indirectly worship only Him—albeit unknowingly—
Interposing their own desires, rites, rituals, lower gods—in between.

But the wise—ah yes the wise!
They worship Him directly—and with full Knowing—
So do thou be that wise one, O pilgrim, be the Wise!

They who see Him in all beings and things—
Those Jnânis of steadfast devotion—become verily Krishna's own.
And they are so very rare—perhaps one in a thousand.

O pilgrim, strive for that highest devotion,
Love for full realization — nothing less, nothing else.
And not just this devotion of emotions—having wants fulfilled.

Remember, O mortal:

Krishna is the harbor where galaxies anchor their silence,
The stillness where stars fold their wings.
Yet most humans stay savoring turbulence,
Whirling in the whirlpool of their ego,
Gyrating in the storm of their endless wants.

O pilgrim, Krishna wants to rest His infinite hull among ye humans—
Alas, He finds no mooring!

Even now His lament drifts like a stranded tide,
Seeking a shore worthy of the Gītā's weight.

A long time ago it was

Krishna entered the world as a Wave of Truth—
Cresting high; Collapsing adharma; Renewing Dharma's rhythm.

But men—ah men—broke the cadence,
Set up discord & adharma, in the very land of Āryāvarta—
where Harmony of Sanātana-Dharma once breathed.

Today Krishna's sorrow rings like a struck bell
Across the oceanic body of existence.

Hear it, O seeker: oscillate back toward Krishna.
Return to thy natural frequency—through the Bhagavad-Gītā of His.

Come—Take the reins of thy era in thy own hands!

Just one wave of Upright-Will can reshape the entire field.
One note of courage will retune the whole crooked civilization.

Come, Let us Hum the Song-Divine with clarity—
let it resonate & crack timid hearts—and the brittle systems of Kali.

When the strong set the frequency—all the rest must adjust.
Arise—become that Dominant Dhārmic Theme of Existence.

Come, Cut through this Haze

Cut the moral laziness that calls itself Tolerance.
Unvanish—wield your mind like a blade.
This age needs a Scalpel—that ends up leaving just the Truth intact.

Come then, Let us enter the Canto-Seven
—where Knowledge becomes Flame.
And let us discover Bhagwān Shri Krishna anew—
Revealed as the Seed, the Sustainer, the Infinite Field of Existence.

सप्तमोऽध्यायः - ज्ञानविज्ञानयोगः
saptamo'dhyāyaḥ - jñānavijñānayogaḥ
:: Canto – VII ::
- The Path of Knowledge and Realization -

ॐ गीता श्लोकः ७.१ – Gītā Verse 7.1

ॐ श्रीमद्भगवद्गीतासूपनिषत्सु ब्रह्मविद्यायां योगशास्त्रे श्रीकृष्णार्जुनसंवादे
om śrīmadbhagavadgītāsūpaniṣatsu brahmavidyāyāṁ yogaśāstre śrīkṛṣṇārjunasaṁvāde
ज्ञानविज्ञानयोगो नाम सप्तमोऽध्यायः श्लोकः १
jñānavijñānayogo nāma saptamo'dhyāyaḥ ślokaḥ 1

— ॐ —

श्रीभगवानुवाच --
śrībhagavānuvāca --

मय्यासक्तमनाः पार्थ योगं युञ्जन्मदाश्रयः ।
mayyāsaktamanāḥ pārtha yogaṁ yuñjanmadāśrayaḥ
असंशयं समग्रं मां यथा ज्ञास्यसि तच्छृणु ॥७-१॥
asaṁśayaṁ samagraṁ māṁ yathā jñāsyasi tacchṛṇu (7-1)

Shri Bhagwān said: "As to how—with absolute dependence on Me, and with your mind intent, and practicing Yoga—you will know Me in entirety, free of doubts, now listen, O Pārtha. **(7.1)**

—: Word-by-Word :—

श्रीभगवानुवाच śrībhagavān uvāca – the Blessed Lord said; मयि mayi – in Me; आसक्तमनाः āsakta-manāḥ – with mind attached; पार्थ pārtha – O son of Pritha (Arjuna); योगम् yogam – yoga; युञ्जन् yuñjan – practicing; मदाश्रयः mat-āśrayaḥ – taking refuge in Me; असंशयम् asaṁśayam – without doubt; समग्रम् samagram – completely; माम् mām – Me; यथा yathā – how; ज्ञास्यसि jñāsyasi – you shall know; तत् tat – that; शृणु śṛṇu – listen.

—: Understanding The Verse :—

— ॐ श्रीकृष्णाय नमः ॐ —

With the advent of the seventh chapter of the Bhagavad-Gītā, Bhagwān Shri Krishna commences a lofty exposition that unites **Jñāna** (knowledge) and **Vijñāna** (realized wisdom).

Bhagwān Shri Krishna shifts from the path of action emphasized in earlier chapters to a **more intimate unveiling of His essential nature**—both immanent and transcendent.

This verse is a sacred invitation—to begin ascending from mere intellectual inquiry to direct realization of the Supreme.

— ॐ श्रीरामाय नमः ॐ —

Having instructed Arjuna on karmas-just-for-dharma and the stillness born of inner renunciation, Bhagwān now opens the door to a more **profound inner vision**—a vision born not of detached speculation but of loving absorption.

The teachings of this chapter are to be grasped not through philosophical reasoning alone, but through unwavering devotion as well—a Yoga that binds the soul to the Eternal, in an utter surrender to Divine Will.

— ॐ विजयाय नमः ॐ —

This introductory verse serves as a clarion call to cultivate an exclusive and undivided heart toward Shri Krishna, the supreme Puruṣa. The path ahead will have emphasis on Bhakti—in directly knowing and perceiving Him.

Bhakti is not as an emotional sentiment, but is a luminous path of transformative union, wherein the seeker, cleaving solely to the Lord, attains a doubtless, complete knowledge of His cosmic and supra-cosmic being.

—: *Key Sanskrit Terms* :—

— ॐ तत् सत् ॐ —

Sanskrit here leans close, intimate yet vast, as though the universe itself were about to whisper a secret. The gentle gravity of मय्यासक्तमनाः mayy āsakta-manāḥ drifts through the breath, and योगम् युञ्जन् yogam yuñjan feels like a quiet gathering of all attention. पार्थ O pārtha glows with tender address.

The verse does not instruct; it invites. Sanskrit becomes a listening posture, a poised stillness in which doubt itself seems to soften, preparing the heart to hear something that has always been waiting.

Now let's begin our inward journey by holding the verse's Sanskrit expressions as one holds sacred flame—with wonder, with care, and with the readiness to be transformed. We will linger with the Sanskrit as with a master's voice inviting closeness. "Hear how, with mind fixed in Me, practicing yoga, you shall know Me completely." Each syllable here is both command and tenderness, a call into intimacy.

— ॐ —

मय्यासक्तमनाः (mayyāsakta-manāḥ):

The phrase draws our vision inward toward the heart of devotion — आसक्ति āsakti denotes deep attachment, yet when directed toward maya (Me, the Divine), it becomes a purifying force rather than a binding one.

The mind (मनाः manas) here is not merely thinking of the Divine, but is riveted, absorbed—as a river that surrenders all its streams to the ocean.

This word reveals that liberation is not attained by dry speculation, but by a luminous, heartfelt surrender wherein mind and heart are yoked to the Divine alone.

— ॐ —

योगं युञ्जन् (yogaṁ yuñjan):

योग Yoga, far from being merely a discipline of postures or meditation, is presented here as the uniting of the finite consciousness with the Infinite Being.

युञ्जन् Yuñjan (practicing, engaging deeply) suggests that the path is dynamic, an inner cultivation requiring effort, steadiness, and ceaseless engagement.

Yoga is the bridge by which the soul crosses from bondage to freedom.

— ॐ —

मदाश्रयः (madāśrayaḥ):

Taking आश्रय āśraya (refuge) in मद् Mad (Me) conveys total reliance.

It is not merely an intellectual acknowledgment but a complete existential resting upon the Divine Reality.

Here, the aspirant surrenders the brittle ego-self and dwells under the eternal protection of the Supreme.

मदाश्रयः Madāśrayaḥ thus implies both shelter and source — to live, move, and have one's being in God.

— ॐ —

असंशयं (asaṁśayam):

असंशयं -- Without doubt. This word pierces the veil of hesitation and intellectual uncertainty. True knowledge of the Divine must come not with tremulous guessing but with a clarity born of direct experience (अपरोक्ष अनुभव aparokṣānubhava).

Doubt is the final chain to be broken before realization dawns.

— ॐ —

समग्रं मां (samagraṁ māṁ):

To know the Supreme "completely" (समग्रं samagram) hints at an integrated vision: not merely knowing an aspect — such as the cosmic form, the impersonal Braham, or the personal Lord — but seeing the indivisible totality of the Divine's essence, manifestation, and transcendence.

It suggests a realization that weaves together the strands of the Divine in all its wondrous expressions.

— ॐ —

ज्ञास्यसि (jñāsyasi):

You shall know. Not merely infer, theorize, or believe — but know in the deepest, most authentic sense.

This is the promise the Lord extends: that through devotion, yoga, and refuge, the aspirant shall attain living knowledge — ज्ञान jñāna that is transformative and salvific.

—: In Brief :—

— ॐ श्रीकृष्णाय नमः ॐ —

In this solemn verse, Bhagwān Shri Krishna, the all-knowing charioteer of Arjuna's destiny, begins His revelation of the supreme wisdom that unites heart and intellect, love and knowledge.

Speaking not to the world but to a surrendered seeker, Krishna sets the foundation for knowing Him in totality—not merely as a concept or a cosmic force, but as the innermost Self of all.

— ॐ रामभद्राय नमः ॐ —

When the Lord speaks of the mind being "मय्यासक्तमनाः mayy āsakta-manāḥ"—attached to Him—He does not imply a fleeting interest or passing thought. This is the mind that has forsaken all entanglements with the perishable, and **like a river losing itself in the ocean, it flows unceasingly toward the Divine.**

Such a mind, like the sādhaka who sustains it, **no longer seeks fulfilment in the evanescent world**, but in the visible embrace of the Eternal.

— ॐ चिरंजीविनमित्राय नमः ॐ —

To practice Yoga **"mad-āśrayaḥ—with absolute dependence on Me"**—is to rest one's entire being upon the foundation of the Divine. It is the inward act of casting off the burden of self-reliance and entrusting oneself wholly to the Supreme Will.

The yogin who lives thus is never bereft; his life becomes a silent yajña, a continuous offering of thought, word, and deed at the altar of Shri Krishna.

And what is the **fruit** of such singleness of heart and steadiness of practice? The Lord declares: "**you shall know Me in entirety, without doubt.**"

Here, to "know" is not mere cognition, but existential realization—a doubtless vision of the Lord as both the manifested world and the transcendent Absolute—as the cause and the sustainer, as the visible and the veiled, as the personal and the impersonal.

Through such knowledge, eventually all dualities dissolve—and **the soul abides in the bliss of Oneness.**

— ॐ सर्वलोकैकनाथाय नमः ॐ —

This verse ushers in the sacred discourse on Bhakti, a sovereign means wherein jñāna is not opposed to devotion but is **fulfilled** by it.

The verse prepares us for the next movement in the Lord's teaching, where He shall reveal His manifested and unmanifested nature, the root of all that is seen and unseen.

Arjuna is thus urged to listen—not merely with the ears, but with the soul awakened to bliss—and so should we -- for the knowledge that is to **follow** is no less than the **esoteric secret of the Divine** Himself.

— ॐ तत् सत् ॐ —

Before moving on, let us once more bow in deep reverence before this sacred verse of the Bhagavad-Gītā, an eternal beacon of wisdom that ceaselessly illumines the path of seekers. Engage with its form—inscribe it with your own hand, let your heart dwell upon its meaning, and raise your voice in its chanting—for within these syllables echoes the undying proclamation delivered millennia ago on the battlefield of Kurukshetra. These words, transmitted unchanged across the unbroken chain of generations, form a living bridge, linking us to that sanctified era when Bhagwāna Shri Krishna Himself walked this earth and bestowed this divine teaching. Through the luminous vibration of these sacred Sanskrit sounds, we are drawn nearer to His timeless presence, touching the very heartbeat of the Eternal.

— ॐ —

श्रीभगवानुवाच --
śrībhagavānuvāca --
मय्यासक्तमनाः पार्थ योगं युञ्जन्मदाश्रयः ।
mayyāsaktamanāḥ pārtha yogaṁ yuñjanmadāśrayaḥ
असंशयं समग्रं मां यथा ज्ञास्यसि तच्छृणु ॥७-१॥
asaṁśayaṁ samagraṁ māṁ yathā jñāsyasi tacchṛṇu (7-1)

श्रीभगवानुवाच -- śrībhagavānuvāca --

मय्यासक्तमनाः पार्थ योगं युञ्जन्मदाश्रयः ।
mayyāsaktamanāḥ pārtha yogaṁ yuñjanmadāśrayaḥ

असंशयं समग्रं मां यथा ज्ञास्यसि तच्छृणु ॥ ७-१ ॥
asaṁśayaṁ samagraṁ māṁ yathā jñāsyasi tacchṛṇu (7-1)

ॐ तत्सदिति श्रीमद्भगवद्गीतासूपनिषत्सु ब्रह्मविद्यायां योगशास्त्रे श्रीकृष्णार्जुनसंवादे
om tatsaditi śrīmadbhagavadgītāsūpaniṣatsu brahmavidyāyāṁ yogaśāstre śrīkṛṣṇārjunasaṁvāde
ज्ञानविज्ञानयोगो नाम सप्तमोऽध्यायः श्लोकः १
jñānavijñānayogo nāma saptamo'dhyāyaḥ ślokaḥ 1

Om-Tat-Sat—Om (Braham) is the sole Reality. In the Yogic Scripture on the Science-of-Braham,
the Shrimada-Bhāgvada-Gītā Upanishad, we hereby conclude Shloka 1 of the Dialogue between
Shrī Krishna and Arjuna entitled Jnana-Vijnana-Yoga, Canto VII.

— ॐ श्रीकृष्णाय नमः ॐ —

I pray, yet know not whom I truly seek,
Alas, my voice is hollow—my faith so weak.

A thousand rites—but none my 'Inner-Flame' could spark or feed;
All my life, I served the shells—I forgot the seed.

I gathered the husk, I forgot the kernel.
Now I just have to cry: where, where art Thou, O Krishna?
Art Thou near? Or far as a Dream?

Alas, I worshipped Thee through my broken thoughts,
Never could I venerate Thee—in an unbroken stream.

Now Thy form eludes; Thy presence fades—
O, but what temple could I have built, to house the Free & Infinite?

O alas, alas—what a sorry fate,
I chanted Thy name, but never found out—where Thou are at.

Alas, alas—for I still know not,
That at the deepest depths—Thou stay hid, in my very own heart.

Behind the flesh. Beneath the breath.
Unmoved, unborn—like a blazing roar without sound—
The Sun within me was always there.
Yes, always. But I knew it not.

Aye, lifetime long, I had it in me—
Yet I lived in the world, begging for candles and wicks.

For none told me—what I must now tell thee.

Feeling Lost?

You believe yourself lost in shadowy corridors?
Soft night drapes ye in sorrows—in silvery hush?
But even this dream carries a hidden tenderness.
For it carries the whispers: तत् त्वम् असि tat-tvam-asi—directly from God.

The One ye seek walks within your own breath,
Moonlight never does wound the sky,
Neither does any grief hurt the Self.

You wander through the mist—thinking it to be Prison,
Yet you are the vast sky above—which ever stays untouched.

O mortal, awaken gently from these dream-identities.
You are That-One – the serene infinite expanse.
And yes—you were never hurt, diminished -- not even once.

Come, in the hush of Silence, allow Krishna to lean toward you,
The Ātmā is not an idea but a Presence—nearer than your self.
Let the Gita-speech arrive—like light through wound in the cloud.

And remember: Krishna is NOT a story—
He is that axis which makes all stories possible.

Feel the presence of Krishna all around ye—
for He is all there is to the world—this Existence.

Stop this trembling—at the demands of the now.
Do not withdraw from world. Just stand more fully within the Self.

Your calm is not retreat; it is clarity gathering shape.
Unvanish—be Sanātana-Dharma itself becomes visible in the world.

O Pilgrim, Cut through the thought: "I suffer."
Cut through the claim: "I am bound in fetters."

Observe the observed. Observe the observing. Observe the observer.
And always know what ye have been told: तत् त्वम् असि tat-tvam-asi.

Remember: You are a being most ancient.
Your beingness is long, long prior to this story here.

You are the Reality beyond words & descriptions.
Pain appears. Pain passes. You are the Witness that stays untouched.
Stand as the Real. Stand Uncut. Stand in Krishna.

ॐ गीता श्लोकः ७.२ – GĪTĀ VERSE 7.2

ॐ श्रीमद्भगवद्गीतासूपनिषत्सु ब्रह्मविद्यायां योगशास्त्रे श्रीकृष्णार्जुनसंवादे
om śrīmadbhagavadgītāsūpaniṣatsu brahmavidyāyāṁ yogaśāstre śrīkṛṣṇārjunasaṁvāde
ज्ञानविज्ञानयोगो नाम सप्तमोऽध्यायः श्लोकः २
jñānavijñānayogo nāma saptamo'dhyāyaḥ ślokaḥ 2

— ॐ —

ज्ञानं तेऽहं सविज्ञानमिदं वक्ष्याम्यशेषतः ।
jñānaṁ te'haṁ savijñānamidaṁ vakṣyāmyaśeṣataḥ
यज्ज्ञात्वा नेह भूयोऽन्यज्ज्ञातव्यमवशिष्यते ॥७-२॥
yajjñātvā neha bhūyo'nyajjñātavyamavaśiṣyate (7-2)

I shall impart to you without reserve that very knowledge, that very realization, knowing which there remains nothing more to be known in this world. (7.2)

—: Word-by-Word :—

ज्ञानम् jñānam – knowledge; ते te – to you; अहम् aham – I; सविज्ञानम् sa-vijñānam – with wisdom; इदम् idam – this; वक्ष्यामि vakṣyāmi – shall declare; अशेषतः aśeṣataḥ – completely; यत् yat – which; ज्ञात्वा jñātvā – having known; न na – not; इह iha – here; भूयः bhūyaḥ – again; अन्यत् anyat – anything else; ज्ञातव्यम् jñātavyam – to be known; अवशिष्यते avaśiṣyate – remains.

—: Understanding The Verse :—

— ॐ श्रीकृष्णाय नमः ॐ —

In this verse, Bhagwān Shri Krishna continues to draw Arjuna into the sanctum of divine wisdom, promising a knowledge that is not merely conceptual but utterly transformative.

This is not the knowledge that fluctuates with the intellect—with more data—nor is it the fleeting insight born of sensory perception. It is **Jñāna**—pure, spiritual understanding—and **Vijnāna**—its direct realization, in an **inner experience lived,** in actuality.

— ॐ श्रीरामाय नमः ॐ —

Our Lord-God here declares that He shall reveal this wisdom fully and without reserve, thereby lifting the veil that separates the finite self from the infinite Reality.

O mortal, rejoice in that promise of the Lord, and know this: Once attained, this knowledge, leaves no residue of doubt, no further quest for truth—for it brings one face to face with the all-encompassing essence of the Divine, in whom all knowledge finds its fulfillment.

Ah, the blessed soul Arjuna! Krishna here is not merely informing Arjuna—He is initiating him into the supreme secret, the heart of all scriptural wisdom.

—: *Key Sanskrit Terms* :—

— ॐ तत सत ॐ —

The cadence deepens, and Sanskrit takes on the warmth of a promise freely given. ज्ञानं तेऽहं सविज्ञानम् Jñānam te aham sa-vijñānam moves like a gift laid gently in open hands. अशेषतः aśeṣataḥ glimmers with a sense of nothing held back. The words do not enumerate what will be known; they simply widen the space for knowing.

The Sanskrit of the Bhagavad-Gītā feels like a clear, generous river, flowing without reserve, carrying the listener toward a horizon where nothing further needs to be sought.

Come, let us imbibe ourselves with the Gītā knowledge, dwell in the verse like in an ancient home—walls lined with Sanskrit echoes, doorways opening onto landscapes of thoughts, where the wind still speaks in ancient tongues.

Let us rest with the Sanskrit as with doors opening one by one. Knowledge and realization both will be declared, nothing further will be left unknown. Each word promises completeness, a circle drawn—closed.

— ॐ —

ज्ञानं (jñānam):

Here ज्ञान jñāna refers not to the collection of empirical or scriptural information, but to the sacred, intuitive knowledge of the ultimate Reality — ब्रह्म Braham.

It is the luminous insight into the eternal truths that lie beyond the senses and mind, encompassing both the knowledge of the Self (आत्म-ज्ञान Ātmajñāna) and the nature of the cosmos as expressions of the Divine.

— ॐ —

सविज्ञानम् (savijñānam):

Not mere theoretical knowledge (ज्ञान jñāna), but सवि-ज्ञान savi-jñāna — knowledge that is confirmed by direct realization (अनुभव anubhava).

विज्ञान Vijñāna is the internalized wisdom wherein knowledge becomes living experience.

It suggests the fullness of understanding: not only knowing Braham as an abstract concept but tasting the essence of ब्रह्म Braham in one's own being.

It is to see God, not merely to think about God.

— ॐ —

अशेषतः (aśeṣataḥ):

Without remainder, nothing held back — total and complete revelation.

The Lord promises to unveil the entirety of the spiritual knowledge, sparing no secret, leaving no veil of ignorance intact.

This completeness is crucial: **half-knowledge binds; whole-knowledge liberates.**

— ॐ —

यज्ज्ञात्वा (yajjñātvā):

"Knowing which" — the knowledge to be given is not fragmented, requiring supplementary learning; rather, it is the master key.

Once known, all else is known by implication, for the Supreme Truth underlies all phenomena.

This reveals the non-dual character of Braham: एकं अद्वितीयम ekam advitīyam — One without a second.

— ॐ —

नेह भूयः अन्यत् ज्ञातव्यम् (neha bhūyo anyat jñātavyam):

"In this world (इह iha), there remains nothing further to be known."

The seeker's thirst is fully quenched. Nothing external can add to the inner plenitude of realization.

Once the substratum of all existence — ब्रह्म Braham — is known, the myriad names and forms are understood as but outer ripples— on its vast, silent ocean of consciousness.

—: In Brief :—

— ॐ श्रीकृष्णाय नमः ॐ —

Bhagwān Shri Krishna proclaims a most gracious assurance—"I shall declare to you that knowledge and realization, knowing which there remains nothing more to be known in this world."

O what great words of benediction!

In the Bhagavad-Gītā, the Lord does not promise partial understanding or scattered glimpses, but one luminous, integral knowledge —**the very crown** of all seeking.

— ॐ श्रीरामाय नमः ॐ —

The word jñāna here refers to the knowledge of the Supreme Reality as it is in its pure, unqualified essence—**nirguṇa Braham**, the formless substratum of all beingness.

Yet the Lord does not stop there. He includes **vijñāna**—the **realized vision** of that same Reality manifesting through name, form, and divine attributes—**the saguṇa aspect**, by which the heart learns to **love and realize what the intellect hitherto perceived**.

Both are to be given together, without withholding, as the total vision of the Lord's integral nature.

— ॐ ब्रजवल्लभाय नमः ॐ —

To know Bhagwān Shri Krishna is both His aspects—as formless Braham and as Krishna of manifest form, is to know the very secret of existence.

How so?

Because **the Lord is the root and substance of all things**. **All sciences, philosophies, and sacred paths converge in Him.**

Just as the knowledge of clay reveals the essence of all clay pots, or the understanding of gold unveils the truth of every ornament, so too the **realization of Bhagwān in His full being—both immanent and transcendent—removes the veil** from the entire field of existence.

Nothing then remains unknown, for all things are fully seen as expressions of the One.

— ॐ जानकीवल्लभाय नमः ॐ —

This verse, prepares us for the solemn truth which follows: that such knowledge is **exceedingly rare**, attained only by the most **steadfast** of seekers.

Nay, it is not gained by cleverness, nor by ritual alone, but by a **purified heart, fixed mind, and unwavering devotion to the Truth**.

Thus, having promised to unveil this supreme truth—complete in knowledge and rooted in direct realization—Bhagwān gently leads Arjuna to the next verse, where He shall speak of the rarity of such attainment, and the greatness of the soul who aspires to it.

Indeed O pilgrim, if thy seeking is sincere—then **feel truly blessed**, and thank thy stars—and above all Bhagwān Shri Krishna.

— ॐ तत् सत् ॐ —

Before we move on, let us bow in reverence to this sacred verse—a timeless beacon of wisdom guiding seekers for ages. Write it by hand, reflect on its meaning, and chant it aloud, for these sounds alone carry the authenticity of that era. The world may have changed but the living vibration of these Sanskrit sounds still remain as original as they were when Bhagwān Shri Krishna Himself walked the earth and imparted these teachings.

— ॐ —

ज्ञानं तेऽहं सविज्ञानमिदं वक्ष्याम्यशेषतः ।
jñānaṁ te'haṁ savijñānamidaṁ vakṣyāmyaśeṣataḥ
यज्ज्ञात्वा नेह भूयोऽन्यज्ज्ञातव्यमवशिष्यते ॥७-२॥
yajjñātvā neha bhūyo'nyajjñātavyamavaśiṣyate (7-2)

ज्ञानं तेऽहं सविज्ञानमिदं वक्ष्याम्यशेषतः ।
jñānaṁ te'haṁ savijñānamidaṁ vakṣyāmyaśeṣataḥ
यज्ज्ञात्वा नेह भूयोऽन्यज्ज्ञातव्यमवशिष्यते ॥७-२॥
yajjñātvā neha bhūyo'nyajjñātavyamavaśiṣyate (7-2)

ॐ तत्सदिति श्रीमद्भगवद्गीतासूपनिषत्सु ब्रह्मविद्यायां योगशास्त्रे श्रीकृष्णार्जुनसंवादे
om tatsaditi śrīmadbhagavadgītāsūpaniṣatsu brahmavidyāyāṁ yogaśāstre śrīkṛṣṇārjunasaṁvāde
ज्ञानविज्ञानयोगो नाम सप्तमोऽध्यायः श्लोकः २
jñānavijñānayogo nāma saptamo'dhyāyaḥ ślokaḥ 2

Om-Tat-Sat—Om (Braham) is the sole Reality. In the Yogic Scripture on the Science-of-Braham,
the Shrimada-Bhāgvada-Gītā Upanishad, we hereby conclude Shloka 2 of the Dialogue between
Shri Krishna and Arjuna entitled Jnana-Vijnana-Yoga, Canto VII.

— ॐ श्रीकृष्णाय नमः ॐ —

The Offered Flame from Krishna
I was offered It—the very Last Knowing.
Not a broken part, not just a single Spark—
But the Entire Flame!

It was offered without reserve. Without any veils. Fully Free.
But I turned instead—
To chatter, glitter, gain, grain, coin, skin.
O what a pathetic Jiva me—a luckless being!

It was a Most Precious Gift! Bestowed Unasked!
Completely priceless! The highest boon! From God Himself!
Free. No Fee. No middleman. No priest.
No price tag. Just the turning inward; Only the still breath.

But the foolish me, I asked instead:
Will it bring me riches? Boost my career?
Ah, did I not already say—I am a pathetic little creature!

The Foolish King who Begged for Trinkets
I was born a King. I was crowned with Fire.
Yet hat in hand, I went around begging in the market of Desires.

I traded Golden Silence—to maunder borrowed words of others.
I forgot the Great Empire—that was right within my own heart.

ॐ गीता श्लोकः ७.३ – GĪTĀ VERSE 7.3

ॐ श्रीमद्भगवद्गीतासूपनिषत्सु ब्रह्मविद्यायां योगशास्त्रे श्रीकृष्णार्जुनसंवादे
om śrīmadbhagavadgītāsūpaniṣatsu brahmavidyāyāṁ yogaśāstre śrīkṛṣṇārjunasaṁvāde
ज्ञानविज्ञानयोगो नाम सप्तमोऽध्यायः श्लोकः ३
jñānavijñānayogo nāma saptamo'dhyāyaḥ ślokaḥ 3

— ॐ —

मनुष्याणां सहस्रेषु कश्चिद्यतति सिद्धये ।
manuṣyāṇāṁ sahasreṣu kaścidyatati siddhaye
यततामपि सिद्धानां कश्चिन्मां वेत्ति तत्त्वतः ॥७-३॥
yatatāmapi siddhānāṁ kaścinmāṁ vetti tattvataḥ (7-3)

Perhaps one in a thousand strives for perfection; and of those that strive, hardly one attains it; and amongst those that reach the ideal—it's a rare soul who knows Me in essence. (7.3)

—: Word-by-Word :—

मनुष्याणाम् manuṣyāṇām – among thousands of men; सहस्रेषु sahasreṣu – among thousands; कश्चित् kaścit – someone; यतति yatati – strives; सिद्धये siddhaye – for perfection; यतताम् yatatām – among those striving; अपि api – even; सिद्धानाम् siddhānām – among the perfected; कश्चित् kaścit – someone; माम् mām – Me; वेत्ति vetti – knows; तत्त्वतः tattvataḥ – in truth.

—: Understanding The Verse :—

— ॐ श्रीकृष्णाय नमः ॐ —

Bhagwān Shri Krishna, having proclaimed the majesty of Jñāna and Vijnāna in the preceding verses, here discloses a solemn truth: one which is revealing of the sacred **rarity** of true spiritual realization. This verse serves as a powerful reflection on the human journey toward the Divine.

While the path is **open to all, few tread it**; among those who strive with sincerity, **fewer still reach its pinnacle**; and among such perfected beings, it is a **rare jewel indeed who realizes the Lord** in His essential nature!

— ॐ श्रीरामाय नमः ॐ —

Here, Shri Krishna does **not discourage but awakens** the seeker to the **gravity of the undertaking.**

Divine realization is no common attainment—it requires more than effort; it calls for unshakable faith, accumulated merit, an undivided longing for the Supreme—and above all the divine grace.

Ultimately it is He, our Maker, who is in charge of the show—not we.

This verse humbles us.
It reminds us that human life is a rare gift not to be squandered;
and that the path to knowing Bhagwān Shri Krishna in His full glory **is not to be walked casually**
—but with the utmost perseverance, caution, and staying in full surrender to Sanātana-Dharma—which is verily **the breath of God.**

—: Key Sanskrit Terms :—

— ॐ तत् सत् ॐ —

Now the verse grows hushed and rarefied. Sanskrit lets सहस्रेषु कश्चित् sahasreṣu kaścid fall like a soft, solitary footstep in a vast hall. यतति सिद्धये yatati siddhaye glimmers faintly, while माम् वेत्ति तत्त्वतः māṃ vetti tattvataḥ shines like a distant star. The language does not lament rarity; it honors it.

Here the Sanskrit of the Gītā feels like a quiet mountain path, where each syllable knows how few will walk it, and therefore speaks with gentle, enduring dignity.

Now let us hear the Sanskrit—for they are like stars rare in the night sky – always there, but **the luckless never even glances** at them.
"Among thousands, few strive for perfection; among the perfected, few know Me truly".
Each syllable glimmers with rarity, a truth both humbling and vast.
Come, let us trace the verse's Sanskrit lifelines—as a reader traces faded ink on sacred parchment—gently, reverently, trusting that even the worn out words are **still speaking directly to him.**

— ॐ —

मनुष्याणां सहस्रेषु (manuṣyāṇāṃ sahasreṣu):
Amongst सहस्रेषु thousands of मनुष्य men—this opening phrase immediately evokes the grandeur and gravity of the spiritual quest.
It suggests that the aspiration for transcendence is rare amidst the countless beings entangled in the webs of worldly life.
The very beginning sets the tone: **the path to realization is walked by but a few.**

— ॐ —

कश्चिद्यतति सिद्धये (kaścid yatati siddhaye):
Among thousands, perhaps कश्चित् kaścit —
"someone," a rare one — यतति yatati,

strives diligently for सिद्धि siddhi, perfection or spiritual accomplishment.

The word सिद्धि Siddhi here does not necessarily mean miraculous powers (siddhis) but denotes 'accomplishment', 'reaching the goal'.

It can be said that it is the attainment of full liberation (मोक्ष-सिद्धि mokṣa-siddhi), the flowering of the soul into its innate divinity.

The stress on यतति yatati (makes the effort) highlights that realization is not a casual occurrence—but far from it.

It is the fruit of intense, focused striving—not just of one life-time but of many prior.

— ॐ —

यततामपि सिद्धानां (yatatām api siddhānām):

Even among those who are striving and have achieved a certain spiritual maturity — सिद्धानां siddhanām — there remains a further, more rarefied attainment.

The Lord indicates that not all who become accomplished in yogic or spiritual practices arrive at the ultimate realization of God in His real essence.

— ॐ —

कश्चिन् मां वेत्ति तत्त्वतः (kaścin māṁ vetti tattvataḥ):

"Rarely does one truly know Me in essence" (tattvataḥ). This phrase is the heart of the verse.

तत्त्व Tattva is the essential reality, the bedrock truth beyond appearances.

Knowing the Lord तत्त्वतः tattvataḥin His very true essence—is not merely to recognize Him as a deity or cosmic power but to realize Him as सच्चिदानन्द ब्रह्म satt-chitt-ānanda braham, the very ocean of existence-bliss-consciousness.

It is 'That' knowing which dissolves the knower into the Known.

—: In Brief :—

— ॐ श्रीकृष्णाय नमः ॐ —

In this deeply sobering verse, Bhagwān Shri Krishna reveals the hidden truth about the soul's journey toward Divine realization:

मनुष्याणां सहस्रेषु कश्चिद्यतति सिद्धये । यततामपि सिद्धानां कश्चिन्मां वेत्ति तत्त्वतः ॥

Among thousands of men, perhaps one strives for perfection; and of those who strive, scarcely one knows Me in truth.

Here, the Lord does not just speak of external devotion or intellectual pursuit.

He refers to that rare spiritual consummation in which the veil of Māyā is fully pierced,
and the seeker beholds Krishna,
—not as an abstract deity, but as the Infinite, the all-sustaining Reality behind the seen and unseen—
who has now become manifest in Form—for us to be able to behold the Formless.

— ॐ श्रीरामाय नमः ॐ —

The reference to मनुष्य manuṣya or "humans" itself bears a deeper implication!

Human birth, the scriptures declare, is a sacred opportunity—a junction where the soul may turn either toward emancipation, or sink further into bondages.

Unlike gods—the alien non-human life-forms, the celestial beings still seen hovering in their vimānas, and who mostly stay intoxicated in pleasures and comforts of their celestial realms, Or—
—the lower beings—the creatures of earth—enmeshed in instinct,
—it is **human alone who holds the potential to strive consciously toward the Supreme.**

Yet, as Shri Krishna bemoans, even among the Jivas invested with this rare chance of human birth, few awaken to the higher calling of realizing who they are—and fewer still are able to persevere until the end.

And what be the end?

This end stands glorified in the mahāvākyas such as अहं ब्रह्मास्मि **aham-braham-āsmi—I am He -- when this little wave called the Jivātmā within us eventually and directly realizes: I am in oneness with the Ocean.**

— ॐ अयोध्याधिपतये नमः ॐ —

But why does the Jiva stay caught—and never wakes up to the Reality? Why is this so?

Because it is the fetters of saṃskāras—the latent impressions from our countless prior births—that entangle our mind in fleeting pleasures and egoic pursuits.

Although born in a human body, **MOST stay inwardly asleep,** held fast by delusion, attachment, ego.

And even among those who seek sincerely,
there remain the obstacles of **inner resistance, false identifications;**
and then there are **worldly distractions** which hinder the ascent—

especially in this day and age of kali.

Only the soul whose devotion is purified through lifetimes,
who stays guided by the sāttvic impulse,
and graced by association with the wise,
is able to walk this path with steadfastness—
and then by the grace of God, fully to its conclusion.

— ॐ श्रीकृष्णाय नमः ॐ —

Even among those rare sādhaka-souls who do reach high levels of spiritual attainment (siddhānām),
the one who truly knows "Me" in essence (mām vetti tattvataḥ)—
who realizes "Me" not merely as the Lord with attributes, but as the One beyond name and form, the very Self of all—
that soul is supremely rare.

Such a soul sees not many, but One;
not the play of multiplicity, but the silent presence of the Eternal behind all phenomena.
To such a one, the universe reveals itself as a spark of His glory—
as Krishna has declared in the Tenth Canto.

— ॐ अनन्तगुणसम्पन्नाय नमः ॐ —

This verse functions as both a revelation and a quiet exhortation.
It invites us not take to this quest casually—but become mindful of its gravity,
to treasure this redemptive human birth,
to renounce complacency—
and to strive with a heart fully of fire, and a mind that stays in surrender to Shri Krishna.

This verse prepares the ground for the next unfolding, where Shri Krishna will disclose the distinction between His lower and higher natures—explaining how all that exists **proceeds from Him**, yet He Himself remains untouched, staying ever beyond, ever the Sovereign.

— ॐ तत सत ॐ —

Before we move on, let us bow in reverence to this sacred verse—a timeless beacon of wisdom guiding seekers for ages. Write it by hand, reflect on its meaning, and chant it aloud, for these sounds alone carry the authenticity of that era. The world may have changed but the living vibration of these Sanskrit sounds still remain as original as they were when Bhagwān Shri Krishna Himself walked the earth and imparted these teachings.

— ॐ —

मनुष्याणां सहस्रेषु कश्चिद्यतति सिद्धये ।
manuṣyāṇāṁ sahasreṣu kaścidyatati siddhaye
यततामपि सिद्धानां कश्चिन्मां वेत्ति तत्त्वतः ॥ ७-३ ॥
yatatāmapi siddhānāṁ kaścinmāṁ vetti tattvataḥ (7-3)

gītā-mūlam 07

मनुष्याणां सहस्रेषु कश्चिद्यतति सिद्धये ।
manuṣyāṇāṁ sahasreṣu kaścidyatati siddhaye
यततामपि सिद्धानां कश्चिन्मां वेत्ति तत्त्वतः ॥७-३॥
yatatāmapi siddhānāṁ kaścinmāṁ vetti tattvataḥ (7-3)

ॐ तत्सदिति श्रीमद्भगवद्गीतासूपनिषत्सु ब्रह्मविद्यायां योगशास्त्रे श्रीकृष्णार्जुनसंवादे
om tatsaditi śrīmadbhagavadgītāsūpaniṣatsu brahmavidyāyāṁ yogaśāstre śrīkṛṣṇārjunasaṁvāde
ज्ञानविज्ञानयोगो नाम सप्तमोऽध्यायः श्लोकः ३
jñānavijñānayogo nāma saptamo'dhyāyaḥ ślokaḥ 3

Om-Tat-Sat—Om (Braham) is the sole Reality. In the Yogic Scripture on the Science-of-Braham,
the Shrimada-Bhāgvada-Gītā Upanishad, we hereby conclude Shloka 3 of the Dialogue between
Shrī Krishna and Arjuna entitled Jnana-Vijnana-Yoga, Canto VII.

— ॐ श्रीकृष्णाय नमः ॐ —

Behold the multitudes—restless as dust in wind.
They chase the baubles of earth,
But never turn their gaze **Within**.

No Sanātana-Dharma. No varna-āshram. No Sanskrit, No Sanskriti,
The 'conditioning-system' of adharma has splintered men into husk.

As aimless-billions they live. Tear-eyed they wander.
They know not whence they came. Know not whither they go.
Benumbed they exist in stupefaction—the Pavlovian hoi-polloi—
Unknown to Sanātana-Dharma. Unknown to the glory of the **Self**.

Yet amongst this ocean of forgetfulness,
One spark awakens. One soul remembers.
And we ask thee, O pilgrim—**Is that** enquiring soul **thee**?

"Who am I? Whither go I? And why?" Yes, some do ask.
And hearing such questions, the rulers of falsehood get distressed,
For they are happy only with the unthinking **Stupes**—bowing to **Ease**.

Conditioning—and bread, spectacle, fights—suffice to chain the masses,
Sticks & carrots, Fear & promises—enough to herd them controlled.
The Elites are scared of **thee—the Thinker, the Awakened**—
For just one "rotten" apple—they know—will spoil all the rest.

Rare is the soul who stops midst the herded flock,
Most rare he, who stops to ask, **"Who indeed am I?"**

Trained to deride such—the world calls him mad for this question,
Yet from up above, **Krishna bends closer**—to hear that lone cry.

ॐ गीता श्लोकः ७.४ – Gītā Verse 7.4

ॐ श्रीमद्भगवद्गीतासूपनिषत्सु ब्रह्मविद्यायां योगशास्त्रे श्रीकृष्णार्जुनसंवादे
om śrīmadbhagavadgītāsūpaniṣatsu brahmavidyāyāṁ yogaśāstre śrīkṛṣṇārjunasaṁvāde
ज्ञानविज्ञानयोगो नाम सप्तमोऽध्यायः श्लोकः ४
jñānavijñānayogo nāma saptamo'dhyāyaḥ ślokaḥ 4

— ॐ —

भूमिरापोऽनलो वायुः खं मनो बुद्धिरेव च ।
bhūmirāpo'nalo vāyuḥ khaṁ mano buddhireva ca
अहङ्कार इतीयं मे भिन्ना प्रकृतिरष्टधा ॥७-४॥
ahaṅkāra itīyaṁ me bhinnā prakṛtiraṣṭadhā (7-4)

Earth, water, fire, air, aether, mind, intellect and egoism—this comprises My eight-fold Prakriti (Nature). (7.4)

—: *Word-by-Word* :—

भूमिः bhūmiḥ – earth; आपः āpaḥ – water; अनलः analaḥ – fire; वायुः vāyuḥ – air; खम् kham – ether; मनः manaḥ – mind; बुद्धिः buddhiḥ – intellect; एव ca – and also; अहङ्कारः ahaṅkāraḥ – ego; इति iti – thus; इयम् iyam – this; मे me – My; भिन्ना bhinnā – divided; प्रकृतिः prakṛtiḥ – nature; अष्टधा aṣṭadhā – into eightfold.

—: *Understanding The Verse* :—

— ॐ श्रीकृष्णाय नमः ॐ —

In this profound verse, Bhagwān Shri Krishna begins to unfold the mystery of His twofold Nature—beginning with the apara-prakṛti, the lower or insentient aspect of His cosmic manifestation.

This eightfold division encompasses both the gross and subtle dimensions of existence, and forms the substratum of the phenomenal world.

— ॐ परब्रह्मणे नमः ॐ —

Here, the Lord enumerates the five gross elements (महा-भूत mahābhūtas)—earth, water, fire, air, and ether—as well as the three subtle components of the antahkarana—mind (manas), intellect (buddhi), and ego-sense (ahaṅkāra).

Together, these eight constitute the field of prakṛti, the mutable, insentient energy through which the Lord creates, sustains, and withdraws the cosmos.

— ॐ श्रीरामाय नमः ॐ —

This delineation marks the beginning of a deeper discourse on the relationship between the Divine and the world.

While these elements constitute the lower nature, they are not apart from the Lord—they are His own śakti, expressed in the field of multiplicity.

The upcoming verses will gradually reveal that beyond this lower nature lies the higher nature (para-prakṛti), the essence of life.

—: Key Sanskrit Terms :—

— ॐ तत् सत् ॐ —

The cadence becomes elemental and resonant. Sanskrit places भूमिरापोऽनलो वायुः bhūmir āpo'nalo vāyuḥ with the steady rhythm of creation itself, and खं मनो बुद्धिरेव च kham mano buddhir eva ca follows like subtle echoes. अहङ्कार ahaṅkāra hums beneath it all.

The words do not list; they assemble gathered together. The Sanskrit feels like a sacred inventory of existence, each syllable carrying the weight of worlds—as if the verse were quietly building the cosmos out of sounds.

Now let us peel back the husk of this śloka, word by blessed Sanskrit word, and find beneath each—a kernel of truth still warm from the lips that first shaped it ages ago.

— ॐ —

भूमिः, आपः, अनलः, वायुः, खम् (bhūmiḥ, āpaḥ, analaḥ, vāyuḥ, kham):
The five महा-भूत mahābhūtas — Earth, Water, Fire, Air, and Ether — represent the gross, elemental constituents of the manifest universe.
Also do note that each element also has a corresponding तन्मात्र tanmātra (subtle essence) and together they govern the realms of form, cohesion, transformation, movement, and space.

— ॐ —

मनो बुद्धिः (mano buddhiḥ):
The manas (मन mind) and buddhi (बुद्धि intellect) belong to the subtle body (सूक्ष्म शरीर sūkṣma-śarīra).
मन Manas is the instrument of thought.
In the human context it is the field where impressions are gathered and emotions arise such as doubt and desire.
बुद्धि Buddhi, higher than the mind, is the faculty of discrimination, judgment, and decisive knowledge.
Together, they orchestrate the drama of human experience, acting as intermediaries between the senses and the Self.

— ॐ —

अहङ्कारः (ahaṅkāraḥ):

अहङ्कार Egoism — the principle of individuation — is the deep-rooted sense of "I" and "mine."

It is a centre of consciousness. It is अहङ्कार ahaṅkāra that falsely identifies the Self with body, mind, and senses, thereby spinning the illusion of separateness.

It binds the eternal spirit (आत्मा Ātmā) to the persona of the Jiva— the transient mask of personality which that centre assumes over time – having become heaped upon the centre called egoism or अहङ्कार.

— ॐ —

इति इयं मे भिन्ना प्रकृतिः अष्टधा (iti iyaṁ me bhinnā prakṛtir aṣṭadhā):

"My Nature divided eightfold."

Thus is described मे -me (mine) भिन्ना-bhinnā (varied/divided) प्रकृतिः-prakṛtiḥ (Nature) अष्टधा -aṣṭadhā (eightfold)

Here, prakṛti is declared to be भिन्ना bhinnā (divided) into eight aspects, yet it remains the Divine's own expression मे-me ("mine").

This division is not a real severance but an apparent manifestation.

The Supreme, through His inscrutable Māyā, differentiates Himself into these eight principles, projecting the cosmos while remaining ever transcendental.

—: In Brief :—

— ॐ श्रीकृष्णाय नमः ॐ —

Bhagwān Shri Krishna unveils here His eightfold apara-prakṛti, the manifest field through which the drama of the universe unfolds.

This eightfold nature—comprising earth, water, fire, air, ether, mind, intellect, and ego—is none other than His own lower energy.

Lower because it is the basic framework.

It is the very matrix of material and mental existence.

Although referred to as "lower,"—because it is at the very base—it is divine in origin, for nothing exists outside the boundless expanse of His being.

These eight elements are not to be seen merely as separate substances but as interwoven aspects of the same cosmic web, infused by the Lord's will.

— ॐ श्रीरामाय नमः ॐ —

The five mahābhutas form the basis of all physical structures, from the solidity of the earth to the subtlety of space.

Yet even more subtle are the inner instruments: the manas that gathers sensory impressions; the buddhi that discerns and decides; and the ahaṅkāra, the ego-principle, which appropriates experience to the fictitious self and veils the awareness of the true Self.

Remember: each महाभूत mahābhūta gross element has respective तन्मात्र tanmātras or subtle essences as follows:
- भूमिः (bhūmiḥ – earth) → गन्धतन्मात्र (gandha-tanmātra – smell)
- आपः (āpaḥ – water) → रसतन्मात्र (rasa-tanmātra – taste)
- अनलः (analaḥ – fire) → रूपतन्मात्र (rūpa-tanmātra – form/vision)
- वायुः (vāyuḥ – air) → स्पर्शतन्मात्र (sparśa-tanmātra – touch)
- खम् (kham – ether/space) → शब्दतन्मात्र (śabda-tanmātra – sound)

So the mahābhutas are not merely physical entities but archetypal forces—become woven from Divine energy.

The अहङ्कार ahaṅkāra is the principle of individuation.
It is the silent architect of bondage, for by it arises the illusion of separateness—of 'I' and 'mine'.
It superimposes finitude upon the Infinite and thus gives rise to saṁsāra, the endless cycle of becoming and dissolution.

— ॐ सेतुकृते नमः ॐ —

These eight aspects, when undisturbed by consciousness, are "inert". Yet enlivened by the presence of the puruṣa—the witnessing Self—they become the theatre of all experience, the vast field (kṣetra) in which karma unfolds and liberation may be sought.

Bhagwān Shri Krishna has revealed here that this entire structure of the known universe—gross and subtle alike—is but His own projected śakti, veiled in māyā, transient and mutable.

Though appearing separate, all and everything arises from God— stays sustained by Him, and eventually dissolve back into Him.

This eightfold prakṛti is the divine play of forms, while the underlying Self, untouched, remains the silent witness behind all transformations.

— ॐ महादेवादिपूजिताय नमः ॐ —

Having thus introduced His lower nature, the Lord shall, in the next verse, distinguish it from His higher nature—para-prakṛti— which is the very life-principle within all beings.

Krishna will now lead us from the seen to the seer, from the changing to the changeless, from prakṛti to the puruṣa—who is Krishna Himself -- as you and I and the innumerous Jivas trapped within these countless life form.

— ॐ —

भूमिरापोऽनलो वायुः खं मनो बुद्धिरेव च ।
bhūmirāpo'nalo vāyuḥ khaṁ mano buddhireva ca
अहङ्कार इतीयं मे भिन्ना प्रकृतिरष्टधा ॥७-४॥
ahaṅkāra itīyaṁ me bhinnā prakṛtiraṣṭadhā (7-4)

— ॐ —

भूमिरापोऽनलो वायुः खं मनो बुद्धिरेव च ।
bhūmirāpo'nalo vāyuḥ khaṁ mano buddhireva ca
अहङ्कार इतीयं मे भिन्ना प्रकृतिरष्टधा ॥७-४॥
ahaṅkāra itīyaṁ me bhinnā prakṛtiraṣṭadhā (7-4)

ॐ तत्सदिति श्रीमद्भगवद्गीतासूपनिषत्सु ब्रह्मविद्यायां योगशास्त्रे श्रीकृष्णार्जुनसंवादे
om tatsaditi śrīmadbhagavadgītāsūpaniṣatsu brahmavidyāyāṁ yogaśāstre śrīkṛṣṇārjunasaṁvāde
ज्ञानविज्ञानयोगो नाम सप्तमोऽध्यायः श्लोकः ४
jñānavijñānayogo nāma saptamo'dhyāyaḥ ślokaḥ 4

Om-Tat-Sat—Om (Braham) is the sole Reality. In the Yogic Scripture on the Science-of-Braham, the Shrimada-Bhāgvada-Gītā Upanishad, we hereby conclude Shloka 4 of the Dialogue between Shrī Krishna and Arjuna entitled Jnana-Vijnana-Yoga, Canto VII.

— ॐ श्रीकृष्णाय नमः ॐ —

God created these beautiful things in order to sport on earth.
But that was then—and this is now:

Mired in adharma, men ravage the very elements they live on.
Earth is seized for greed,
Water poisoned for profit,
Fire harnessed for destruction,
Air thickened with smoke of folly,
Ether filled with waves and noise of endless chatter.

Mind is yoked to serve as beast of burden,
Reason is bent into cunning,
And as King Tyrant—it is man's ego that reigns on earth.

But be warned O cruel human creature—
For thy destruction is now well nigh.

ॐ गीता श्लोकः ७.५ – Gītā Verse 7.5

ॐ श्रीमद्भगवद्गीतासूपनिषत्सु ब्रह्मविद्यायां योगशास्त्रे श्रीकृष्णार्जुनसंवादे
om śrīmadbhagavadgītāsūpaniṣatsu brahmavidyāyāṁ yogaśāstre śrīkṛṣṇārjunasaṁvāde
ज्ञानविज्ञानयोगो नाम सप्तमोऽध्यायः श्लोकः ५
jñānavijñānayogo nāma saptamo'dhyāyaḥ ślokaḥ 5

— ॐ —

अपरेयमितस्त्वन्यां प्रकृतिं विद्धि मे पराम् ।
apareyamitastvanyāṁ prakṛtiṁ viddhi me parām
जीवभूतां महाबाहो ययेदं धार्यते जगत् ॥७-५॥
jīvabhūtāṁ mahābāho yayedaṁ dhāryate jagat (7-5)

This is My lower Nature—the material. Different from that, O mighty-armed, know My higher Prakriti—in the form of Jīva, the individual soul; and in this duality of my Prakriti, the world is held existent. (7.5)

—: Word-by-Word :—

इयम् अपरा iyam aparā – this is inferior; इतः itaḥ – besides this; तु tu – but; अन्याम् anyām – another; प्रकृतिम् prakṛtim – nature; विद्धि viddhi – know; मे me – My; पराम् parām – superior; जीवभूताम् jīva-bhūtām – the life-giving; महाबाहो mahābāho – O mighty-armed; यया yayā – by which; इदम् idam – this; धार्यते dhāryate – is sustained; जगत् jagat – the world.

—: Understanding The Verse :—

— ॐ श्रीकृष्णाय नमः ॐ —

Having described the apara-prakṛti—the lower, insentient nature composed of the eightfold matrix of elements and mental faculties—Bhagwān Shri Krishna now reveals a higher truth.

He introduces para-prakṛti, His supreme nature, the Consciousness —now manifest in the form of the jīva-bhūta, the individual self who enlivens and sustains the world from within.

— ॐ श्रीरामाय नमः ॐ —

This higher prakṛti is not another entity divorced from the Lord; it is His own eternal radiance, His cit-śakti, the conscious that knows, experiences, and upholds the cosmos.

This para-prakṛti is **the indwelling Self in all beings**—the puruṣa, the kṣetrajña, the knower of the field—through whom the universe is energized, and held animated through beings.

Together, these two prakṛtis—**the lower, mutable matrix of matter, and the higher, immutable essence of life**—form the totality of the Lord's cosmic manifestation.

The world, as we experience it, rests on this sacred duality.

—: Key Sanskrit Terms :—

— ॐ तत् सत् ॐ —

The verse here lifts into a higher register. Sanskrit lets अपरा परा प्रकृति apara and parā prakṛti glow like two interwoven flames, while जीवभूताम् jīva-bhūtām flickers with living presence. महाबाहो mahā-bāho anchors the vastness in human breath.

The language does not divide; it reveals a subtle duality within one great field. The Sanskrit feels like a bridge between seen and unseen —with matter and life listening to each other through syllables.

Gaining knowledge is always a spiral—ever stay circling in tighter pattern—eventually honing in to the centre;
and here too we will continue to circle closer,
breath by breath, word by blessed word of the Bhagavad-Gītā—
into the still, glowing heart of the meaning of existence.

— ॐ —

अपरा इयम् (apara iyam):
"This is inferior."
Shri Bhagwān marks a clear distinction: the eightfold prakṛti, though vast and wondrous, is अपरा apara — the lower nature.
Though it constitutes all forms and forces, it lacks self-luminosity; it is dependent, mutable, and perishable.
In the context of Gītā chapter 13, it is the field (क्षेत्र kṣetra)— rather than the higher entity: the knower of the field (क्षेत्रज्ञ kṣetrajña).

— ॐ —

इतः तु अन्यां प्रकृति विद्धि (itastvanyāṁ prakṛtiṁ viddhi):
"But different from this, know another prakṛti of Mine."
इतः Itas तु tu अन्यां anyām — besides this; but; another—But besides this exists another -- which is "different and higher."
There exists another dimension of My being, the परा प्रकृति parā prakṛti, which is not tainted into inertness—like the eightfold अपरा apara—but is pristine consciousness, self-aware, and paramount and vital.

— ॐ —

मे परम् (me parām):

"My supreme nature."

Here the Lord claims ownership not merely of the material matrix but of the conscious soul-substance itself.

परम् Parām signals transcendence — a higher order of being that is not subject to decay, division, or ignorance.

— ॐ —

जीवभूतां (jīvabhūtām):

"In the form of the Jīva."

This higher prakṛti manifests as the living souls — the jīvas, individual sparks of consciousness. Though seemingly many, each is an expression of the one indivisible Spirit, temporarily encased within the veils of mind and matter.

— ॐ —

यया इदं धार्यते जगत् (yayedaṁ dhāryate jagat):

"By which यया इदं this world जगत् is upheld धार्यते."

The world, though composed of inert matter, is animated, sustained, and enlivened by the presence of the living souls. It is through the jīva-śakti that the lifeless prakṛti is quickened into the dance of life.

Without the animating consciousness, the universe would be but a heap of machinery in motion—fully automatic, no free-will.

—: *In Brief* :—

— ॐ श्रीकृष्णाय नमः ॐ —

Bhagwān Shri Krishna here completes the vision of His cosmic nature by revealing its twofold principle.

While the earlier verse enumerated Lord's **apara**-prakṛti—
the insentient energies that compose the material and mental universe;
here Shri Krishna speaks of His **para**-prakṛti,
the supreme conscious essence:
the jīva-bhūtaḥ,
the living self that illumines and animates all things.

— ॐ श्रीरामाय नमः ॐ —

This introduces a profound metaphysical duality within the Divine's manifestation: the interplay of the so-called "unconscious" nature and "conscious" spirit.

Do know: the "unconscious" is merely an appearance.

When we go deep – everything is found to be conscious.
But when that consciousness becomes imbued with inertness
—operating strictly mechanically, displaying no free-will—
then it has become molded into what we call "dead" matter—
which of course too is very much alive.

This apara is the lower matrix of Braham
—very much conscious—but mechanical,
bereft of free-will;
and such of these waves of consciousness— in the ocean of
consciousness satt-chitt-ānanda braham—are called the lower अपरा
aparā prakriti.

In contrast to the lower **aparā** is the higher, the **parā**.
This para-prakṛti is none other than the immortal spark of Divinity
residing in each being.

It is the soul, the Jiva—within each and everyone.
It witnesses. It has a will.
It does not merely enact like matter—with zero degrees of
freedom—it lives, it learns, it exercise choices.

And these choices may not be free—as within creatures who are
driven by instincts encoded in their dna—but these are choices
still—which makes them move hither, thither driven by experiences
and their wants.

Remember: this Jiva or soul is the eternal witness, untouched by
the fluctuations of matter—and yet the very ground upon which all
movement occurs.

Though often veiled by ignorance and ego, the essence of the Jiva
remains ever-pure, ever-luminous, and ever-free, having as its
centre: **the Ātmā pure.**

**Never forget: There is Jiva in all—in each and every creature;
and that Jīva is not a separate distinct entity;
but he is verily the ray of the One Divine Sun—
he is a fragment (aṁśa) of Bhagwān Himself, timeless and
indivisible.**

The lower nature, aparā-prakṛti, operates through the laws of
cause and effect, driven by guṇas, constantly in flux.
But it does not operate just for itself—what avail this show if there
is none watching?

There is the parā—the observer, the witness, for which the aparā weaves this show.

It is jaḍa, inert—no free-will of its own. It stays dependent on the parā—the purusha—whom he serves.

The show goes on for the pleasure of the Witness, the Observer.

Parā is the conscious principle—the higher prakṛti—which lends vitality, meaning, and purpose to this cosmic show going on.

— ॐ भवरोगस्य भेषजाय नमः ॐ —

Just as a puppet cannot move without the guiding hand, so too prakṛti cannot weave these shows without the animating presence of the Self.

The world of names and forms is a shadow-play held together by the silent light of consciousness.

Thus, Shri Krishna declares: अपरेयमितस्त्वन्यां प्रकृतिं विद्धि मे पराम् apareyam-itastvanyāṁ prakṛtiṁ viddhi me parām, "Know this other prakṛti of Mine, higher than the previous one."

The entire creation, from the gross to the subtle, from the inert to the aware, is sustained by this interplay between the objective and the subjective, the seen and the seer, the mutable and the eternal.

Lord-God is sporting, and this cosmos is like a gargantuan yajña being performed for His pleasure by the play of parā and aparā prakṛti; a sacred offering composed of His own dual energies—matter and spirit, body and soul, form and formless.

— ॐ परमानन्दाय नमः ॐ —

It is with this comprehensive vision that Shri Krishna now prepares to lead Arjuna—and through him all of us—into a more penetrating understanding of the mysteries of creation.

In the verses that follow, Shri Krishna will reaffirm that beyond these prakṛtis stands He Himself: the Supreme-Self, the ultimate absolute, the substratum, the sovereign source of all beings and things.

We shall hear how the cosmos and all beings arise from Him—and eventually rest in Him. Remember: **He alone is. Other than Him, there exists nothing else.**

— ॐ तत् सत् ॐ —

Before we move on, let us bow in reverence to this sacred verse—a timeless beacon of wisdom guiding seekers for ages. Write it by hand, reflect on its meaning, and chant it aloud, for these sounds alone carry the authenticity of that era. The world may have changed but the living vibration of these Sanskrit sounds still remain as original as they were when Bhagwān Shri Krishna Himself walked the earth and imparted these teachings.

— ॐ —

अपरेयमितस्त्वन्यां प्रकृतिं विद्धि मे पराम् ।
aparēyamitastvanyāṁ prakṛtiṁ viddhi me parām
जीवभूतां महाबाहो ययेदं धार्यते जगत् ॥७-५॥
jīvabhūtāṁ mahābāho yayedaṁ dhāryate jagat (7-5)

अपरेयमितस्त्वन्यां प्रकृतिं विद्धि मे पराम् ।
aparēyamitastvanyāṁ prakṛtiṁ viddhi me parām
जीवभूतां महाबाहो ययेदं धार्यते जगत् ॥७-५॥
jīvabhūtāṁ mahābāho yayedaṁ dhāryate jagat (7-5)

ॐ तत्सदिति श्रीमद्भगवद्गीतासूपनिषत्सु ब्रह्मविद्यायां योगशास्त्रे श्रीकृष्णार्जुनसंवादे
om tatsaditi śrīmadbhagavadgītāsūpaniṣatsu brahmavidyāyāṁ yogaśāstre śrīkṛṣṇārjunasaṁvāde
ज्ञानविज्ञानयोगो नाम सप्तमोऽध्यायः श्लोकः ५
jñānavijñānayogo nāma saptamo'dhyāyaḥ ślokaḥ 5

Om-Tat-Sat—Om (Braham) is the sole Reality. In the Yogic Scripture on the Science-of-Braham, the Shrimada-Bhāgvada-Gītā Upanishad, we hereby conclude Shloka 5 of the Dialogue between Shrī Krishna and Arjuna entitled Jnana-Vijnana-Yoga, Canto VII.

— ॐ श्रीकृष्णाय नमः ॐ —

The ancient verses in Krishna's voice—pulsate like the hidden Flames.
O thou flaming One! O breath behind all breathing!
O thou Âtmâ concealed in all forms—men & creatures—
May we never stay forgetful of Thee.

But alas! Men of this age, stay bowed before outer forms & glitter—
They remain forgetful of the Âtmâ—the inner sustainer.

They stay praising the outer garment,
They ignore the living wearer neath the garb.

The Rishis' hearts bend in quiet anguish remembering how—
—The higher nature, the secret Sun beneath the skin—
Which once shone bright in every heart—now lies forgotten.

O Living Light, return to memory,
Lest the world mistake itself for dead matter.

I Too Didst Feel the "Memory" Stir in Me—Once Upon
Aye, once upon. A long time ago 'twas.
A soft ache. A flicker of 'I' that was pristinely pure.
But then—the "system" forced me to return back to its arms.

Aye, I turned. I returned. Back to the endless running on treadmill.
Back to pats-on-back. Back to dust. Back to applause. Back to the earthly.
I let the Soul fall down—and it has been silent ever since.

ॐ गीता श्लोकः ७.६ – GĪTĀ VERSE 7.6

ॐ श्रीमद्भगवद्गीतासूपनिषत्सु ब्रह्मविद्यायां योगशास्त्रे श्रीकृष्णार्जुनसंवादे
om śrīmadbhagavadgītāsūpaniṣatsu brahmavidyāyāṃ yogaśāstre śrīkṛṣṇārjunasaṃvāde
ज्ञानविज्ञानयोगो नाम सप्तमोऽध्यायः श्लोकः ६
jñānavijñānayogo nāma saptamo'dhyāyaḥ ślokaḥ 6

— ॐ —

एतद्योनीनि भूतानि सर्वाणीत्युपधारय ।

etadyonīni bhūtāni sarvāṇītyupadhāraya

अहं कृत्स्नस्य जगतः प्रभवः प्रलयस्तथा ॥ ७-६ ॥

ahaṃ kṛtsnasya jagataḥ prabhavaḥ pralayastathā (7-6)

Know, O Arjuna, that all beings have evolved from this twofold nature of Mine. I am the origin of this whole creation, and into Me again everything submerges in the end. (7.6)

—: *Word-by-Word* :—

एतत् etat – this; योनीनि yonīni – as the origin; भूतानि bhūtāni – all beings; सर्वाणि sarvāṇi – all; इति iti – thus; उपधारय upadhāraya – understand; अहम् aham – I; कृत्स्नस्य kṛtsnasya – of the entire; जगतः jagataḥ – universe; प्रभवः prabhavaḥ – the origin; प्रलयः pralayaḥ – the dissolution; तथा tathā – as well.

—: *Understanding The Verse* :—

— ॐ श्रीकृष्णाय नमः ॐ —

With this verse, Bhagwān Shri Krishna brings forth a sublime revelation: that all beings—animate and inanimate, high and low— emerge from and are sustained by His twofold prakṛti, the lower material nature (apara-prakṛti) and the higher conscious principle (para-prakṛti).

These twin energies are the womb of the universe, from which all forms arise and into which they return.

— ॐ श्रीरामाय नमः ॐ —

Krishna affirms that He is the ādibhūta—the primal source of all creation—and the antabhāva—the final resting place of all beings.

In this vision, the universe is not a mechanical occurrence but a living manifestation of the Divine.

All of existence, with its rhythms of birth, growth, dissolution, and rebirth, is but the outward play of His own being.

To know this is to rise above the illusion of separation and perceive the sacred unity of all things within the eternal, indivisible presence of the Lord.

—: *Key Sanskrit Terms* :—

— ॐ तत सत ॐ —

The cadence gathers toward origin and return. Sanskrit whispers एतद्योनीनि भूतानि etad-yonīni bhūtāni as if naming countless births, while अहं कृत्स्नस्य जगतः प्रभवः aham kṛtsnasya jagataḥ prabhavaḥ glows with quiet sourcefulness. प्रलय pralayaḥ drifts like a soft dusk. The verse does not dramatize creation; it breathes it. Sanskrit becomes the tide itself, carrying all beings out of and back into the same vast, resonant depth.

Remember pilgrim: The verses of Gītā do not hide or resist us—they are waiting to be discovered by the earnest. The Sanskrit within this verse awaits too—not to be conquered, but to be seen. To be met. And to then be **remembered**.

— ॐ —

एतद्योनीनि (etadyonīni):
"These are the wombs" —
Here, योनि yoni is a profoundly evocative word. It means womb, source, matrix.
एतत्-etat योनि -yoni indicates that all beings arise from the twofold प्रकृति prakṛti — the lower material (अपरा aparā) and the higher conscious (अपरा parā) natures — already introduced.
Thus, the entire universe is born of the Divine's own Nature, not external to Him.

— ॐ —

भूतानि सर्वाणि (bhūtāni sarvāṇi):
"सर्वाणि All भूतानि beings."
Not a single creature exists outside this sacred emanation.
From the smallest insect to the non-human beings soaring in vimāna, the highest celestial (देव devas)—all exist within this Lord's dual play of nature -- all rooted in His consciousness.
सर्वाणि Sarvāṇi emphasizes totality: no existence lies apart from His manifest existence.

— ॐ —

उपधारय (upadhāraya):
"Understand deeply, grasp well."

The Lord urges Arjuna—and all of us—not merely to hear, but to realize this truth in the depths of our beingness.

Remember: **Upadhāraya** is an intimate, contemplative absorption, where knowledge becomes a living certainty.

— ॐ —

अहं कृत्स्नस्य जगतः प्रभवः (ahaṁ kṛtsnasya jagataḥ prabhavaḥ):

"I am the source of the whole universe."

प्रभवः Prabhavaḥ — the original arising, the primal emergence.

Shri Bhagwān declares Himself the fountainhead from which all existence flows.

The totality (कृत्स्नस्य जगतः kṛtsnasya jagataḥ) — seen and unseen, gross and subtle — springs from His Being.

— ॐ —

प्रलयस्तथा (pralayas tathā):

"And also the dissolution."

Just as He is the origin (प्रभव prabhava), so too is He the final absorption (प्रलय pralaya).

The cycle of creation and destruction, the ceaseless rhythm of सृष्टिः sṛṣṭi (creation), स्थिति sthiti (sustenance), and लय laya (dissolution), is entirely contained within His infinite reality.

—: *In Brief* :—

— ॐ श्रीकृष्णाय नमः ॐ —

In this verse, Bhagwān Shri Krishna discloses the majestic continuity of creation and dissolution, holding that all beings (भूतानि bhūtāni) arise from the union of His two prakṛtis and return into Him at the close of the cosmic cycle.

This is not a distant metaphysical abstraction but the living truth of all existence.

— ॐ श्रीरामाय नमः ॐ —

The term bhūtāni encompasses every grade of being—celestial, terrestrial, and sub-terrestrial; conscious and unconscious; gross and subtle.

From the simplest atom to the highest god, all are born through the interplay of the inert matrix of matter (apara-prakṛti) and the life-giving principle of consciousness (para-prakṛti).

These two are not independent; they are Bhagwān Shri Krishna's own divine energies, seamlessly woven into the fabric of creation.

Just as water vapor condenses to form clouds, drifts across the sky, and finally returns as rain to the earth, so too this diversity of the universe—
- **arises from the Lord,**
- dances **for a time within the realm of manifest** forms and names,
- and then, at the **destined** moment, **dissolves back into Him.**

The Lord is both the beginningless origin and the timeless dissolution.

He is the unmoved mover—the silent ground from which all movement emerges and into which it subsides—submerges, gets dissolved at the **designated time ordained.**

Aye—the designated time is fixed, unchanged
—in line with our karmas and Daiva, our Destiny—
and the human so-called "self-will" really counts for nix.

That which does come to pass by the force of alleged human-will was in fact established there by the will of God.

The human heart beats, or even a blade of grass stirs—only because He so allowed it.

All is Bhagwān but He however is not transformed or diminished by creation—despite this play of transformations going on.

The Consciousness does not perish with the "perishable" matter— merely changes form.

The play of changes does not exhaust God. He is inexhaustible.

All this is merely manifestations—a play of His śaktis, a divine sport (līlā).

Although the Lord pervades all things, He remains ever beyond them—unchanging, complete, and eternal.

ॐ पूर्णमदः पूर्णमिदं पूर्णात् पूर्णमुदच्यते । पूर्णस्य पूर्णमादाय पूर्णमेवावशिष्यते ।
om pūrṇamadaḥ pūrṇamidaṁ pūrṇāt pūrṇamudacyate,
pūrṇasya pūrṇamādāya pūrṇamevāvaśiṣyate ,

That One is infinite, complete, entire.

This entire manifest universe has emerged from the Fullness of His entireness.

The Manifest universe does not become subtracted from the Unmanifest Braham .

The waves still remain as the Ocean—albeit defiled into forms.

This universe is humungous, but even the vastness of the visible cosmos is still minuscule.

The Ocean, our source—satt-chitt-ānanda braham, the waveless ocean of existence-bliss-consciousness—can never be fathomed or known.

— ॐ विश्वभावनाय नमः ॐ —

This vision dissolves the illusion of autonomy.

The cosmos is not separate from its source,

nor is the jīva—this little wave—isolated in its plays of endeavoring, striving, straining.

Despite its smallness, this flickering little wave remains very much one within the ocean.

And for that reason Sanātana-Dharma declares: तत् त्वम् असि tat-tvam-asi— you too are He.

To see the world as springing from, resting in, and returning to the Supreme is to behold the great unity that underlies all diversity.

It is to see that birth and death, appearance and disappearance, are but the waves rising and falling upon the ocean of the Lord's beingness.

— ॐ श्रीकृष्णाय नमः ॐ —

Having declared that He is the origin and final repose of all that exists, Shri Krishna prepares next to speak of His immanence—the way in which He pervades all beings, yet remains transcendent.

This will further deepen the vision—preparing the heart to receive the ultimate Truth: that **He alone is the cause and effect, the essence and substratum—within and behind each and everything.**

In the next unfolding, Bhagwān Shri Krishna reveals how all beings, things, forces, are sustained by Him, yet He remains unentangled.

— ॐ तत् सत् ॐ —

Before we move on, let us bow in reverence to this sacred verse—a timeless beacon of wisdom guiding seekers for ages. Write it by hand, reflect on its meaning, and chant it aloud, for these sounds alone carry the authenticity of that era. The world may have changed but the living vibration of these Sanskrit sounds still remain as original as they were when Bhagwān Shri Krishna Himself walked the earth and imparted these teachings.

— ॐ —

एतद्योनीनि भूतानि सर्वाणीत्युपधारय ।
etadyonīni bhūtāni sarvāṇītyupadhāraya
अहं कृत्स्नस्य जगतः प्रभवः प्रलयस्तथा ॥७-६॥
ahaṁ kṛtsnasya jagataḥ prabhavaḥ pralayastathā (7-6)

— ॐ —

एतद्योनीनि भूतानि सर्वाणीत्युपधारय ।
etadyonīni bhūtāni sarvāṇītyupadhāraya
अहं कृत्स्नस्य जगतः प्रभवः प्रलयस्तथा ॥७-६॥
ahaṁ kṛtsnasya jagataḥ prabhavaḥ pralayastathā (7-6)

ॐ तत्सदिति श्रीमद्भगवद्गीतासूपनिषत्सु ब्रह्मविद्यायां योगशास्त्रे श्रीकृष्णार्जुनसंवादे
om tatsaditi śrīmadbhagavadgītāsūpaniṣatsu brahmavidyāyāṁ yogaśāstre śrīkṛṣṇārjunasaṁvāde
ज्ञानविज्ञानयोगो नाम सप्तमोऽध्यायः श्लोकः ६
jñānavijñānayogo nāma saptamo'dhyāyaḥ ślokaḥ 6

Om-Tat-Sat—Om (Braham) is the sole Reality. In the Yogic Scripture on the Science-of-Braham,
the Shrimada-Bhāgvada-Gītā Upanishad, we hereby conclude Shloka 6 of the Dialogue between
Shrī Krishna and Arjuna entitled Jnana-Vijnana-Yoga, Canto VII.

— ॐ श्रीकृष्णाय नमः ॐ —

Hearken O child of fleeting breaths, of stardust & noise—
Let the truth now ring—in Krishna's sonorous voice:
"All beings arise from Me; they play; then submerse back in Me."
Dust becomes **tree**; falls on forest floor as **leaf**; then re-becomes **Dust**.

It's not chance & chaos that stirs the world into forms and names—
But the sacred Divine-Will—of the one & only—Bhagwan Shri Krishna.

Creation's breath is drawn from Him alone,
And when Life stills down into Death—it rests in that Same Womb.

Mark, O Jiva, this Dance thou jive is not thy own—
Despite thyself, thou just stay Waltzing—within the rhythm of Whole.

All beings arise from that Solitary Silence.
Yet men worship only the noise of names & shapes.

Men stay bowed before the multitudes of beings & things—
Yet ignore the Source, the common origin—which incredibly is One & Only.

The Param-Ātmā is the hidden womb,
From Him alone every form is born.

Mostly He watches, Stays aloof;
Yet at times He mourns the scattered vision of the worldly fools,
For whom their very own Origin remains forgotten.

God 'laments'—as it were:
" He was born of Me. He cried into My air.
He walked by My strength. He laughed in My delights.
He moved around on My earth. He ate what I provided.
And as to Me, God?—he has totally forgotten! "

Man stays forgetful of the Hand that holds his life, his stars.
Man runs about—and wherever he turns, there is just only He—
And yet the ingrate fool—stays blind and oblivious to God!

ॐ गीता श्लोकः ७.७ – Gītā Verse 7.7

ॐ श्रीमद्भगवद्गीतासूपनिषत्सु ब्रह्मविद्यायां योगशास्त्रे श्रीकृष्णार्जुनसंवादे
om śrīmadbhagavadgītāsūpaniṣatsu brahmavidyāyāṁ yogaśāstre śrīkṛṣṇārjunasaṁvāde
ज्ञानविज्ञानयोगो नाम सप्तमोऽध्यायः श्लोकः ७
jñānavijñānayogo nāma saptamo'dhyāyaḥ ślokaḥ 7

— ॐ —

मत्तः परतरं नान्यत्किञ्चिदस्ति धनञ्जय ।
mattaḥ parataraṁ nānyatkiñcidasti dhanañjaya
मयि सर्वमिदं प्रोतं सूत्रे मणिगणा इव ॥ ७-७ ॥
mayi sarvamidaṁ protaṁ sūtre maṇigaṇā iva (7-7)

Besides and beyond Me, O Dhananjaya, there exists nothing else. Within Me alone is this universe strung—like gems threaded on a string. (7.7)

—: *Word-by-Word* :—

मत्तः mattaḥ – beyond Me; परतरम् parataram – superior; न na – not; अन्यत् anyat – anything else; किञ्चित् kiñcit – whatsoever; अस्ति asti – exists; धनञ्जय dhanañjaya – O Dhananjaya (Arjuna); मयि mayi – in Me; सर्वम् sarvam – all this; इदम् idam – this; प्रोतम् protam – is pervaded; सूत्रे sūtre – on a thread; मणिगणाः mani-gaṇāḥ – pearls; इव iva – like.

—: *Understanding The Verse* :—

— ॐ श्रीकृष्णाय नमः ॐ —

With this verse, Bhagwān Shri Krishna makes a bold and all-encompassing declaration of His supreme non-dual nature.
He affirms that **there exists nothing beyond or apart from Him**—
He is both the **ultimate substratum**;
and He is the **indwelling presence in all.**

Just as a thread holds together a string of gems—unseen yet the vital requisite—God upholds and permeates the entire cosmos, which is strung upon Him.

This metaphor—the connecting thread running through the pearls—evokes the intimate immanence of the Divine.

— ॐ श्रीरामाय नमः ॐ —

While the manifold names and forms of the universe shine with individuality, they are all bound by and dependent upon the unchanging presence of the Lord.

This verse stands as a majestic proclamation of the Unity that underlies all apparent multiplicity.

It paves the way for a deeper recognition of Bhagwān as the inner essence of all that exists.

—: Key Sanskrit Terms :—

— ॐ तत् सत् ॐ —

Now the verse becomes a final, luminous binding.

Sanskrit lets मयि सर्वमिदं प्रोतं mayi sarvam idaṁ protam stretch like a subtle thread through the breath, and मणिगणा इव सूत्रे maṇi-gaṇā iva sūtre shimmers with delicate precision. धनञ्जय Dhanañjaya holds the image in place.

The language does not assert supremacy—it quietly displays cohesion. The Sanskrit itself feels like the invisible string upon which the words—the shining jewels of the Bhagavad-Gītā—rest -- glinting in silent ordered wonder.

Let us linger with the Sanskrit as with pearls strung on an invisible thread. "There is nothing higher than Me; all rests upon Me". Each syllable glistens like jewel resting upon a string now unseen.

— ॐ —

मत्तः परतरं न अन्यत् (mattaḥ parataram nānyat):
"There is nothing higher than Me."

This proclamation is absolute. Final.
Game over. Finito. The-End.
End of the road. The buck stops right here. Period.

Higher?
There doesn't even exist anything beyond, let alone higher.
Singularity reached. The Absolute End.

मत्तः Mattaḥ — from Me;

परतरं parataram — superior, beyond;

न अन्यत् na anyat — none exists.

Shri Bhagwān declares that He is the supreme pinnacle, the ultimate substratum (adhiṣṭhāna) upon which all things rest.
Beyond Him, no other realm or reality abides.
All existence is encompassed within Krishna's Beingness.

— ॐ —

धनञ्जय (dhanañjaya):
"O Dhananjaya" — "O conqueror of wealth."
Arjuna, addressed by this noble epithet, is reminded that true conquest is not the winning of earthly riches but the acquisition of the supreme wealth of Self-knowledge.

The Lord beckons Arjuna toward this higher triumph.

— ॐ —

मयि सर्वम् इदं प्रोतम् (mayi sarvam idaṁ protaṁ):
"In Me, all this is strung."
प्रोतम् Protam evokes the image of threading — an intimate, hidden binding together.

It is not that the Lord merely surrounds or supports the universe from outside; rather, He pervades it from within, secretly holding all forms and movements in the unity of His own Self.

— ॐ —

सूत्रे मणिगणाः इव (sūtre maṇigaṇā iva):
"Like pearls on a string."
Ah, what an exquisite simile that!
Pearls appear discrete and beautiful, but it is the invisible thread that holds them in order and gives them coherence.
Similarly, the Lord is the unseen thread weaving the manifold universe into a single, living Unity.

Without the thread, the pearls scatter and lose their meaning; without the Lord, the universe would dissolve into chaos—**nay, the universe wouldn't even exist. Nothing will.**

—: In Brief :—

— ॐ श्रीकृष्णाय नमः ॐ —

Bhagwān Shri Krishna utters a truth so profound that it resounds through the core of Vedānta and echoes the vision of unity seen by the sages: **"There exists nothing whatsoever apart from Me, O Dhananjaya. All this world is strung upon Me, like pearls on a string."**

— ॐ श्रीरामाय नमः ॐ —

The Lord here has removed every vestige of duality and declares His all-encompassing, all-pervading reality.

In saying that nothing exists beyond Him, Krishna does not deny the world's appearance, but affirms that its very essence is none other than Himself.

The world is not other than God.
All this is He—the Singularity of the Absolute.
The universe is in Him—and is by Him -- and is made of Him.

— ॐ बलरामाग्रजाय नमः ॐ —

The analogy of pearls on a thread is exquisitely chosen. The gems represent the multitude of forms—variegated, beautiful, distinct—yet each is sustained by a subtle reality hidden from view.

The thread is unseen, but without it, the entire garland collapses. So too, while the names and forms of the world may dazzle the eyes, they are all upheld by the unseen presence of the Lord, who pervades them silently, intimately, and completely.

— ॐ धर्मसंस्थापकाय नमः ॐ —

Mark well mortal: As the potter's clay, though shaped into vessels of a million kinds, remains but the one substance; similarly all that exists are different forms of the One Supreme-Reality—varied in their outer guises, yet of and from Him alone.

All is the One without a second: satt-chitt-ānanda braham—whose manifest form in Bhagwān Shri Krishna.

— ॐ विश्वामित्रप्रियाय नमः ॐ —

A subtle philosophical harmony is achieved in this verse.

In the previous verse, Krishna had spoken of the universe arising from and dissolving into His twofold prakṛti.

One might be led to imagine the Lord as distinct from His creation—as a potter from the pot. But here, He corrects that notion: nānyat kiñcit asti, "There is nothing else besides Me."

This is not a mere poetic sentiment, but a declaration of non-duality (advaya-tattva).

The Lord is both the material cause (upādāna-kāraṇa) and the efficient cause (nimitta-kāraṇa), the creator and the creation, the thread and the beads, the unseen essence and the visible form.

— ॐ शाकटासुरभञ्जनाय नमः ॐ —

Just as water, when frozen, appears as ice, yet remains water in essence; or gold, fashioned into ornaments, never ceases to be gold—so too, this manifold universe is but the Lord, appearing in countless guises.

It is not illusion in the sense of falsehood, but illusion in the sense of misapprehension—**the reality is One, though His forms are many.**

— ॐ यज्वने नमः ॐ —

This verse stands as a pillar in the edifice of divine philosophy of Sanātana-Dharma: the unity of all that exists in the being of Bhagwān.

There is no within or without, no other or second. To realize this truth is to transcend all fragmentation, all fear, all bondage.

To bring this abstract vision into concrete perception, Shri Krishna shall, in the following verses, illustrate how He is present in all that sustains and enlivens the universe.

It is **just He** manifesting in nature, in qualities, in experiences, as the essence behind each and everything.

Moving forward we shall descend into that radiant unfolding.

— ॐ तत् सत ॐ —

Before we move on, let us bow in reverence to this sacred verse—a timeless beacon of wisdom guiding seekers for ages. Write it by hand, reflect on its meaning, and chant it aloud, for these sounds alone carry the authenticity of that era. The world may have changed but the living vibration of these Sanskrit sounds still remain as original as they were when Bhagwān Shri Krishna Himself walked the earth and imparted these teachings.

— ॐ —

मत्तः परतरं नान्यत्किञ्चिदस्ति धनञ्जय ।
mattaḥ parataraṁ nānyatkiñcidasti dhanañjaya
मयि सर्वमिदं प्रोतं सूत्रे मणिगणा इव ॥ ७-७॥
mayi sarvamidaṁ protaṁ sūtre maṇigaṇā iva (7-7)

मत्तः परतरं नान्यत्किञ्चिदस्ति धनञ्जय ।
mattaḥ parataraṁ nānyatkiñcidasti dhanañjaya
मयि सर्वमिदं प्रोतं सूत्रे मणिगणा इव ॥ ७-७॥
mayi sarvamidaṁ protaṁ sūtre maṇigaṇā iva (7-7)

ॐ तत्सदिति श्रीमद्भगवद्गीतासूपनिषत्सु ब्रह्मविद्यायां योगशास्त्रे श्रीकृष्णार्जुनसंवादे
om tatsaditi śrīmadbhagavadgītāsūpaniṣatsu brahmavidyāyāṁ yogaśāstre śrīkṛṣṇārjunasaṁvāde
ज्ञानविज्ञानयोगो नाम सप्तमोऽध्यायः श्लोकः ७
jñānavijñānayogo nāma saptamo'dhyāyaḥ ślokaḥ 7

Om-Tat-Sat—Om (Braham) is the sole Reality. In the Yogic Scripture on the Science-of-Braham, the Shrimada-Bhāgvada-Gītā Upanishad, we hereby conclude Shloka 7 of the Dialogue between Shrī Krishna and Arjuna entitled Jnana-Vijnana-Yoga, Canto VII.

— ॐ श्रीकृष्णाय नमः ॐ —

Man loves the worldly gems. He clutches at the beads.
Family, flesh, riches, fame—entire throng strung on the fabric of space-time.
So bright, so tangible—yet so evanescent—fluxing wave-like.
But man never stops to ask—What binds them?
What's their common thread?
Whence their beginning? Their beingness?

Listen O world: All is One. There is nothing else here other than HE.
No second. No other Reality. No other light. No one but HE.

All things dance upon His presence—He, Krishna.

Even the illusion that hangs upon thee—is by dint of the Māyā of His.

God wishes to keep the sport ongoing, continue playing out—
And so His Māyā keeps ye in Ignorance. Ye stay befooled.

But there are no barriers to the Exit-Door, to Quit the play.
So be the Wise one who leaves the sporting arena altogether—
To verily join God in the gallery.

Yes, gain thy oneness in Him—re-become the God ye are.

O Pilgrim, look far—across the panoptic line of time,
See Bhagwān Shri Krishna standing: steady, radiant, horizon-born.

To lead us out—Krishna arrived as a fiery new Dawn,
Yet humans stay swarmed in their own little fights, petty storms.

Krishna's lament is not anger, but the exhaustion of Eternity—
Watching small minds—His lil fragments—stunt themselves into nothing.

Come, O wanderer, widen thy gaze.
Meet God Krishna in the Gitā—where the soul gets to meet the Sky.

On the ridge where old winds recite the Law of Great Heights,
I hear the Gitā—like drumstone under thunderfoot.
There Krishna stands—ridge-king—sky-hinged—world-still.
He does not appeal to humans. He commands the horizon.

Rise—tells the ridge. Arise—says the skyline.
Let every fear fall down the cliff -- like loose gravel.

Arise, O mortal, let Sanātana-Dharma be your Stance, not a slogan.
Unvanish. Be the Mountain. Remain no more a mere wisp of smoke.

Once, a man tried to become mist—
Thinking mist is safe from stones and arrows.
But a kingdom rotted while he faded.

Then Krishna rode into his dream with the Gita in His palm,
Not as a minstrel, but as Time with eyes like dawn-iron.
"Be the lion who need not roar," said Krishna,
"Yet whose presence the forest always remembers."

So the man returned as a Boundary—
And adharma found the road blocked—by just that single soul!

O mortal, lift thy face to the inner Sun!
Let its Brilliance scatter the Night of Ignorance and Sin!

O man, thou art not a trembling spark in hostile winds!
Thou art the Radiant Source itself!
Come, aver: अहं ब्रह्मास्मि aham-braham-asmi.

The Light by which sorrow is seen—is greater than sorrow.
The Flame by which fear is known—is greater than fear.

Shine in the certainty of the Self—the Ātmā
—of which Ātmā, Bhagwān Krishna Himself came down to teach!

Let no shadow persuade thee of smallness!
Even right now, ye are fragment of the Luminous Being Himself;

And who knows what more is there to thy destiny?
No more just a wave—but the entireness of Ocean could be thee!

<u>Carved upon the eternal lintel of Truth:</u>
इदम् प्रोतं सूत्रे मणिगणा इव idam protam sūtre maṇigaṇā iva
In me is everything strung—like pearls joined by unseen thread!

O world, hear the decree carried upon the ancient flames:
सर्वं खल्विदं ब्रह्म sarvam-khalvidam-braham, प्रोतं सूत्रे मणिगणा protam sūtre maṇigaṇā
All is a Oneness. There really is no fragmentation in the Infinite Sea.

Empires rise and fall beneath these inscriptions.
Worlds are born and dissolve—yet these lines endure.
Neither time nor decay can erode the clarity of Sanātana-Dharma.

O human, all that you call your joys and sorrows,
It all shimmers just within that indivisible Being; Braham!

The desert and the river, the wound and the balm,
The cry and the answer — all is the One Essence: Braham—
Whose manifest form is Bhagwān Shri Krishna.

O mortal, cease dividing the Indivisible,
See Unity where small minds invent ruptures,

That-One alone appears as the many,
Awaken into the wholeness of Bhagwān Shri Krishna!

O mortal, read the sacred engraving within the heart of Gitā:
The Knower stands beyond all changes and appearances.
That Witness is not subject to birth-death—and That-One thou art.

To recognize this is liberation. To abide in it is tranquility.
Thus speaks the Timeless Temple of Wisdom: Krishna's Bhagavad-Gitā.

ॐ गीता श्लोकः ७.८ – GĪTĀ VERSE 7.8

ॐ श्रीमद्भगवद्गीतासूपनिषत्सु ब्रह्मविद्यायां योगशास्त्रे श्रीकृष्णार्जुनसंवादे
om śrīmadbhagavadgītāsūpaniṣatsu brahmavidyāyāṁ yogaśāstre śrīkṛṣṇārjunasaṁvāde
ज्ञानविज्ञानयोगो नाम सप्तमोऽध्यायः श्लोकः ८
jñānavijñānayogo nāma saptamo'dhyāyaḥ ślokaḥ 8

— ॐ —

रसोऽहमप्सु कौन्तेय प्रभास्मि शशिसूर्ययोः ।
raso'hamapsu kaunteya prabhāsmi śaśisūryayoḥ
प्रणवः सर्ववेदेषु शब्दः खे पौरुषं नृषु ॥७-८॥
praṇavaḥ sarvavedeṣu śabdaḥ khe pauruṣaṁ nṛṣu (7-8)

Hearken, O Kuntī-son, I am all: in water, I am its sapidity; I am the radiance in the sun and moon; I am the sacred syllable Om of the Vedas; and I am the sound in aether, and the endeavor in men. (7.8)

---: *Word-by-Word* :---

रसः rasaḥ – taste; अहम् aham – I am; अप्सु apsu – in water; कौन्तेय kaunteya – O son of Kunti (Arjuna); प्रभा prabhā – light; अस्मि asmi – I am; शशि- सूर्ययोः śaśi-sūryayoḥ – of the moon and the sun; प्रणवः praṇavaḥ – the syllable Om; सर्ववेदेषु sarva-vedeṣu – in all the Vedas; शब्दः śabdaḥ – sound; खे khe – in the ether; पौरुषम् pauruṣam – the prowess; नृषु nṛṣu – in men.

---: *Understanding The Verse* :---

— ॐ श्रीकृष्णाय नमः ॐ —

Having declared that nothing exists apart from Him and that the universe is strung upon Him as pearls on a string, Bhagwān Shri Krishna now begins to illumine how His presence may be directly perceived in the world around us in the best possible way.

God does stay pervaded throughout the Creation, but He remains hidden to the world because He abides transcendent, aloof. He never does advert His presence—but unto the wise, He is within direct reach and easily ascertained.

He manifests as the very essence within things—for instance the taste in water, the radiance in the celestial orbs, the sacred resonance of the Vedas, the vibration within space, and the heroic impulse in humans.

The Lord—who is indeed everything in existence—gives, in this verse and the following, a short list to help us conceive of Him.

Mind it: The list is only illustrative, touching on the immediate relatable happenings of life—serving as hint unto the wise sādhaka (spiritual aspirant).

— ॐ श्रीसीतारक्षाय नमः ॐ —

This verse opens a luminous doorway for us—offering a vision of the Divine not merely as a remote Absolute, but as the immediate and intimate reality immanent in the most fundamental experiences of life.

Through such contemplative insight, devotion no longer stays confined to ritual or temple—it becomes the very act of perceiving, tasting, hearing, striving -- with Him alone as the essence of everything.

Lord-God Bhagwān Shri Krishna now begins to teach us how to see Him in all of Creation.

—: Key Sanskrit Terms :—

— ॐ तत सत ॐ —

Sanskrit here begins to shimmer like water itself, holding flavor inside the sounds of its vibrations. The soft glow of रसः rasaḥ moves through the breath, while प्रभास्मि शशिसूर्ययोः prabhāsmi śaśi-sūryayoḥ glints like light on rippling waves. प्रणवः praṇavaḥ, the sound of Oṃkāra rises quietly from the depths of sound; even खे khe seems to open into space.

The verse does not describe the Lord's immanence present throughout—it saturates the air with it. The Sanskrit becomes taste, light, and resonance at once, inviting the listener to feel divinity as sensation. So then let us sip the nectar of this śloka slowly, drop by golden drop, beginning with the Sanskrit blossoms from which its ambrosial essence is drawn.

— ॐ —

रसः अहम् अप्सु (rasaḥ aham apsu):
"अहम् I am the रसः sapidity in अप्सु water."
रस Rasa — the essence, taste, savor — is the vital sweetness that makes water life-giving and delightful.
अप्स Water, the most nurturing element, conceals within it the Lord's presence, tasted through its very रस rasa.

Thus, even the simplest act of drinking water becomes a hidden communion with the Divine.

— ॐ —

प्रभा अस्मि शशि-सूर्ययोः (prabhāsmi śaśi-sūryayoḥ):

"अस्मि I am the प्रभा radiance in the शशि moon and the सूर्य sun."

प्रभा Prabhā — light, effulgence — is the glory by which the सूर्य-शशि sun and moon shine.

The brilliance that illuminates day and night is none other than the Lord's own splendor.

This reveals that the celestial lights—seen worshipped across many cultures—are but reflections of His supreme radiance.

— ॐ —

प्रणवः सर्ववेदेषु (praṇavaḥ sarvavedeṣu):

"I am the syllable Om (प्रणव) in सर्व all the वेद Vedas."

प्रणव Praṇava, the sacred syllable Om, is the very seed of all Vedic wisdom. It encapsulates the cosmic vibration, the primal sound from which the universe unfolds.

That which is sung in the स्तुति hymns, chanted in the मंत्र mantras, and meditated upon in the heart — is but God's very own resonance.

— ॐ —

शब्दः खे (śabdaḥ khe):

"I am शब्द sound in the ख ether."

शब्द Śabda — sound — in खम् kham (space or ether) signifies the subtlest manifestation.

Please see verse 7.4 also which briefly talk of the महाभूत mahābhūta gross element and their respective तन्मात्र tanmātras.

In case of the elemental space, its subtle essence manifests as sound: खम् (kham – ether/space) → शब्दतन्मात्र (śabda-tanmātra – शब्द Śabda sound).

Sound—born as the subtle element of space—marks the invisible thread of existence, the unseen stirring before form arises.

The very possibility of communication is through the Lord having become manifest as Sound—शब्द the sacred pulse within vast silence.

— ॐ —

पौरुषं नृषु (pauruṣaṃ nṛṣu):

"I am the पौरुष virility, the strength in नृषु men."

पौरुष Pauruṣam — the heroic strength, vitality, spirit of endeavor — is not merely brute force but the noble vigor of striving, courage, and creativity.

In human beings (नर nara), it is the inner dynamism by which greatness is achieved, and it too is but a manifestation of the Lord.

—: *In Brief* :—

— ॐ श्रीकृष्णाय नमः ॐ —

रसोऽहमप्सु कौन्तेय प्रभास्मि शशिसूर्ययोः । प्रणवः सर्ववेदेषु शब्दः खे पौरुषं नृषु ॥

The Lord-God declares: "I am the rasa in water, the light of the moon and sun, the sacred syllable Om in the Vedas, the sound in space, and the virility, the heroic striving, in man."

In this exquisite verse, Bhagwān Shri Krishna unveils the Divine not in abstraction, but as the living essence within the most elemental experiences of life.

Each word presses divinity into the senses.
The tastes, scents, and echoes of the world are manifestations of the divine.
Dost thou have the eye, tongue, ear to perceive that O mortal?

— ॐ श्रीरामाय नमः ॐ —

Here, rasaḥ—the sapidity or essence in water—represents more than taste; it is that which quenches, refreshes, and gives vitality.

In this most immediate and life-sustaining element, Krishna reveals His presence. Every drop of water, when rightly seen, is not mere matter, but a touch of the Divine.

The tejas of the sun and moon—their radiance—is not merely physical brilliance, but the symbolic light of consciousness, of guidance, of life.

The sun dispels darkness without and the moon soothes the restlessness of the within mind. In both, the seeker may contemplate the ever-shining glory of the Lord, who is the eternal light behind all appearances.

— ॐ महादेवाय नमः ॐ —

प्रणवः सर्ववेदेषु 'Pranavaḥ sarva-vedeṣu'—Shri Krishna declares Himself to be Om, the primal sound of the Vedas.

Om is not just a syllable but the mystic vibration from which the cosmos itself emerged.
It is the sound-body of the Absolute, the seed of all mantra, and the spiritual pulse of the sacred word.
In chanting Om, one touches the threshold where name dissolves into formless Being.

The शब्दः खे śabdaḥ khe—sound in space—is another subtle revelation. Kha, or ākāśa (ether), is the subtlest of the five elements, and sound is its defining quality.

Every vibration, every spoken word, every resonance that travels through space is, in essence, a movement of the Divine.

The voice of the cosmos is none other than the voice of the Lord.

— ॐ योगीश्वराय नमः ॐ —

And finally, पौरुषं नृषु pauruṣaṁ nṛṣu—the energy of manhood, or the vital force of endeavor in humanity.

This is not limited to gendered virility, but signifies the noble impulse to strive, to overcome, to rise, to stand firm in dharma.

In every act of heroic will, in the flame of aspiration, Krishna reveals His presence as the inner mover of all karmas—and even more so in our actions driven by dharma.

— ॐ अहल्या शाप शमनाय नमः ॐ —

Thus, in this single verse, the Lord offers a sacred key: the world is not to be feared or renounced in despair, but to be penetrated with awakened vision.

To the wise, every experience becomes a pointer toward the Divine. The ordinary becomes extraordinary, the visible becomes the veil of the Invisible.

In the verses that follow, Shri Krishna shall continue to draw back the veil, naming further expressions of His divine presence in the manifest world.

Through this divine litany, the devotee in us is taught to see, not with the eyes of separation, but with the heart of Unity.

— ॐ बालकृष्णाय नमः ॐ —

As we proceed further, we shall behold more of the **sacred manifestations** through which God is to be remembered.

Remember: Though all is Braham, but it is **only** through the beautiful, sacred, divine, that we should venerate God.

Aye, not the profane but the sacred—for that is what Sanātana-Dharma is all about: a system which worships the beautiful, lasting, divine—and through that, to have sacred, beauty, permanence in our own life as well.

The other way round is also possible—which we see in these modern times—where it is **adharma that is venerated and has become institutionalized -- as a system that majorly brings just pain and suffering all around -- in people's life, and on earth and her creatures** —and which could end soon with the death of our species.

— ॐ रघुपतये नमः ॐ —

Yes, everything is indeed He: Braham,
but to be reminded of Him—whom we know of as the Lord-God --
we should dwell on the sacred, redeeming, emancipating, blissful
aspects of His
—and not on the dark that has been institutionalized by the stupid,
selfish, greedy few—
which though too is He, but which will have the exact reverse effect
in life on earth.

— ॐ करुणासागराय नमः ॐ —

The One consciousness Braham:
He is the saint—as well the sinner;
He is man—as well as the creatures and insects.
He is blissful joy—as well as pain and suffering.

Aye, all is Braham's sport, but at no time on history has ugliness,
wicked, evil, vileness become so much institutionalized than at
present times.

And this is a warning sign O human—indicating that your time on
earth may soon be up!

O human: Venerate the ugly, evil, bad, and that's what you will get
in life—along with the ensuing pain and suffering, **which always
remain conjoined with the dark and evil.**

Venerate the good, beautiful, divine; and that's what you will get in
life—blissful joy – **which ever remain conjoined with the sacred and
divine.**

But alas, O humans, thy ways have become dark and ugly.
Thou have forsaken Sanātana-Dharma—given to thee as the Vedas,
the breath of Bhagwān Shri Krishna -- the manifest form of satt-chitt-
ānanda braham, the ocean of existence-bliss-consciousness.
It is tragic that thou have abandoned Sanātana-Dharma and chosen
to follow adharma, and now worship the vile and profane.
Pain, suffering, annihilation—that then is thy inevitable destiny, O
luckless beings.

— ॐ सत्यभामापतये नमः ॐ —

All is indeed Braham—but be prepared also for the consequences
of the path thou take, and be ready for the sufferings that follow in
the wake of evil mode of life.

The formless Braham, contains in Him both the good and bad—
but **His manifest divine form is that of the beautiful and redeeming:
Bhagwān Shri Krishna.**

Worship Him in His sacred divine aspects—which Shri Bhagwān has enumerated throughout the Bhagavad-Gītā—and be saved, and live a blissful happy life as a collective.

Worship the evil—and then pain, suffering will be thy lot in life. Take they pick.

This is a subtle point, not to be over-stressed, but one we should ever stay cognizant of, within our hearts.

— ॐ तत सत ॐ —

Before we move on, let us bow in reverence to this sacred verse—a timeless beacon of wisdom guiding seekers for ages. Write it by hand, reflect on its meaning, and chant it aloud, for these sounds alone carry the authenticity of that era. The world may have changed but the living vibration of these Sanskrit sounds still remain as original as they were when Bhagwān Shri Krishna Himself walked the earth and imparted these teachings.

— ॐ —

रसोऽहमप्सु कौन्तेय प्रभास्मि शशिसूर्ययोः ।
raso'hamapsu kaunteya prabhāsmi śaśisūryayoḥ
प्रणवः सर्ववेदेषु शब्दः खे पौरुषं नृषु ॥७-८॥
praṇavaḥ sarvavedeṣu śabdaḥ khe pauruṣaṁ nṛṣu (7-8)

रसोऽहमप्सु कौन्तेय प्रभास्मि शशिसूर्ययोः ।
raso'hamapsu kaunteya prabhāsmi śaśisūryayoḥ
प्रणवः सर्ववेदेषु शब्दः खे पौरुषं नृषु ॥७-८॥
praṇavaḥ sarvavedeṣu śabdaḥ khe pauruṣaṁ nṛṣu (7-8)

ॐ तत्सदिति श्रीमद्भगवद्गीतासूपनिषत्सु ब्रह्मविद्यायां योगशास्त्रे श्रीकृष्णार्जुनसंवादे
om tatsaditi śrīmadbhagavadgītāsūpaniṣatsu brahmavidyāyāṁ yogaśāstre śrīkṛṣṇārjunasaṁvāde
ज्ञानविज्ञानयोगो नाम सप्तमोऽध्यायः श्लोकः ८
jñānavijñānayogo nāma saptamo'dhyāyaḥ ślokaḥ 8

Om-Tat-Sat—Om (Braham) is the sole Reality. In the Yogic Scripture on the Science-of-Braham, the Shrimada-Bhāgvada-Gītā Upanishad, we hereby conclude Shloka 8 of the Dialogue between Shri Krishna and Arjuna entitled Jnana-Vijnana-Yoga, Canto VII.

— ॐ श्रीकृष्णाय नमः ॐ —

Seeing the Divine in All Creation

Awake, O soul! The world is no exile—it is His hymn.
The taste in water is not only refreshment—it's a caress of Divine.

The sun's blaze, the moon's balm—they are His eyes upon us.
Each ray, a thread of His glory; each drop, a pearl of His bliss.

ॐ Aum—rises not from lips, but from the heart of the cosmos.
The sound through air, though unseen—
Is the Lord-God Himself in motion.

And what of that striving within thee—the strength to rise again?
That too is only He—and not simply thy own making.

To see thus is to fall in love anew with life—Krishna Himself.
Remember: Ye live not apart from God—but inside His very pulse.

But most humans stay as thankless wretches.
They drink water. Praise its chill.
They Praise the glass. Praise the spring.
But never Him—the Real thing!

O mortal, it is HE who is the taste—the life in water—
Which God, goes unnamed, unnoticed by the ingrate human.

Sun on the skin, Moon through the trees—I wake up to the light.
But then I look away, without acknowledging—or even saying Hi—
Because Light is so humdrum, so mundane.

Alas, I failed to realize: it was Krishna Himself who stood there.
Krishna is everywhere, in every ray—just not in my thoughts, alas.

Once upon, a long time ago—Krishna walked upon earth
Step by step Krishna passed the crooked roads of men—
From Vrindāvan's dust to Dvārakā's gold to the war-field's hush.
At every threshold He waited for mankind to rise—in **Dharma**,
But we humans—we who should have ascended—
Stayed crawling in our own little circles of selfishness & desires.

Krishna's journey became His grief:
That even after revealing the Self and the Supreme-Self,
Few dared to walk as the Gītā demanded.

In fact—some even outright blasphemed that great God
Who chose to descend midst us undeserving men!

With silly silken threads—the fools veiled the Flaming One.
Endless stories of Krishna, the Lover, were spun by cravenly poets—
Who fear Fiery-Gods—come arrived to decimate comfy human delusions.

They softened the Infinite; covered Him with embroidered illusions.
They hid the sword-edge of His smile in garish colors—
Soaked further in an over-sweet amative stench.

But as soon as the Wise tug away the gaudy embroidered threads
woven upon Krishna—they get to see:
Krishna was not just the painted delicate youth of little festivals,
He was a Thunder of Lightning—wearing a human face.
Come, let's pull away the veils—let Krishna blaze forth in all His fiery glory.

Yes, He sat with the cowherds, tended cows, walked barefoot,
Touched the earth as any man would
—And the simple dust of the path knew Him truer than did kings—
Yet even in this quiet guise, His Fiery Presence alone was enough—
To rearrange the air wherever He moved.

Krishna's lament is simple too—a dust-soft whisper:
"O Âryâs, why did ye become cowardly and fearful—
When it was I Myself—verily God—who walked besides ye?"

O humans, wake up; Arise as the Flame

Fear is sin. It is ignorance & forgetfulness of Âtmâ. It is not thy fate.
Krishna taught: Ye are the Âtmâ rooted in Me—
The Âtmâ which is unborn, undying, untouched by loss & gain.

O humans of Âryâvarta,

Why didst ye forget the Bhagavad-Gitâ? Forget the Real Krishna?
Why did ye distort the smile of Krishna?

In the Gita, Krishna's smile is Lightning contained—
A benign sky in which the Dhârmic live in dignity and freedom—
But trained to strike what must be struck—destroy Adharma.
He never did say: Be imbecilic. Grin & Clap. Embrace thy enemies.

Your calm must be: deep river-bed stone, immovable under flood.
Your action must be: clean, unspiteful—but Terror to Adharma.

Come arise—stand in Sanâtana-Dharma like a pillar in storm.
Unvanish—let adharma shatter on the bright wall of your Beingness.

Come O Sanâtani

From the ashes of despair, let a new flame awaken within,
Let new wings of Gitâ's fire unfold thy radiant ascent.

O mortal, do not fear the burning of illusions—let them rupture.
What perishes was never your true nature.
Dare to hear the true call of Gitâ: तत् त्वम् असि tat-tvam-asi.

Remember: Ye can never be consumed by sorrow or time.
After every fall of the unreal, let arise—a deeper realization of the Real.
Let each ending of non-Self—become a gateway to clarity of the Self.

Come rise—not as ego reborn, but as an awakened Being.
Ignite your spirit in the fearless recognition: aham-braham-âsmi.
You are the Fire that none—let alone Death—can extinguish.

ॐ गीता श्लोकः ७.९ – GĪTĀ VERSE 7.9

ॐ श्रीमद्भगवद्गीतासूपनिषत्सु ब्रह्मविद्यायां योगशास्त्रे श्रीकृष्णार्जुनसंवादे
om śrīmadbhagavadgītāsūpaniṣatsu brahmavidyāyāṁ yogaśāstre śrīkṛṣṇārjunasaṁvāde
ज्ञानविज्ञानयोगो नाम सप्तमोऽध्यायः श्लोकः ९
jñānavijñānayogo nāma saptamo'dhyāyaḥ ślokaḥ 9

— ॐ —

पुण्यो गन्धः पृथिव्यां च तेजश्चास्मि विभावसौ ।
puṇyo gandhaḥ pṛthivyāṁ ca tejaścāsmi vibhāvasau
जीवनं सर्वभूतेषु तपश्चास्मि तपस्विषु ॥ ७-९ ॥
jīvanaṁ sarvabhūteṣu tapaścāsmi tapasviṣu (7-9)

I am the pure odor of the earth; and the brightness of the fire; and I am the life in all beings; and of the ascetics—I am their austerity. (7.9)

—: *Word-by-Word* :—

पुण्यः puṇyaḥ – pure; गन्धः gandhaḥ – fragrance; पृथिव्याम् pṛthivyām – in the earth; च ca – and; तेजः tejaḥ – the brilliance; च asmi – I am; अस्मि ca – also; विभावसौ vibhāvasau – in fire; जीवनम् jīvanam – life; सर्वभूतेषु sarva-bhūteṣu – in all beings; तपः tapaḥ – austerity; च asmi – I am; तपस्विषु tapasviṣu – among the ascetics.

—: *Understanding The Verse* :—

— ॐ श्रीकृष्णाय नमः ॐ —

Continuing His luminous exposition of divine immanence, Bhagwān Shri Krishna further reveals how He pervades both the natural world and the inner life of beings.

In this verse, He declares Himself as the puṇya-gandha, the pure and sacred fragrance of the earth, the brilliance (tejas) of fire, the jīvanam—the vital force that animates all living beings—and the tapas or ascetic fervor found in the hearts of those engaged in spiritual austerity.

Through these revelations the Lord deepens our understanding—that divinity is not necessarily to be sought apart from the world, but within the sacred in it.

— ॐ श्रीरामाय नमः ॐ —

Remember O pilgrim: Unto the wise, every aspect of creation is a portal to the Supreme.

Earth, fire, life, and asceticism—elements both of the outer and inner cosmos—are not self-existent but derive their very being from the presence of the indwelling within the Divine.

By contemplating these manifestations, the wise is drawn to the vision of Unity—wherein the world becomes not an obstacle, but a sacred mirror reflecting the Lord's immanence: सर्वं खल्विदं ब्रह्म sarvam-khalvidam-braham.

—: Key Sanskrit Terms :—

— ॐ तत सत ॐ —

Now the cadence deepens into earth and flame. Sanskrit carries पुण्यो गन्धः puṇyo gandhaḥ like a subtle fragrance, while तेजः tejaḥ glows beneath the words. जीवनं सर्वभूतेषु jīvanaṁ sarva-bhūteṣu hums with quiet continuity, and तपः tapaḥ stands like a steady inner fire. The language feels elemental and intimate at once. Here Sanskrit does not merely name life—it breathes it into the verse, filling the syllables with a living warmth that lingers on the tongue.

Let us, for a moment, forget analysis, and let the Sanskrit words sing as they once did in days of yore: unburdened, bright, each note echoing in the chamber of the soul.

— ॐ —

पुण्यः गन्धः पृथिव्यां च (puṇyaḥ gandhaḥ pṛthivyāṁ ca):
"I am the pure fragrance in the earth."

As what beautiful expressions Bhagwān Shri Krishna comes up with, throughout the Gitā! And here the Lord-God uses the term पुण्यः गन्धः to describe the गन्धः aroma of earth as being पुण्य—sacred!

पुण्यः गन्धः Puṇya-gandha — the sacred, sanctified aroma — is not merely the physical scent of soil but the life-essence, the sweet subtlety hidden within matter.

The scent of earth after rain, the fragrance of life emerging from dust — these are whispers of the Divine's own presence in the material world.

Only those who live in Āryāvarta and recognize the lovely aroma of earth which comes with rains can appreciate the term पुण्य sacred mentioned in reference to aroma.

It's a most beautiful scent, unlike anything man-made!

Of course with the earth itself become defiled from human touch and the blood of slaughtered animals—this पुण्यः गन्धः too has mostly disappeared from the land of Āryāvarta

— ॐ —

तेजः च अस्मि विभावसौ (tejaś cāsmi vibhāvasau):

"च and अस्मि I am the तेजः radiance in the fire विभावसौ ."

तेजः Tejas is the dynamic, shining power — the brilliance that flames in fire, the light that transforms and purifies.

विभावसौ Vibhāvasu — fire, in its elemental form — embodies this luminous, devouring, purifying energy. The Lord is the inner splendor, the invisible force behind the visible flame.

— ॐ —

जीवनं सर्वभूतेषु (jīvanaṁ sarvabhūteṣu):

"I am जीवन life in all beings सर्वभूतेषु."

जीवनं Jīvanam — the vital principle, the animation that breathes in every creature — is the direct expression of the Lord's own life-energy.

It is the sacred life-breath that moves unseen within plants, animals, and human beings alike, affirming the unity of all life in His being.

— ॐ —

तपः च अस्मि तपस्विषु (tapaś cāsmi tapasviṣu):

"च and अस्मि I am तप austerity among तपस्वि ascetics."

तपः Tapas — the heat of spiritual striving, the fire of inner purification — is not mere mortification but a sacred transformation of the soul.

In those who undertake austerity (तपस्या tapasyā) to burn away ignorance and impurities, the Lord reveals Himself as the very force of their aspiration and endurance.

—: In Brief :—

— ॐ श्रीकृष्णाय नमः ॐ —

Bhagwān Shri Krishna, following the sacred rhythm established in the preceding verses, now continues to unveil the truth of His pervasiveness. He declares: "I am the pure fragrance in the earth, the radiance in fire, the life in all beings, and the austerity in ascetics."

This verse, like a polished jewel, reflects multiple facets of divine presence—subtle, vital, and transformative. Each word like freshness of rain on soil; each syllable showcasing His presence even in the ordinary.

The **पुण्यो गन्धः पृथिव्यां** puṇya-gandhaḥ pṛthivyām—the pure scent in the earth—is not a mere sensory phenomenon, but the subtle tanmātra (elemental essence) of fragrance.

Krishna is the essence that gives earth its rootedness and sanctity. It is the inner principle that defines the nature of earth itself.

This sacred quality evokes not just the physical fragrance of soil after rain, but the deeper spiritual grounding and nourishment that the earth symbolizes.

Ah... how gently the Lord reveals Himself— not just in thunder, but in the soft perfume that rises when rain kisses the waiting soil;

and in that first breath after the clouds break, the heart remembers the yore days of innocence;

it was as if Krishna Himself was there, moving as aroma through the clay.

— ॐ परमात्मने नमः ॐ —

But today the earth exhales a different story.

Once, the earth offered a lovely odor in her soil—

but today she produces malodor—for she is forced to breathe the acrid smoke of chemicals, the iron smell of blood and industry, the reek of sewage and waste.

The earth's sacred body—gored out from the touch of savage hands—now weeps through all her pores—producing a stench.

And today's men, grown accustomed to these lesions, no longer even notice the stink. The nostrils of the modern mind have forgotten what the purity of earth smells like.

Perhaps beneath the grime, the holy fragrance remains in some parts. Waiting.

Come O human, give up the brute. Return to stillness;

and perhaps even now you may yet catch the faint sweetness of the Eternal rising from the dust of the earth after the rains.

— ॐ करुणासागराय नमः ॐ —

तेजश्चास्मि विभावसौ Tejaś cāsmi vibhāvasau—"I am the brilliance in fire." Fire is not merely a physical element, but a sacred presence revered since the Vedic age.

In yajña, fire is the mouth of the gods, the carrier of offerings, the purifier.

The brilliance here signifies both its physical light and the metaphysical illumination that it imparts.

That light which guides, purifies, and transforms—that is Krishna.

— ॐ दयानिधानाय नमः ॐ —

जीवनं सर्वभूतेषु Jīvanam sarva-bhūteṣu—"I am the life in all beings."
This is no ordinary biological animation, but the sacred life-principle (prāṇa) that distinguishes the living from the inert.

It is the same life-current that pulses in the bird and the sage, in the tree and the ascetic.

The Lord is not merely the giver of life; He is the life itself, the secret flame of vitality within every breath, the unseen force that animates the cosmos.

— ॐ अनिरुद्धाय नमः ॐ —

And finally, **तपश्चास्मि तपस्विषु** tapas cāsmi tapasviṣu—"I am the austerity in ascetics."

Tapas is not self-denial for its own sake, but the sacred fire of inner discipline, the concentrated will that burns away impurity and kindles spiritual illumination.

Wherever there is true penance, purity, and determined striving for truth, there resides the presence of Krishna, who is the very essence of that divine striving.

— ॐ गोवर्धनधराय नमः ॐ —

In all these expressions—fragrance, light, life, and discipline—Bhagwān teaches that He is not only the distant Absolute but the intimate, sustaining essence of all that is noble, beautiful, and vital in creation.

The seeker who meditates upon these manifestations begins to perceive the world not as fragmented, but as a sacred whole held together by the Divine presence in all things.

This verse invites us to cultivate divya-dṛṣṭi—the divine eye—which sees beyond form into essence. Krishna, as the soul of the world, dwells in every fragrance, every flame, every breath, and every act of sincere spiritual effort.

In the verses to follow, the Lord will continue to unfold this vision, showing how He abides in the forces of nature and in the qualities of mind and character, gradually leading us from outer perception to inner realization.

— ॐ तत् सत् ॐ —

Before we move on, let us bow in reverence to this sacred verse—a timeless beacon of wisdom guiding seekers for ages. Write it by hand, reflect on its meaning, and chant it aloud, for these sounds alone carry the authenticity of that era. The world may have changed but the living vibration of these Sanskrit sounds still remain as original as they were when Bhagwān Shri Krishna Himself walked the earth and imparted these teachings.

— ॐ —

पुण्यो गन्धः पृथिव्यां च तेजश्चास्मि विभावसौ ।
puṇyo gandhaḥ pṛthivyāṁ ca tejaścāsmi vibhāvasau
जीवनं सर्वभूतेषु तपश्चास्मि तपस्विषु ॥७।९॥
jīvanaṁ sarvabhūteṣu tapaścāsmi tapasviṣu (7-9)

— ॐ —

पुण्यो गन्धः पृथिव्यां च तेजश्चास्मि विभावसौ ।
puṇyo gandhaḥ pṛthivyāṁ ca tejaścāsmi vibhāvasau
जीवनं सर्वभूतेषु तपश्चास्मि तपस्विषु ॥ ७-९ ॥
jīvanaṁ sarvabhūteṣu tapaścāsmi tapasviṣu (7-9)

ॐ तत्सदिति श्रीमद्भगवद्गीतासूपनिषत्सु ब्रह्मविद्यायां योगशास्त्रे श्रीकृष्णार्जुनसंवादे
om tatsaditi śrīmadbhagavadgītāsūpaniṣatsu brahmavidyāyāṁ yogaśāstre śrīkṛṣṇārjunasaṁvāde
ज्ञानविज्ञानयोगो नाम सप्तमोऽध्यायः श्लोकः ९
jñānavijñānayogo nāma saptamo'dhyāyaḥ ślokaḥ 9

Om-Tat-Sat—Om (Braham) is the sole Reality. In the Yogic Scripture on the Science-of-Braham, the Shrimada-Bhāgvada-Gītā Upanishad, we hereby conclude Shloka 9 of the Dialogue between Shrī Krishna and Arjuna entitled Jnana-Vijnana-Yoga, Canto VII.

— ॐ श्रीकृष्णाय नमः ॐ —

You, O human, crushed the soil. Ye tilled it. Bought it. Sold it.
But never inhaled it. Never knelt before the Divine.

" The scent of earth—that ancient musk—that is Me."
Humans assume: God is "any elsewhere but here"—
But Krishna's presence is, in fact, **everywhere**.

His Presence is in the scent rising from the soil,
It is in the shimmer that dances in fire.

The breath of beasts, the surge of sap,
The sparkle of colors in butterfly—
All that, and everything else too, is just that "I".

"And in those who burn away darkness with discipline—
I am that burning.
Not afar, not above—I am in the very act of becoming.

Where there is life, there am I;
Where there is austerity, I am the silent flame that feeds it. "

This then is the immanence of Bhagwân Shri Krishna.
Such is the blazing intimacy of the Bhagavad-Gitâ.

ॐ गीता श्लोकः ७.१० – Gītā Verse 7.10

ॐ श्रीमद्भगवद्गीतासूपनिषत्सु ब्रह्मविद्यायां योगशास्त्रे श्रीकृष्णार्जुनसंवादे
om śrīmadbhagavadgītāsūpaniṣatsu brahmavidyāyāṁ yogaśāstre śrīkṛṣṇārjunasaṁvāde
ज्ञानविज्ञानयोगो नाम सप्तमोऽध्यायः श्लोकः १०
jñānavijñānayogo nāma saptamo'dhyāyaḥ ślokaḥ 10

— ॐ —

बीजं मां सर्वभूतानां विद्धि पार्थ सनातनम् ।

bījaṁ māṁ sarvabhūtānāṁ viddhi pārtha sanātanam

बुद्धिर्बुद्धिमतामस्मि तेजस्तेजस्विनामहम् ॥७-१०॥

buddhirbuddhimatāmasmi tejastejasvināmaham (7-10)

O Pārtha, know Me to be the eternal seed of all beings; I am the intelligence of the intelligent—and the glory of the glorious. (7.10)

—: Word-by-Word :—

बीजम् bījam – the seed; माम् mām – Me; सर्वभूतानाम् sarva-bhūtānām – of all beings; विद्धि viddhi – know; पार्थ pārtha – O Partha (Arjuna); सनातनम् sanātanam – eternal; बुद्धिः buddhiḥ – intelligence; बुद्धिमताम् buddhimatām – of the intelligent; अस्मि asmi – I am; तेजः tejaḥ – brilliance; तेजस्विनाम् tejasvinām – of the brilliant; अहम् aham – I am.

—: Understanding The Verse :—

— ॐ श्रीकृष्णाय नमः ॐ —

In this verse, Bhagwān Shri Krishna further illuminates His immanent nature by declaring Himself to be the सनातन बीज sanātana bīja—the eternal seed—from which all beings arise.

Shri Krishna affirms that He is not only the origin of life, but also the animating intelligence in those who possess understanding, and the splendor in those who shine with greatness.

Through these affirmations, Krishna reveals that all human capacities which evoke wonder—be it wisdom, strength, or nobility—are but partial reflections of His own infinite being.

— ॐ श्रीरामाय नमः ॐ —

This verse continues the thread of divine immanence that runs through this chapter.

Remember: the Lord is not merely the creator who set the cosmos in motion from afar, He is the very essence that pulses within it—the origin, the sustaining force, and the final goal.

By recognizing that the light of intelligence and glory in the world is but the radiance of Krishna Himself, we are led toward a sacred vision of Unity and reverence for all life.

—: Key Sanskrit Terms :—

— ॐ तत् सत् ॐ —

The verse grows seedlike and radiant. Sanskrit lets बीजं मां सर्वभूतानां bījaṃ māṃ sarva-bhūtānām settle with ancient weight, while बुद्धिर्बुद्धिमताम् buddhiḥ buddhimatām glimmers like intelligence recognizing itself. तेजस्तेजस्विनाम् tejas tejasvinam pulses softly beneath.

The language of the Bhagavad-Gītā feels fertile, as though each syllable were capable of unfolding worlds, carrying within it the quiet potency of endless becoming.

Nothing needs explaining; everything is sown. Still let us turn gently to the verse; let us reflect on the weight and whisper of its key Sanskrit terms; let us linger with the Sanskrit as with seeds resting in our palm. "I am the eternal seed of all beings, intelligence of the intelligent, splendor of the splendid"; and soon we shall find each word to begin germinating in our heart, swelling with hidden power.

— ॐ —

बीजं मां सर्वभूतानां (bījaṃ māṃ sarvabhūtānām):
"Know Me मां as the बीजं seed of सर्वभूतानां all beings."
बीज Bīja — seed — evokes the idea of the primal cause, the subtle origin from which all manifest forms arise. The seed is unseen, humble, yet contains within it infinite potential.
By declaring Himself as the बीज bīja of सर्वभूतानां sarvabhūtānām (all beings), the Lord reveals that He is the hidden source and secret energy behind all life — not merely its creator, but its central core.

— ॐ —

सनातनम् (sanātanam):
"Eternal."
This word सनातन shines with profound depth.
Sanātana implies that the Divine Seed is not of time, nor subject to decay; it is beginningless and endless, ever unchanging amidst the changing currents of manifestation.
It hints at the eternal continuity of life and spirit — all arising from the timeless Source.

The word itself reminds us of एकम् सनातन धर्म Ekam-Sanātana-Dharma—the one true religion, the only and only, the cosmic order since times eternal.

— ॐ —

बुद्धिः बुद्धिमताम् अस्मि (buddhir buddhimatām asmi):
"I am the बुद्धिः intelligence, बुद्धिमताम् of the intelligent."
बुद्धिः Buddhi here is not merely intellect but the higher faculty of discernment (विवेक viveka), clarity, understanding.

Among the wise and discerning, their very intelligence is the radiance of the Lord shining through them.

It is not self-generated but a gift, a reflection of Divine consciousness.

— ॐ —

तेजः तेजस्विनामहम् (tejaḥ tejasvinām aham):
"The तेजः splendor, तेजस्विनाम of the splendid, अहम I am."
तेजः Tejas — brilliance, energy, spiritual effulgence — is the inner luminosity that empowers greatness, valor, and dynamic presence.

Wherever true radiance, strength, or noble energy is seen, it is none other than the Lord's own majesty (mahattva) manifest.

—: In Brief :—

— ॐ श्रीकृष्णाय नमः ॐ —

बीजं मां सर्वभूतानां विद्धि पार्थ सनातनम् । बुद्धिर्बुद्धिमतामस्मि तेजस्तेजस्विनामहम् ॥

In this sacred verse, Bhagwān Shri Krishna declares:
"O Pārtha, know Me to be the eternal seed of all beings; I am the intelligence of the intelligent and the splendor of the glorious."

The word bīja, meaning "seed," signifies the origin—the subtle cause from which the gross form emerges; but here Krishna qualifies it further as sanātana-bīja, the "eternal seed."

Unlike a perishable material seed, which is born and destroyed in time, the Lord is beginningless and deathless.

He is not a 'one cause among many', but the uncaused cause—the very primordial root of all beings and things.

All life, whether of gods, men, animals, plants, arises from this eternal seed which is Krishna Himself.

— ॐ श्रीरामाय नमः ॐ —

And yet, Krishna is not merely the source from which beings emerge; He is also the buddhi—the discerning intelligence in those who are wise.

The intellect (buddhi) is the luminous faculty by which truth is discerned, dharma upheld, and clarity born midst even confusions of life.

That faculty, subtle and penetrating, is not an independent property of the mind; it is but a reflection of the Lord's own consciousness.

When a being displays wisdom of the highest kind—it is Krishna who is shining through that faculty.

The intelligence of the intelligent is a ray of clarity—having its source in satt-chitt-ānanda braham, the ocean of existence-bliss-consciousness – whose manifest form is Krishna.

— ॐ सर्वदेवतामयाय नमः ॐ —

Likewise, Skri Krishna declares: तेजस्तेजस्विनामहम् tejas tejasvinām aham—"I am the glory, the brilliance, of the glorious." Tejas here refers not only to physical radiance or prowess, but to the inner power to inspire, to lead, to influence, to uplift.

It is the majestic quality that commands reverence, the force that burns with moral or spiritual authority.

In the context of Sanātana-Dharma, wherever we encounter true grandeur, heroism, magnetism —there it is Krishna who is present, radiating His hidden essence through that being, spreading the aroma of goodness, bringing joy to the world.

The same raw power may be seen in adharma too—but it comes out as barbarism, savagery, raw brute power—and becomes the cause of suffering to others,

— ॐ आत्मारामाय नमः ॐ —

Wherever true nobility arises —where courage stands without cruelty, where a quiet charisma warms rather than burns—there Krishna is breathing through a human form.

It is verily **His** hidden light—moving through heroes and healers—which makes the world feel momentarily whole.

Yet power itself is a double-edged flame.
The same force that crowns the noble—when severed from Dharma—falls into the dark shadows of adharma.

And then the same intensity becomes barbarism,

strength hardens into savagery,
radiance forgets its source—and begins to devour.

Krishna does not withdraw the fire—
He reveals its true home.

When tejas bows to Dharma—it illumines the path, and should be revered;
when it rebels, it scorches the earth—and should be spurned.

Thus the Gītā speaks quietly to the heart:
Power is divine.
Its direction decides, whether it becomes a lamp—
or a wildfire.

— ॐ कौलिनाय नमः ॐ —

Thus, with each line of this verse, the Lord reveals Himself in ever subtler and more intimate ways. He is not merely in the elements or cosmic forces—He is in the living qualities of beings, in their highest faculties and finest expressions.

Wisdom, vitality, brilliance—all these are but the bright rays of the same one sun.

— ॐ अर्जुनप्रियाय नमः ॐ —

This teaching is not merely philosophical—it is deeply transformative.

To see the intelligence in others as Krishna, to recognize greatness not as personal achievement but as divine manifestation, is to dissolve the human ego and open the heart to humility and wonders of existence.

It cultivates in the seeker samadarśitva—equal vision—and deepens devotion, for all beauty and greatness become occasions to remember the Lord.

Thusly, Shri Krishna continues to lead Arjuna from the outer perception of the world to the inner recognition of the Divine in all.

The thread of manifestation continues in the verses that follow, where the Lord will further illustrate how He abides in the very energies that move the world—sustaining, animating, and guiding all.

— ॐ तत् सत् ॐ —

Before we move on, let us bow in reverence to this sacred verse—a timeless beacon of wisdom guiding seekers for ages. Write it by hand, reflect on its meaning, and chant it aloud, for these sounds alone carry the authenticity of that era. The world may have changed but the living vibration of these Sanskrit sounds still remain as original as they were when Bhagwān Shri Krishna Himself walked the earth and imparted these teachings.

— ॐ —

बीजं मां सर्वभूतानां विद्धि पार्थ सनातनम् ।
bījaṁ māṁ sarvabhūtānāṁ viddhi pārtha sanātanam
बुद्धिर्बुद्धिमतामस्मि तेजस्तेजस्विनामहम् ॥७-१०॥
buddhirbuddhimatāmasmi tejastejasvināmaham (7-10)

— ॐ —

बीजं मां सर्वभूतानां विद्धि पार्थ सनातनम् ।
bījaṁ māṁ sarvabhūtānāṁ viddhi pārtha sanātanam
बुद्धिर्बुद्धिमतामस्मि तेजस्तेजस्विनामहम् ॥७-१०॥
buddhirbuddhimatāmasmi tejastejasvināmaham (7-10)

ॐ तत्सदिति श्रीमद्भगवद्गीतासूपनिषत्सु ब्रह्मविद्यायां योगशास्त्रे श्रीकृष्णार्जुनसंवादे
om tatsaditi śrīmadbhagavadgītāsūpaniṣatsu brahmavidyāyāṁ yogaśāstre śrīkṛṣṇārjunasaṁvāde
ज्ञानविज्ञानयोगो नाम सप्तमोऽध्यायः श्लोकः १०
jñānavijñānayogo nāma saptamo'dhyāyaḥ ślokaḥ 10

Om-Tat-Sat—Om (Braham) is the sole Reality. In the Yogic Scripture on the Science-of-Braham,
the Shrimada-Bhāgvada-Gītā Upanishad, we hereby conclude Shloka 10 of the Dialogue between
Shrī Krishna and Arjuna entitled Jnana-Vijnana-Yoga, Canto VII.

— ॐ श्रीकृष्णाय नमः ॐ —

Speech begins not from sound—but Silence.
Movement stems not from motion—but Stillness.
"All begins in Me—Krishna.
I am the eternal seed. Before root. Before form. Before name."

But look at the Ingrate who forgot God: man.
He eats the fruits—that are from Him.
He clutches the flower—that are His.
He builds his empires upon the branches of His Tree—
And yet the Stupe forgets: the-Seed.

Man never bows to God, the hidden One—the core, the vital essence.
He bows only to the bloom. And bloom, alas, is brief.

The "Wise" guy who wears Pride
" I lent him wit, clarity, vision, brain.
But he built high towers for himself—not temples to the Supreme-Self."

He Spoke so cleverly.
Yet the fool knew not—whose tongue he used!

The Glory? Man hogged it all for himself.

It was God's—the fire, the voice, the power, the glory.
But man claimed it as his own.
He stamped it. Branded. Leased. Sold it. Resold it.

But then one day he became dimmed—*"Because I withdrew"*
And now he lies collapsed—as dust and ash.

— ॐ श्रीकृष्णाय नमः ॐ —

From the vantage of eternity Krishna stays watching us—
Puny little figures of men—running around, scrambling, fornicating,

Stuporous flock, practicing sham men-made-sects in the name of God
—With two evil creeds full of inanities, calling themselves "religions"
—having taken over half the world!

These supposed "religious" people, talk so glibly of God, mercy, love,
And yet slaughter & devour God's creatures—their own kindred.

They blatantly ravage, rapine the earth—which is the body of God.
And yet these vile, ugly, cruel creatures
—Who have never known: All is Oneness; All creatures have soul—
Have the temerity to take the high moral ground—To decimate
Sanātana-Dharma—To break its temples, idols, people, varna-āshram
—To mock Krishna and His Gitā!

But why blame the world—when it was my "own" who first betrayed,
They who stopped reading the Gitā—abandoned Sanātana-Dharma.

Krishna's hawk-sight pierces through the Ages:
He is looking for any Arjunas, Pāndavas that are there to be saved,
But all God sees is a species celebrating—while devouring itself,
A naked dance of sense madness—playing out in all its gory details.

Alas, the people of the holy land of Āryāvarta themselves
Have forgotten of God, of the all pervasive glory of the Ātmā;
The land that once sanctified life—is now known for its beef-exports!

Aye, Krishna didst say: I will keep Sanātana-Dharma protected—
But fools, it could well be though another species—
For ye humans, have NOT proven worthy of His grace.

O fools, there well could be some time—beg forgiveness of Krishna!
Let the Gitā lift thee skyward—and perhaps ye could yet be saved.

Or a BROB event—Big-Reset-of-Braham—stands yonder on horizon—
Ready to devour cruel humans—ravaging & raping Earth & Her creatures.

ॐ गीता श्लोकः ७.११ – Gītā Verse 7.11

ॐ श्रीमद्भगवद्गीतासूपनिषत्सु ब्रह्मविद्यायां योगशास्त्रे श्रीकृष्णार्जुनसंवादे
om śrīmadbhagavadgītāsūpaniṣatsu brahmavidyāyāṁ yogaśāstre śrīkṛṣṇārjunasaṁvāde
ज्ञानविज्ञानयोगो नाम सप्तमोऽध्यायः श्लोकः ११
jñānavijñānayogo nāma saptamo'dhyāyaḥ ślokaḥ 11

— ॐ —

बलं बलवतां चाहं कामरागविवर्जितम् ।
balaṁ balavatāṁ cāhaṁ kāmarāgavivarjitam
धर्माविरुद्धो भूतेषु कामोऽस्मि भरतर्षभ ॥७-११॥
dharmāviruddho bhūteṣu kāmo'smi bharatarṣabha (7-11)

I am that strength of the strong which is free of passion and attachment; and O Bhārata, in beings I am that concupiscence which is unopposed to virtue and scriptural injunctions. (7.11)

—: Word-by-Word :—

बलम् balam – strength; बलवताम् balavatām – of the strong; च ca – and; अहम् aham – I am; कामरागविवर्जितम् kāma-rāga-vivarjitam – free from desire and attachment; धर्म-अविरुद्धः dharma-aviruddhaḥ – not opposed to righteousness; भूतेषु bhūteṣu – in beings; कामः kāmaḥ – desire; अस्मि asmi – I am; भरतर्षभ bharatarṣabha – O best of the Bharatas (Arjuna).

—: Understanding The Verse :—

— ॐ श्रीकृष्णाय नमः ॐ —

In this profound verse, Bhagwān Shri Krishna continues to illumine the subtle presence of the Divine in human experience—not only in attributes such as wisdom or brilliance, but even in primal forces like strength and desire.

Yet, He offers a crucial distinction: strength must be free from attachment and selfish craving, and desire must be aligned with Dharma—sanctioned by virtue and śāstra—to stay divine in its essence.

— ॐ श्रीरामाय नमः ॐ —

Here the Lord teaches that even the lower human impulses stay impure no more—when they become alignment with the principles of Sanātana-Dharma—for righteousness and for higher purpose.

Strength that is rooted in ego, or desire that violates virtue, does not reflect the beautiful and Divine any longer. But when purified, disciplined, and guided by Dharma, even these potent raw forces become expressions of the Divinity Himself.

This verse thus expands our vision, encouraging the sanctification of life rather than its outright rejection. Even the carnal instincts, when become refined through the śāstric teachings of Sanātana-Dharma—turn into spiritual expressions.

—: Key Sanskrit Terms :—

— ॐ तत सत ॐ —

Now the cadence steadies into strength without strain. Sanskrit offers बलं बलवतां balaṁ balavatāṁ with a calm, rooted gravity, and कामरागविवर्जितम् kāma-rāga-vivarjitam glides through the breath with gentle restraint. भरतर्षभ bharatarṣabha anchors the tone in human listening.

The verse feels neither indulgent nor severe—only poised. Here Sanskrit becomes a disciplined flame, holding power and harmony in the same glowing syllables.

Now let us turn to these terms not as something foreign, but as something remembered—each term a soft bell calling us back to what we already do know, quietly, beneath the surface, in our heart of hearts – but which may have become outwardly forgotten!

— ॐ —

बलं बलवतां चाहं (balaṁ balavatāṁ cāham):
"च and अहम् I am, the बलं strength of the बलवतां strong."
Here, बल bala (strength) must be understood not merely as brute physical prowess, but as the innate power that upholds Dharma righteousness—forbearance, steadfastness, and noble action.
बलवतां Balavatām (of the strong) refers to those in whom this force naturally abides, yet Krishna teaches that even this strength must be recognized as Divine in origin — not something born of ego or ambition.

— ॐ —

कामरागविवर्जितम् (kāma-rāga-vivarjitam):
"विवर्जितम् Free from काम desire and राग attachment."
काम Kāma (desire) and राग rāga (attachment) are twin forces that bind the soul to the realm of becoming.
Desire ignites longing, while attachment fetters the heart to fleeting objects.
True strength, says the Lord, is utterly purified of these taints — it is power that emanates not from craving but from pure Beingness.

— ॐ —

धर्माविरुद्धः (dharma-aviruddhaḥ):

"अविरुद्धः Unopposed to धर्म Dharma."

Dharma is the sustaining order, the eternal righteousness that aligns individual conduct with cosmic truth.

विरुद्ध Viruddha (opposed) signifies deviation or rebellion.

Thus, Krishna declares that certain forms of काम kāma — such as the procreative urge of householders or their worldly desire towards virtuous aspirations — when harmonious with their grahastha-āshrama dharma, are not chains but expressions of His own will.

— ॐ —

भूतेषु कामः (bhūteṣu kāmaḥ):

"कामः Desire, भूतेषु in beings."

भूतेषु Bhūteṣu (in beings) suggests the universal presence of impulse and vitality within living creatures.

Krishna reveals that even this fundamental force of life, when rightly directed, is none other than His own divine energy sustaining the wheel of existence.

— ॐ —

भरतर्षभ (bharatarṣabha):

O bull among the Bhāratas.

This address to Arjuna signifies not merely praise but a summons to heroic virtue. As the noblest scion of a dharmic lineage, Arjuna is called to discern between passion that binds and sacred will that liberates.

—: In Brief :—

— ॐ श्रीकृष्णाय नमः ॐ —

बलं बलवतां चाहं कामरागविवर्जितम् । धर्माविरुद्धो भूतेषु कामोऽस्मि भरतर्षभ ॥

Here is a verse of strength and passion—tempered with discipline.

In this subtle and deeply ethical teaching, each syllable refines energy into purity as Bhagwān Shri Krishna proclaims:

"I am that strength of the strong which is free from desire and attachment; and in beings, O Bhārata, I am that desire which is not opposed to Dharma."

The Lord is reveals that He is manifest not just in serene detachment or transcendental vision—but is also manifest in dynamic qualities such as bala—strength—and kāma—desire—when these remain purified and harmonized with Sanātana-Dharma.

The divine does not outright reject power, lust; but He would rather that they stay sanctified by alignment with the principles of Sanātana-Dharma—by following what the śāstra have stipulated as what man should or should not do.

Remember: All existence is just the sport of Braham—but this sport remains beautiful and lasting only if we play by the rules of Sanātana-Dharma—the cosmic code breathed by Braham in the shape of the Vedas and by which all higher life-forms should live in their respective realms.

Live by thy Dharma—thusly God has ordained.

The Dharma for all lower life-forms is encoded in their dna.

The Dharma for higher life-forms is encoded in the Vedic Sanātana-Dharma. Live not by it—and ye perish.

— ॐ श्रीरामाय नमः ॐ —

The beautiful varna-āshram system was created expressly for this purpose. This system exists so that even the debasing urges of man become sanctified and remain no longer as hindrances on the spiritual path—rather become even an easier path to the divine.

When one enters the gṛhastha-āśrama—the sacred householder's path— the soul does not flee the world—he learns how to walk **within it without being owned**.

Slowly, gently, the basal **instincts are tamed by Dharma.**
Hunger learns restraint.
Desire learns reverence.
The need for shelter becomes the art of sheltering others.
The need for power becomes the art of protecting sanātana-dharma.
The need for nurturing becomes the art of nurturing one's dharma.
 The need for love becomes the way of bhakti—devotion for dharma and one's chosen deity within sanātana-dharma.

What were once raw cravings—are refined into vessels for duty and dharma.

A seeker does **not necessarily** reach God by abandoning life,
but he **certainly can do so** by consecrating powers of life to God through activity performed in the cause of Sanātana-Dharma.

As a Karma-Yogi, following one's dharma—for instance in grahastha-āshrama, through daily bread and shared love, through work, children, and sacred obligations, duties fulfilled—one is able to reach the Divine—

because as Bhagwān Shri Krishna has revealed, the divine is not beyond the world—but is shining quietly through it.

Of course the caution has already been given in earlier chapters: Do not become attached to the external; be not slave to sense-delights; stay inwards; remain trenched just only to Bhagwān Shri Krishna and His Sanātana-Dharma; crave no fruits; always consecrate the fruits at the feet of Krishna; remain happy doing what He has ordained—the varna-āshram duties lined up for us.

— ॐ योगीश्वराय नमः ॐ —

In Sanātana-Dharma—there is a time and place for everything—hence the four Varnas, Āshrams.

It is not our birth that binds us, nor the weight of our past that stays crowning or condemning us—for no karma arrives already pure or stained.

The solution is simple: sanctify the karmas by consecrating them through dharma—what the śāstras ordain.

It is through the lens of Sanātana-Dharma—the same quiet law of His that also holds the stars in their courses—by which the truth of human life is revealed—by which we know the Truth.

O human: walk in the eternal rhythm of Sanātana-Dharma,
and thy life will become sanctified,
and even what once seemed small and soiled—will become gently lifted into the light.
And now work will become worship,
and breath will become prayer,
and even the ordinary will turn translucent with God and His sanātana-dharma—which He bequeathed to us humans.

Krishna whispers this truth into our heart: **Nothing is sacred or profane by its own nature; It is you, O human, who make it sacred or profane.**

When our acts get aligned with Dharma, then our every step
—even upon the dirty dust of the world—
will move us toward God, towards the Infinite—towards our emancipation.

And vice-verse.

Following the path of adharma—even otherwise noble acts, births, circumstances—become transfigured into malefic evil;

and then we fall down into even deeper bondages;
and we stay revolving in this birth-death cycle of sorrows.

We are fortunate to be born in this human body this time around.
Who knows which skin we will find ourselves in, in our next life?
 O human, ever stay in the embrace of Sanātana-Dharma—if thou knowest what is good for thee.

— ॐ यज्ञेश्वराय नमः ॐ —

बल Bala—or strength—can manifest in various forms: physical, moral, intellectual, or spiritual. Yet, when such strength is driven by ego, aggression, or selfish ambition, it becomes a demoniacal force, as later described in Chapter Sixteen as well.

True strength, Krishna says, is कामरागविवर्जितम् kāma-rāga-vivarjitam—free from selfish desire and possessive attachment. It is the inner power that upholds and protects sanātana-dharma, protects the good, speaks the truth, and remains firm even in adversity.

Aye, this is the बल strength of sages and of warriors-of-dharma and of ascetics—and it is the **reflection of Krishna Himself.**

— ॐ यज्ञप्रियाय नमः ॐ —

Likewise, काम kāma—desire—is often vilified in spiritual discourse, and rightly so when it degenerates into uncontrolled craving or sensual indulgence.

But here, Krishna makes a crucial distinction. He says, "कामोऽस्मि भूतेषु धर्माविरुद्धो kāmaḥ asmi bhūteṣu dharma-aviruddhaḥ"—I am that desire of beings which is unopposed to Dharma.

This then is the sacred longing inherent in beings—the desire to uphold life, to fulfill righteous duties, to seek knowledge, to strive toward the Divine.

— ॐ वन्दे सूर्यं शशाङ्क वह्निनयन वन्दे मुकुन्द प्रियम् ॐ —

Remember:
Even fierce desire—when fully yoked to the chariot of Dharma—will cease to bind. It will in fact become the road itself.

Desire, when purified by śāstra, is no longer a chain around the soul, but becomes a flame having been lit in its lamp; and now it:
- becomes the quiet fire that moves noble deeds,
- becomes the ache that draws the heart toward Truth.

From its intensity—great devotion becomes born.
From it—creation unfolds.
From it flows that sacred joy—that does not darken the mind

but widens it.

Krishna does not exile kāma from the holy house.

In the gr̥hastha's dwelling—where children are conceived and bread is earned, where discipline shelters love, and sanctity crowns labor—**this very desire comes to shine as a holy power.**

काम **kāma is the Divine's own urge to become.**
To come into existence. To continue into the next generation.

If kāma were only a dark shadow to be spurned,
then how would the sun of life rise generation after generation?

Once cleansed in the river of the great Varna-Āshram system of Sanātana-Dharma, Desire becomes the river through which the will of God enters the world.

Never forget: all this is Braham sporting, and the rules of the game are spelled out in the śāstra of sanātana-dharma;
    and when we play by the rules—the play stays elysian -- **with us eventually reaching our own divinity;**
    or if we go against God's rules, live in adharma—then we will get plucked out from the earth and be placed in the dustbin of history – as the also-rans, a failed species.

— ॐ सत्यमूर्तये नमः ॐ —

By addressing Arjuna as Bhārata, the scion of a noble and dharmic lineage, Krishna implies that Arjuna possesses the inner refinement to recognize and embody this higher form of strength and desire.

The Lord gently corrects the notion that spiritual life must mean the suppression of all natural impulses. Rather, Shri Krishna invites us to align them with dharma—sanctify them by acting in accordance with the sacred laws of the śāstras.

— ॐ पितृभक्ताय नमः ॐ —

O mortal: **Be natural—but stay under the discipline of Dharma.**
Just as the Lord does not ask the river to forget its current, nor the fire to cease its warmth, so too, the soul is not commanded to strangle its own nature in the name of holiness.

Read the verses again—for Krishna speaks softly but clear;
quietly He unties the knots within the heart:
Do not war against the life I have placed within thee.
Lift thyself above the impulses, He says—do not bury them.

Refine them through the laws of varna-āshram dharma.
Let desire be washed in right conduct.
Let thy strength be guided by the sacred order: Sanātana-Dharma.

Then, in all that is noble, steady, and beautiful,
you will feel **just Him, Bhagwān Shri Krishna, moving.**
Not as an idea,
but as the living breath of dharma pulsing through thy being.

— ॐ परात्पराय नमः ॐ —

Thus, with this verse, the Lord continues weaving together the seen and the unseen, the inner and the outer, the passive and the active—showing that all forces in creation, when purified, are none other than He Himself Lord-God Bhagwān: He who is satt-chitt-ānanda braham and whose manifest presence in the world is in the shape of Krishna.

This paves the way for the concluding thought of this section next—wherein the Lord will reveal that all qualities, all states, all beings emerge from His prakṛti, constituted by the three guṇas.

— ॐ तत् सत ॐ —

Before we move on, let us bow in reverence to this sacred verse—a timeless beacon of wisdom guiding seekers for ages. Write it by hand, reflect on its meaning, and chant it aloud, for these sounds alone carry the authenticity of that era. The world may have changed but the living vibration of these Sanskrit sounds still remain as original as they were when Bhagwān Shri Krishna Himself walked the earth and imparted these teachings.

— ॐ —

बलं बलवतां चाहं कामरागविवर्जितम् ।
balaṁ balavatāṁ cāhaṁ kāmarāgavivarjitam
धर्माविरुद्धो भूतेषु कामोऽस्मि भरतर्षभ ॥७-११॥
dharmāviruddho bhūteṣu kāmo'smi bharatarṣabha (7-11)

बलं बलवतां चाहं कामरागविवर्जितम् ।
balaṁ balavatāṁ cāhaṁ kāmarāgavivarjitam
धर्माविरुद्धो भूतेषु कामोऽस्मि भरतर्षभ ॥७-११॥
dharmāviruddho bhūteṣu kāmo'smi bharatarṣabha (7-11)

ॐ तत्सदिति श्रीमद्भगवद्गीतासूपनिषत्सु ब्रह्मविद्यायां योगशास्त्रे श्रीकृष्णार्जुनसंवादे
om tatsaditi śrīmadbhagavadgītāsūpaniṣatsu brahmavidyāyāṁ yogaśāstre śrīkṛṣṇārjunasaṁvāde
ज्ञानविज्ञानयोगो नाम सप्तमोऽध्यायः श्लोकः ११
jñānavijñānayogo nāma saptamo'dhyayaḥ ślokaḥ 11

Om-Tat-Sat—Om (Braham) is the sole Reality. In the Yogic Scripture on the Science-of-Braham, the Shrimada-Bhāgvada-Gītā Upanishad, we hereby conclude Shloka 11 of the Dialogue between Shri Krishna and Arjuna entitled Jnana-Vijnana-Yoga, Canto VII.

— ॐ श्रीकृष्णाय नमः ॐ —

<u>Strength Misnamed</u>
Man thought it to be "My" strength.
He called it "My" power—
The striving, the swelling, the rise, the roar—
All that loud ascent—magnate, lordship, baron, mogul.

Tacitly man thundered: "O world, look at me. The Great me. I."
But I was not there. For I burn without smoke.

Krishna is Steadfastness
He is the silent power—even of the little.
He is the strength which is in **stillness**, in **self-control**.

Not passion's roar nor anger's flame, nor wrathful warrior's rage—
Strength is only in the **Master-of-the-self**—
One who does **Not** seek, claim, proclaim.

Inside each steadfast mind—it is Krishna who stands descended—
Not as comfort, but as confrontation—of non-real, falseness, untruth.

Krishna's Gitā is the surgery of the soul,
He is the scalpel—who cuts illusion from Truth.

Yet men stay stitching their wounds with denials,
They drown their troubles in alcohol, drugs, inanities, hobbies, games,
And when they do turn inward—it is only to hide their head.

Come O seeker, start anew,
Descend again within the Self—
But this time meet the Krishna of Gitā—
Who will reshape thy inner architecture altogether.

Let Krishna speak to thee in the silence of thy soul
Let the Fiery words of Gitā spring forth -- coil, uncoil.
Let them rise, circle, tighten around delusions—like cosmic serpents.
Let the splendor of Gitā spiral through thy Consciousness,
Let it crush all illusions—until it's all torn asunder.

But alas, most people slither away from true transformation.
They prefer wanton comfort to real metamorphosis.

O pilgrim rise—Dare the Self again,
Let that long buried lament—wrap thee into a New Awakening.

O come, discover thy true inner strength,
Let thy within heaven—split with blazing illumination!

Let the Gitā's Lightning inscribe Truth across thy inner firmament.
O mortal, come hear that thunder—which shatters all illusions:
तत् त्वम् असि **tat-tvam-asi**
—Which is not a metaphor—but the greatest Revelation!

ॐ गीता श्लोकः ७.१२ – Gītā Verse 7.12

ॐ श्रीमद्भगवद्गीतासूपनिषत्सु ब्रह्मविद्यायां योगशास्त्रे श्रीकृष्णार्जुनसंवादे
om śrīmadbhagavadgītāsūpaniṣatsu brahmavidyāyāṁ yogaśāstre śrīkṛṣṇārjunasaṁvāde
ज्ञानविज्ञानयोगो नाम सप्तमोऽध्यायः श्लोकः १२
jñānavijñānayogo nāma saptamo'dhyāyaḥ ślokaḥ 12

— ॐ —

ये चैव सात्त्विका भावा राजसास्तामसाश्च ये ।
ye caiva sāttvikā bhāvā rājasāstāmasāśca ye
मत्त एवेति तान्विद्धि न त्वहं तेषु ते मयि ॥७-१२॥
matta eveti tānviddhi na tvahaṁ teṣu te mayi (7-12)

All these three—the Sattvika, Rājasika, and Tāmasika states—know these to be born of Me; I am not in them, though they abide in Me. (7.12)

—: *Word-by-Word* :—

ये ye – whatever; च eva ca – and indeed; सात्त्विकाः sāttvikāḥ – arising from goodness; भावाः bhāvāḥ – states of being; राजसाः rājasāḥ – arising from passion; तामसाः tāmasāḥ – arising from ignorance; च ca – and; ये ye – whatever; मत्तः mattaḥ – from Me; एव iti – indeed; तान् tān – them; विद्धि viddhi – know; न na – not; तु tu – but; अहम् aham – I; तेषु teṣu – in them; ते te – they; मयि mayi – in Me.

—: *Understanding The Verse* :—

— ॐ श्रीकृष्णाय नमः ॐ —

In this esoteric verse most deep, Bhagwān Shri Krishna draws a crucial distinction between Himself and the three guṇas—Sattva, Rajas, and Tamas—which are the primary constituents of apara-prakṛti, His lower, material nature.

While these three modes are responsible for all diversity, movement, and experience in the phenomenal world, the Lord reveals that He, although their origin, remains ever transcendent and untouched.

— ॐ श्रीरामाय नमः ॐ —

Krishna affirms that all beings and their various states—whether of clarity, restlessness, or delusion—arise from these guṇas, and that these guṇas, in turn, have their origin in Him.

However, though the guṇas exist in and through Him, He does not dwell in them, nor are they intrinsic to His true nature.

This verse thus establishes the Lord's immanence and transcendence simultaneously—He is both within all things as their source and yet beyond all things as their unchanging Self.

—: *Key Sanskrit Terms* :—

— ॐ तत् सत् ॐ —

The sound widens into subtle complexity. The Sanskrit weaves सत्त्व रजस् तमस् sattva-rajas-tamas like three strands of a single cord, and तेषु ते मयि teṣu te mayi hums quietly beneath them.

The verse does not sort or judge; it simply holds. Here Sanskrit feels like a vast loom of being, where every state of existence is threaded through one silent, sustaining presence.

Let us now rest awhile at the threshold of this verse—attending to its foundational Sanskrit terms. Let us hear the Sanskrit as with colors blending on canvas. "All states of sattva, rajas, tamas—know them as born of Me, yet I am not in them." Each word both mingles and withdraws. Wisdom here lies coiled—like wick in an unlit lamp. What we need is the flint of ancient Sanātana understanding to ignite the spark.

— ॐ —

सात्त्विका भावा (sāttvikā bhāvā):
The सात्त्विक Sāttvika भाव states.
Sattva represents luminosity, purity, harmony, and knowledge.
भावा Bhāvā (states or dispositions) are modes of being—the inner tendencies of mind and heart.
सात्त्विक भाव Sattvic bhāvas incline the soul towards clarity, compassion, truthfulness, and serene joy — all reflections of the higher nature of the Self, yet still within the realm of change.

— ॐ —

राजसाः (rājasāḥ):
The Rājasic states.
राजस Rajas signifies activity, passion, restlessness, and striving.
It is the principle that propels movement, ambition, and desire.
राजसि भाव Rājasic bhāvas bind the soul through ceaseless craving for results, leading outward into the flux of worldly pursuits.

— ॐ —

तामसाः (tāmasāḥ):
The Tāmasic states.

तमस Tamas is the principle of darkness, inertia, ignorance, and confusion.

तामसि भाव Tāmasic bhāvas obscure the light of knowledge—binding the soul to delusion, error, sloth, heedlessness, and moral decline.

— ॐ —

मत्त एव (matta eva):

From मत्त Me एव alone.

Here, मत्त matta (from Me) underscores that all these guṇa-born states, whether luminous, active, or dark, have their origin in the Supreme.

They are expressions of the Lord's माया Māyā, not alien to Him, but born of His inscrutable power.

— ॐ —

न त्वहं तेषु (na tu ahaṁ teṣu):

"But I am not in them."

न na – not; तु tu – but; अहम् aham – I; तेषु teṣu – in them.

Although the guṇas arise from the Lord's potency, He remains untouched by them.

The Self is not modified by the movements of nature; it is the silent Witness साक्षी beyond all transformation.

— ॐ —

ते मयि (te mayi):

"ते They are in मयि Me."

While the guṇas and their evolutes dwell within the field of the Lord's manifestation, they do not affect His essential nature.

The entire phenomenal universe abides in Him as waves rest upon the ocean, without ever disturbing its fathomless depths.

—: In Brief :—

— ॐ श्रीकृष्णाय नमः ॐ —

ये चैव सात्त्विका भावा राजसास्तामसाश्च ये । मत्त एवेति तान्विद्धि न त्वहं तेषु ते मयि ॥

Here, the Lord reaffirms a subtle truth that is central to understanding the nature of reality: that all conditioned states, all tendencies of thought, feeling, and behavior—be they luminous, agitated, or inert—are products of the three guṇas.

These guṇas, like threads woven into the fabric of prakṛti, create the manifold appearances of the cosmos.

Whether one is inclined toward knowledge and purity (sattva), passion and striving (rajas), or inertia and ignorance (tamas), these states do not arise independently—they are but the unfolding of the Lord's own creative energy.

— ॐ श्रीरामाय नमः ॐ —

Yet—and this is the crux—Shri Krishna simultaneously also proclaims that He is not in them. Though they arise from Him, they do not bind or define Him.

The guṇas belong to prakṛti, which is His power, but not His essence.

He is the substratum, the unchanging witness (sākṣin) who remains untouched by the movements of nature, just as the sky is never stained by the clouds that float within it.

— ॐ बालकृष्णाय नमः ॐ —

To illustrate, the ancient Rishis give the analogy of the atmosphere and the cloud.

The cloud appears within the atmosphere, is supported by it, and cannot exist apart from it. Yet the atmosphere is never within the cloud, nor is it altered by its passing presence.

Likewise, though all conditioned states appear within the domain of prakṛti—and prakṛti itself is inseparable from the Lord—the Lord remains free, unaffected, eternally beyond.

This is the mystery of divine immanence and transcendence.

— ॐ सत्यनन्दाय नमः ॐ —

This teaching is not merely metaphysical; it is of immense practical significance to the spiritual aspirant. The Jiva may be influenced by the guṇas, but at the core, the Self is not.

The ego, the mind, the senses—these are molded by prakṛti, but the Ātmā is untouched. To realize this distinction is to begin the process of liberation.

By knowing the guṇas to be transient, and their source to be the unconditioned Lord, one begins to transcend identification with their play.

— ॐ दशग्रीव शिरोहराय नमः ॐ —

Thus, the Lord has now clarified that all forms, qualities, and temperaments arise from Him, yet He is ever beyond them.

This prepares the way for a deeper inquiry: if the Divine is so near, so all-pervading, why do beings fail to recognize Him? Why does the world, permeated by God, remain blind to God?

In the next verse, Bhagwān shall answer this very question— exposing the veil that obscures human vision and binds us souls to ignorance.

— ॐ तत् सत ॐ —
Before we move on, let us bow in reverence to this sacred verse. Write it by hand, reflect on its meaning, chant it aloud, make it your own.

— ॐ —

ये चैव सात्त्विका भावा राजसास्तामसाश्च ये ।
ye caiva sāttvikā bhāvā rājasāstāmasāśca ye
मत्त एवेति तान्विद्धि न त्वहं तेषु ते मयि ॥७-१२॥
matta eveti tānviddhi na tvahaṁ teṣu te mayi (7-12)

— ॐ —

ये चैव सात्त्विका भावा राजसास्तामसाश्च ये ।
ye caiva sāttvikā bhāvā rājasāstāmasāśca ye
मत्त एवेति तान्विद्धि न त्वहं तेषु ते मयि ॥७-१२॥
matta eveti tānviddhi na tvahaṁ teṣu te mayi (7-12)

ॐ तत्सदिति श्रीमद्भगवद्गीतासूपनिषत्सु ब्रह्मविद्यायां योगशास्त्रे श्रीकृष्णार्जुनसंवादे
om tatsaditi śrīmadbhagavadgītāsūpaniṣatsu brahmavidyāyāṁ yogaśāstre śrīkṛṣṇārjunasaṁvāde
ज्ञानविज्ञानयोगो नाम सप्तमोऽध्यायः श्लोकः १२
jñānavijñānayogo nāma saptamo'dhyāyaḥ ślokaḥ 12

Om-Tat-Sat—Om (Braham) is the sole Reality. In the Yogic Scripture on the Science-of-Braham, the Shrimada-Bhāgvada-Gītā Upanishad, we hereby conclude Shloka 12 of the Dialogue between Shrī Krishna and Arjuna entitled Jnana-Vijnana-Yoga, Canto VII.

— ॐ श्रीकृष्णाय नमः ॐ —

Daily the same dance. In three primary colors. Gold, crimson, black.
Three veils. Three primary moods. Three shimmering lies of Light—
But infinite their chromaticities & combinations.

Sattva, Rajas, Tamas—endless mingling hues upon the horizon—
Stay draped upon me—day in, day out. And I wear them all night.

There's no escape—it seems.
Robes of glittering sky—bright, burning, blind—
Braid a trammeling network—through our breath, marrow, mind.

The dream keeps turning; it keeps swirling—
Has swallowed me complete.
I can no longer see the Dreamer—who once, I think, was me.

ॐ गीता श्लोकः ७.१३ – Gītā Verse 7.13

ॐ श्रीमद्भगवद्गीतासूपनिषत्सु ब्रह्मविद्यायां योगशास्त्रे श्रीकृष्णार्जुनसंवादे
om śrīmadbhagavadgītāsūpaniṣatsu brahmavidyāyāṁ yogaśāstre śrīkṛṣṇārjunasaṁvāde
ज्ञानविज्ञानयोगो नाम सप्तमोऽध्यायः श्लोकः १३
jñānavijñānayogo nāma saptamo'dhyāyaḥ ślokaḥ 13

— ॐ —

त्रिभिर्गुणमयैर्भावैरेभिः सर्वमिदं जगत् ।
tribhirguṇamayairbhāvairebhiḥ sarvamidaṁ jagat
मोहितं नाभिजानाति मामेभ्यः परमव्ययम् ॥ ७-१३ ॥
mohitaṁ nābhijānāti māmebhyaḥ paramavyayam (7-13)

Deluded by the three *Gunas* of Nature this whole creation fails to recognize Me—who am the immutable Primal Cause which is beyond the three. (7.13)

—: *Word-by-Word* :—

त्रिभिः tribhiḥ – by the three; गुणमयैः guṇamayaiḥ – consisting of the modes (qualities); भावैः bhāvaiḥ – by states of being; एभिः ebhiḥ – by these; सर्वम् sarvam – all; इदम् idam – this; जगत् jagat – world; मोहितम् mohitam – deluded; न na – not; अभिजानाति abhijānāti – knows; माम् mām – Me; एभ्यः ebhyaḥ – beyond these; परमम् paramam – supreme; अव्ययम् avyayam – imperishable.

—: *Understanding The Verse* :—

In this poignant verse, Bhagwān Shri Krishna turns to the root cause of humanity's spiritual blindness. Despite His all-pervading presence, the world fails to recognize Him—not because He is distant or concealed, but because beings are deluded by guṇa-mayī māyā, the veil draped upon the Self—which obscureness is woven by the three modes of nature: Sattva, Rajas, and Tamas.

These guṇas, while arising from the Lord's own prakṛti, have the peculiar power to obscure the very source from which they come.

— ॐ सत्यधर्मपरायणाय नमः ॐ —

The guṇas are not inherently evil; rather, they are the dynamic forces that shape experience, perception, and thought.

But when one becomes identified with their fluctuating manifestations—be it the pleasure of Sattva, the restlessness of Rajas, or the inertia of Tamas—**one forgets the substratum, the niyamya, the one who is beyond all movement and change: the Self.**

This verse reveals a profound psychological and metaphysical truth: ignorance of the Divine arises not from lack of access to God, but from misidentification with the transient evolutes of prakṛti.

The way back lies in transcending these guṇas, and recognizing the unchanging Lord who is their source but remains ever beyond them.

—: Key Sanskrit Terms :—

— ॐ तत् सत् ॐ —

Now the cadence dims and glows at once. त्रिभिः मोहितम् जगत् tribhiḥ mohitaṃ jagat drifts like a soft veil across the hearing, while परमम् अव्ययम् paramam avyayam shines faintly behind it.

The Sanskrit lets obscuration and transcendence rest in the same breath. The verse feels like a twilight of awareness, where the unseen is not absent, only gently hidden within the folds of sound.

Now let us continue on, not chasing the verse but walking with it—like pilgrims, poets, and wanderers always have. And if the path is winding, so be it. The Bhagavad-Gītā was never meant to be a straight road to the summit—but a gentle less-tiring circling path.

— ॐ —

त्रिभिः गुणमयैः भावैः (tribhiḥ guṇamayaiḥ bhāvaiḥ):
"By the त्रिभिः threefold गुणमयैः guṇa-imbued भावैः states."
गुणमय Guṇamaya (composed of the guṇas) indicates that the modes of existence — whether of Sattva, Rajas, or Tamas — are pervaded, conditioned, and shaped entirely by these primal forces.
The भावैः bhāvāḥ (states or dispositions) thus are not intrinsic to the pure Self, but are modifications of Prakṛti, woven by the interplay of the guṇas गुण.

— ॐ —

एभिः सर्वमिदं जगत् (ebhiḥ sarvam idaṃ jagat):
"एभिः By these, सर्वमिदं जगत् this whole world."
The जगत् jagat — the moving, mutable universe — is wholly under the influence of the three गुण guṇas.
From the subtlest thought to the densest matter, all phenomena arise from these qualities, and thus all of conditioned existence is immersed in their sway.

— ॐ —

मोहितं (mohitam):
"Deluded."

मोह Moha signifies deep confusion or bewilderment, a condition wherein the true nature of reality is obscured.

The world, मोहितं mohitam, stands bewildered by the ever-shifting play of the guṇas, unable to perceive the underlying eternal Reality.

— ॐ —

न अभिजानाति (na abhijānāti):

"Does न not अभिजानाति recognize."

The ignorance born of moha is not mere intellectual unawareness; it is a profound failure of vision — a spiritual blindness that prevents beings from recognizing their own immortal essence and the Supreme Source behind all appearances.

— ॐ —

माम् एभ्यः परम् अव्ययम् (mām ebhyaḥ param avyayam):

"Me, who is beyond these—and imperishable."

एभ्यः Beyond these, माम् Me—who am परमम् the supreme अव्ययम् imperishable.

The Lord is here revealing His own transcendent nature: परम param (beyond) the गुण guṇas, अव्ययम् avyayam (imperishable, immutable), untouched by the vicissitudes of the manifested cosmos.

Though the guṇas arise from Him, He remains ever free, the changeless substratum of all which is seen fluxing.

Alike the unwavering ocean deep—beneath its heaving waves!

—: In Brief :—

— ॐ श्रीकृष्णाय नमः ॐ —

त्रिभिर्गुणमयैर्भावैरेभिः सर्वमिदं जगत् । मोहितं नाभिजानाति मामेभ्यः परमव्ययम् ॥

"The whole world, deluded by the objects born of the three guṇas, fails to recognize Me, who am the immutable absolute, beyond the guṇas."

We beings stay lost in the forest mist. **Deluded by the guṇas we know not Him—who abides beyond this manifest mist.**

Each Gītā word speaks to us of great truths—but ignorance lurks in our hearts, and **ensnared in the web of māyā, we stay sighing behind veils of delusions.**

— ॐ श्रीरामाय नमः ॐ —

The vision of this verse is at once philosophical and compassionate. The Lord, having revealed His presence in the forces of nature and in the noble qualities of beings, now explains why, despite His nearness, He is not known. **It is moha—delusion, born of attachment to the guṇas—that veils the truth.**

The word **गुणमयैः** guṇa-mayaiḥ indicates that all phenomena in this world—both external objects and internal experiences—are constituted by the guṇas.

— ॐ चतुर्भुजाय नमः ॐ —

The jagat, the world of living beings, becomes enchanted by these phenomena.

Sattva tempts with peace and knowledge;

Rajas agitates with desire and ambition;

Tamas seduces with sleep and forgetfulness—

and in all cases, the Jiva—having become entranced by these shifting forces—loses sight of his own eternal source.

— ॐ अग्निजन्मने नमः ॐ —

Though the guṇas arise from Him, Bhagwān asserts that He is not bound by them. He is avyayaḥ—imperishable, beyond all mutation, standing ever as the silent witness (sākṣin) behind prakṛti's play.

He is not touched by the qualities that emanate from Him, just as light illumines objects of all colors without being altered by any.

— ॐ त्रिलोकात्मने नमः ॐ —

The analogy, often given by sages, is that of gold and ornaments.

All ornaments—bracelets, rings, necklaces—are but modifications of gold. Yet, if one is mesmerized by the shape, one forgets the substance.

So too, those who are drawn only to the surface of creation—the effects of Sattva, Rajas, and Tamas—fail to perceive the gold-like essence, the ātmā-rūpa of Bhagwān, that pervades and supports all.

— ॐ भक्तप्रियाय नमः ॐ —

And yet, this verse carries no tone of condemnation. It is not a verdict, but a diagnosis.

Krishna, as the Divine Teacher, gently points out that those who are caught in the glamour of prakṛti mistake the transient for the eternal, the conditioned for the Absolute. And in this misidentification, they lose sight of the very goal of life—realization of the Self, gaining one's union with the Lord – becoming one in the waveless ocean of existence-bliss-consciousness.

— ॐ यज्ञप्रियाय नमः ॐ —

This verse subtly prepares us for transition to the next teaching: how one may transcend the delusion of the guṇas.

Arjuna's unspoken question—"Is there a way beyond this delusion?"—rises naturally in the heart. Compassionate and ever-gracious, the Lord anticipates this and will now reveal the way to cross beyond this guṇa-bound world into the light of the Eternal.

Next we shall hear how the veils are lifted and the path to the Supreme is revealed.

— ॐ तत् सत् ॐ —

Before moving on, let us once more bow in deep reverence before this sacred verse of the Bhagavad-Gītā, an eternal beacon of wisdom that ceaselessly illumines the path of seekers. Engage with its form—inscribe it with your own hand, let your heart dwell upon its meaning, and raise your voice in its chanting—for within these syllables echoes the undying proclamation delivered millennia ago on the battlefield of Kurukshetra. These words, transmitted unchanged across the unbroken chain of generations, form a living bridge, linking us to that sanctified era when Bhagwāna Shri Krishna Himself walked this earth and bestowed this divine teaching. Through the luminous vibration of these sacred Sanskrit sounds, we are drawn nearer to His timeless presence, touching the very heartbeat of the Eternal.

— ॐ —

त्रिभिर्गुणमयैर्भावैरेभिः सर्वमिदं जगत् ।
tribhirguṇamayairbhāvairebhiḥ sarvamidaṁ jagat
मोहितं नाभिजानाति मामेभ्यः परमव्ययम् ॥७-१३॥
mohitaṁ nābhijānāti māmebhyaḥ paramavyayam (7-13)

त्रिभिर्गुणमयैर्भावैरेभिः सर्वमिदं जगत् ।
tribhirguṇamayairbhāvairebhiḥ sarvamidaṁ jagat
मोहितं नाभिजानाति मामेभ्यः परमव्ययम् ॥७-१३॥
mohitaṁ nābhijānāti māmebhyaḥ paramavyayam (7-13)

ॐ तत्सदिति श्रीमद्भगवद्गीतासूपनिषत्सु ब्रह्मविद्यायां योगशास्त्रे श्रीकृष्णार्जुनसंवादे
om tatsaditi śrīmadbhagavadgītāsūpaniṣatsu brahmavidyāyāṁ yogaśāstre śrīkṛṣṇārjunasaṁvāde
ज्ञानविज्ञानयोगो नाम सप्तमोऽध्यायः श्लोकः १३
jñānavijñānayogo nāma saptamo'dhyāyaḥ ślokaḥ 13

Om-Tat-Sat—Om (Braham) is the sole Reality. In the Yogic Scripture on the Science-of-Braham, the Shrimada-Bhāgvada-Gītā Upanishad, we hereby conclude Shloka 13 of the Dialogue between Shrī Krishna and Arjuna entitled Jnana-Vijnana-Yoga, Canto VII.

— ॐ श्रीकृष्णाय नमः ॐ —

Behold the tragedy of human kind —
God who came down to sport—yet now walking in chains,

Spirit become drunk—on the spirit of his own becoming—
Rather unbecoming. From god→to man. And in this age→back to brute!

The guṇas three? They decorate his prison wall.
Darkness? He sleeps on that bed of Tamas all night long.

Desire? He likes the whipping of Rajas lacerating his heart.
Virtue? Aye—even Sattva's goodness stays a noose upon his soul.

All the while, Krishna stands nigh—the Supreme One, beyond three!
Yet man see Him not—remaining bedazzled by the Guna's plays.
He stays forgetful of the Gītā—the fire that unmasks all illusions,

Awaken O mortal to the Gītā verses—
That are like the iron clang upon the sleeping soul.
Wake up human—to Krishna and His Gītā—
And save thyself from certain Death—the upcoming BROB event.

In our minds, the world hangs like a Tapestry:
Threads of gold, shadow, blood, and dawn.
Woven by Prkriti—in three primary colors of Gunas Three,
And Krishna is the immutable Primal-Cause behind all weavings,

But humans of this age have kept slashing at the threads
They have sliced the Tapestry—loosened the ends, created imbalance
And now the whole pattern is about to unravel

Listen sharply, O human—
Do ye hear the footsteps of Kāla approaching yonder from Hell?
Krishna's lament flickers through the broken weave:
"Ye humans unmade My design—
Now walk the jagged frayed edges ye created."

O human fools, Do ye feel God's pain?
He God is nearer and dearer than breath,
Yet farther than the edge of Aloofness—for He doesn't really care.
He weeps without sorrow, burns without heat,
He laments but without despair—to Him human is just a gnat, a yawn.

Krishna's paradox is simple:
"Ye are Me—
Yet ye refuse to be me."
Yes, we humans have become the very opposite of God & goodness.
O seeker, understand this paradox—and awaken even now.

God will **not** let the whole tapestry be ruined—
Just because a single thread has gone rogue.
He would rather surgically excise this cancerous abscess forever.

Aye, God **will let go** of the gangrene sore called Homo-sapiens—

Rather than let the whole Earth die—due to follies of one species.

God appears to us as an Entity most Strange—
Until we remember: God is not human-centric at all.
Sometimes even His shadow teaches,
Sometimes even His presence destroys.
Birth & Death. Both are Truth. Both are His mercy.

It was humans who abandoned the **Light** of **Sanâtana-Dharma**.
And now stand scared of **Darkness**—that inevitably descends with **adharma**.

God laments—and yet He yawns aloof—looking at us Stupes:
"I gave to thee Sanâtana-Dharma—
The beautiful path to worldly happiness and Nirvana, both—
And yet you chose neither—but embraced adharma instead!
It is for that reason—that I have withdrawn from midst thee,
And I allow the light of the world to now grow dim."

O Bedazed Foolish Humans
You know Nothing at all of Bhagwân Krishna
You mistook the Infinite for an anecdote,
You took His teachings to be some kind of joke.

You took His Fire to be a festival lamp,
You took Krishna, the Axis of Dharma, for a dancing boy.

Hear now the thunder that rips apart this man-made charade:
Krishna is not a butter-thief who come to amuse you—
To charm you with tales of romance, song, dance.

He came to remind you of your Dharma.
He came to redeem, to enlighten—to tell us right from wrong.

But we shrank that great God to fit our comforts—
Rather than detonate our awakening, realize our oneness in God.

But never mind the world—
For the Wise always remains awake in the **Real Krishna**.
The wise recognizes the immutable **Primal-Cause** beyond Three Gunas.
He stays bowed before the blazing Sun of Consciousness: Bhagwân Krishna.

The wise does not tremble before the mirage of death.
He knows: I am the radiant Âtmâ, unborn, undying.

In the orbit of Gitâ's wisdom I stand firm.
ॐ तत्सत् Om Tat Sat — He, Bhagwân Krishna, alone is The-One.

ॐ गीता श्लोकः ७.१४ – Gītā Verse 7.14

ॐ श्रीमद्भगवद्गीतासूपनिषत्सु ब्रह्मविद्यायां योगशास्त्रे श्रीकृष्णार्जुनसंवादे
om śrīmadbhagavadgītāsūpaniṣatsu brahmavidyāyāṁ yogaśāstre śrīkṛṣṇārjunasaṁvāde
ज्ञानविज्ञानयोगो नाम सप्तमोऽध्यायः श्लोकः १४
jñānavijñānayogo nāma saptamo'dhyāyaḥ ślokaḥ 14

— ॐ —

दैवी ह्येषा गुणमयी मम माया दुरत्यया ।

daivī hyeṣā guṇamayī mama māyā duratyayā

मामेव ये प्रपद्यन्ते मायामेतां तरन्ति ते ॥७-१४॥

māmeva ye prapadyante māyāmetāṁ taranti te (7-14)

This most enchanting Māyā of mine, constituted of the *Gunas*, is indeed most difficult to overcome; only those who take refuge in Me are able to get across Māyā. (7.14)

—: *Word-by-Word* :—

दैवी daivī – divine; हि hi – indeed; एषा eṣā – this; गुणमयी guṇamayī – consisting of the modes of nature; मम mama – My; माया māyā – illusory energy; दुरत्यया duratyayā – difficult to overcome; माम् mām – to Me; एव eva – alone; ये ye – those who; प्रपद्यन्ते prapadyante – surrender; मायाम् एतां māyām etāṁ – this illusion; तरन्ति taranti – cross beyond; ते te – they.

—: *Understanding The Verse* :—

— ॐ श्रीकृष्णाय नमः ॐ —

In this revealing verse, Bhagwān Shri Krishna discloses the formidable power of His Māyā—the divine illusion composed of the three guṇas: Sattva, Rajas, and Tamas.

This Māyā is not a mere mental error or a trick of perception, but an all-encompassing cosmic force, subtle and vast, most formidable —and which causes us souls to identify with the fleeting world of names and forms rather than with the eternal Self—the source.

Through this veil, the Infinite appears as finite, the Self appears as body, and the fleeting appears permanent, and the unchanging appears to be dull, dead, void—vacuous.

— ॐ श्रीरामाय नमः ॐ —

Yet even as the Lord proclaims its power and the near impossibility of overcoming it by human effort alone, He offers a clear path to transcendence: those who take exclusive refuge in Him do get to cross this ocean of illusion, this भवसागर bhavasāgara.

Thus, while the world may stay bewildered, Krishna stands as the ever-accessible harbor of liberation—the gracious refuge for those who turn to Him in complete surrender.

This verse forms a pivotal moment in the Gītā, where the doctrine of surrender (शरणागति śaraṇāgati) is unveiled as the highest means to freedom from bondages.

—: Key Sanskrit Terms :—

— ॐ तत सत ॐ —

Now let us hearken the sounds. Let us begin, as though for the first time—like tracing the hush of early morning on a still lake. Feel each Sanskrit word here as a ripple, soft and sure, expanding into the vast quiet of meaning.

The language turns quiet and formidable. Sanskrit lets देवी हि एषा daivī hy eṣā guṇa-mayī rise like a luminous barrier, and माया māyā flickers with enchanting gravity. मामेव ये प्रपद्यन्ते mām eva ye prapadyante glows like a narrow, radiant crossing.

The verse does not struggle; it stands. Here Sanskrit becomes both veil and passage, casting a spell that only surrender seems able to loosen.

— ॐ —

देवी हि एषा (daivī hi eṣā):
"देवी Divine एषा this हि indeed is."
The adjective देवी daivī (divine) immediately uplifts the understanding of Māyā from a mere illusory trap to a sacred, cosmic force.
Though माया Māyā veils reality, it is a power of the Lord Himself — not separate from Him, but manifesting His inscrutable will.
The particle हि hi (indeed) lends emphasis, affirming the profound mystery of this माया Māyā.

— ॐ —

गुणमयी (guṇamayī):
"Made of the guṇas."
गुणमयी Guṇamayi suggests that माया Māyā is constituted and woven from the threads of सत्त्व रजस तमस Sattva, Rajas, and Tamas. It is through the modulation of these threefold qualities that Māyā shapes all forms, experiences, and states of consciousness.

— ॐ —

मम माया (mama māyā):

"मम My माया Māyā."

Here, Krishna reveals His own intimate relationship to Māyā — it is not an independent or external principle, but His own शक्ति śakti (divine potency).

Thus, even while Māyā deludes, it remains under the supreme sovereignty of the Lord.

— ॐ —

दुरत्यया (duratyayā):

"Difficult to cross."

The term दुरत्यया duratyayā conveys the formidable strength of Māyā.

For the ordinary being, bound by ignorance and desire, the crossing over this vast ocean of delusion is all but impossible through mere personal effort.

— ॐ —

मामेव ये प्रपद्यन्ते (mām eva ye prapadyante):

माम् to Me एव alone ये those who प्रपद्यन्ते surrender—"Those who surrender unto Me alone."

The phrase प्रपद्यन्ते prapadyante (from prapatti, surrender) signifies an act of complete self-offering, a placing of one's entire being at the feet of the Divine, acknowledging one's helplessness before Māyā and one's sole reliance upon the Supreme.

— ॐ —

मायामेतां तरन्ति ते (māyām etāṁ taranti te):

मायाम् this illusion तरन्ति cross over ते they—"They cross beyond this Māyā."

Through surrender, by Divine grace, the aspirant is carried beyond the shoreless sea of Māyā.

The verb तरन्ति taranti (they cross) evokes the image of a soul ferried across the treacherous ocean of becoming into the realm of immortal Beingness.

—: In Brief :—

— ॐ श्रीकृष्णाय नमः ॐ —

दैवी ह्येषा गुणमयी मम माया दुरत्यया । मामेव ये प्रपद्यन्ते मायामेतां तरन्ति ते ॥

We rest with this verse as with net woven strong. Bhagwān Shri Krishna declares with gravity and compassion: "Truly, this Māyā of Mine—composed of the three guṇas—is divine and most difficult to overcome; but those who take refuge in Me alone, they cross over this Māyā." Each word here is a challenge—but which comes with the key.

This Māyā is not a simple illusion born of ignorance, but daivī māyā—God's own inscrutable, divine power. It is the Lord's cosmic shakti, through which He conceals Himself even while pervading all. Remember this is all a sport of Braham.

It is by this Māyā that the One appears as many, the Formless takes form, and the Immutable plays amidst change.

Through it arise all dualities—pleasure and pain, success and failure, bondage and apparent freedom.

— ॐ ब्रह्मरूपिणे नमः ॐ —

The phrase दुरत्यया duratyayā—"most difficult to cross"—conveys the vastness and subtlety of this divine veil.

No mere human effort, intellectual pursuit, or ritual alone can pierce it. Even Sattva, though luminous, is still a chain if not transcended.

Therefore, the Lord reveals the only sure path: मामेव ये प्रपद्यन्ते mām eva ye prapadyante—"those who take refuge in Me alone."

Not half-heartedly, not in part, but eva—exclusively, unreservedly.

— ॐ जानकीवल्लभाय नमः ॐ —

To take refuge in Krishna is not simply to seek Him in distress, but to surrender the very ego that claims separation.

It means to offer one's body, mind, and heart into His hands, to see Him as the ultimate protector, beloved, guide, and goal.

Such surrender is not a mark of weakness but the highest strength, for it transcends the fragmented self and aligns the soul with the infinite.

— ॐ अद्भुतचरित्राय नमः ॐ —

The devotee who thus surrenders ceases to be bewildered by Māyā, for he no longer sees the world as disconnected from the Divine. **Instead, he sees all as belonging to Krishna, and everything as His līlā;**
and now the sense of "mine" and "not mine," the fever of desire and fear, fall away;
and the devotee lives in the world—and yet remains untouched, just like the lotus leaf on water.

— ॐ जगदेकधारिणे नमः ॐ —

Thus, the Lord establishes here a great spiritual truth:

while Māyā is indeed overpowering, surrender to the Supreme—śaraṇāgati—is the master key that dissolves its hold.

It is by His grace alone that the veil is lifted and the truth of the Self is revealed.

And yet, this profound gift of refuge is not embraced by all! Why?

The question naturally arises: if surrender is the only way across, what keeps humans from seeking it? **Why do they persist in clinging to that which binds them?**

Anticipating this question, the all-compassionate Lord now turns to expose the inner condition that causes beings to turn away from Him—the subtle forces that veil one's will itself.

We shall now listen to the Lord unveiling a great truth—shedding light on the inner **root of resistance to the Divine.**

— ॐ तत् सत् ॐ —

Before moving on, let us once more bow in deep reverence before this sacred verse of the Bhagavad-Gītā, an eternal beacon of wisdom that ceaselessly illumines the path of seekers. Engage with its form—inscribe it with your own hand, let your heart dwell upon its meaning, and raise your voice in its chanting—for within these syllables echoes the undying proclamation delivered millennia ago on the battlefield of Kurukshetra. These words, transmitted unchanged across the unbroken chain of generations, form a living bridge, linking us to that sanctified era when Bhagwāna Shri Krishna Himself walked this earth and bestowed this divine teaching. Through the luminous vibration of these sacred Sanskrit sounds, we are drawn nearer to His timeless presence, touching the very heartbeat of the Eternal.

— ॐ —

दैवी ह्येषा गुणमयी मम माया दुरत्यया ।
daivī hyeṣā guṇamayī mama māyā duratyayā
मामेव ये प्रपद्यन्ते मायामेतां तरन्ति ते ॥७-१४॥
māmeva ye prapadyante māyāmetāṁ taranti te (7-14)

— ॐ —

दैवी ह्येषा गुणमयी मम माया दुरत्यया ।
daivī hyeṣā guṇamayī mama māyā duratyayā
मामेव ये प्रपद्यन्ते मायामेतां तरन्ति ते ॥७-१४॥
māmeva ye prapadyante māyāmetāṁ taranti te (7-14)

ॐ तत्सदिति श्रीमद्भगवद्गीतासूपनिषत्सु ब्रह्मविद्यायां योगशास्त्रे श्रीकृष्णार्जुनसंवादे
om tatsaditi śrīmadbhagavadgītāsūpaniṣatsu brahmavidyāyāṁ yogaśāstre śrīkrṣṇārjunasaṁvāde
ज्ञानविज्ञानयोगो नाम सप्तमोऽध्यायः श्लोकः १४
jñānavijñānayogo nāma saptamo'dhyayaḥ ślokaḥ 14

Om-Tat-Sat—Om (Braham) is the sole Reality. In the Yogic Scripture on the Science-of-Braham, the Shrimada-Bhāgvada-Gītā Upanishad, we hereby conclude Shloka 14 of the Dialogue between Shrī Krishna and Arjuna entitled Jnana-Vijnana-Yoga, Canto VII.

— ॐ श्रीकृष्णाय नमः ॐ —

A shimmering veil fully spun of gold—
Ah, that charming net was so beautiful, so adorable.

Māyā—the wench made of stunning lights,
Was not fearsome at all—but bold, lovely, bright.

Nothing coarse—only fine silken clothes, silver, jewel, gold,
Her aura so enchanting—I could do nothing else but simply bow.

And so ever since then—
I have stayed bound to these beautiful chains. Still am.
O Māyā—sweetness doused in wine, women, dance, song,
Thou have wrapped me so soft—I am nothing now but thy pet hound.

Trammeled—with thy sparkle, froth, lust, power, gold—
I stay so enthralled—I call **thy chains** my love, my life, my soul.

Thou wearest these masks: of love, success, friends, aura, fame—
O lady, ye stay veiling our True Lord—behind thy shifting face.

Alas, I followed thy sparkling dreams, drank thy wine—and I slept.
I forgot—there was a harsh tempest raging outside.
And now I am all alone. And belatedly I realize—
It was Lord-God Krishna, the Savior, I had left behind.

Then, of a Sudden—Krishna's Unannounced Grace!
Lo—for Silence suddenly blooms within my chest—
Not thought—but something beyond -- something supremely blessed,
The kind that does not shout or shine—
Simply whispers: "O child, you still are very much Mine."

The storms outside have not yet fully ceased—
But something in me—a tranquil within stillness—has now increased.

It's a Knowing—that I need no longer fight—
But simply flow unconcerned—into the very Arms-of-Light.

The Woven Māyā's Net was all My Doing—all Mine.
Yes—mine, not Thine. I was the culprit, I admit.
It was I who wove the threads with such gusto, so much relish.

The charms, the songs & dance—and then going back to sleep.
Daily. Day after day. Everyday. Without delay.
You could have seen—and simply passed on unconcerned.
And yet You stayed!
O Thank You, Thank You, Bhagwān Shri Krishna. I am so fortunate.

ॐ गीता श्लोकः ७.१५ – Gītā Verse 7.15

ॐ श्रीमद्भगवद्गीतासूपनिषत्सु ब्रह्मविद्यायां योगशास्त्रे श्रीकृष्णार्जुनसंवादे
om śrīmadbhagavadgītāsūpaniṣatsu brahmavidyāyāṁ yogaśāstre śrīkṛṣṇārjunasaṁvāde
ज्ञानविज्ञानयोगो नाम सप्तमोऽध्यायः श्लोकः १५
jñānavijñānayogo nāma saptamo'dhyāyaḥ ślokaḥ 15

— ॐ —

न मां दुष्कृतिनो मूढाः प्रपद्यन्ते नराधमाः ।

na māṁ duṣkṛtino mūḍhāḥ prapadyante narādhamāḥ

माययापहृतज्ञाना आसुरं भावमाश्रिताः ॥७-१५॥

māyayāpahṛtajñānā āsuraṁ bhāvamāśritāḥ (7-15)

Wretches among men, the wicked and the ignorant, do not take refuge in Me—betaking themselves to their demoniacal nature, and being deprived of their discrimination and discernment by dint of Māyā. (7.15)

—: *Word-by-Word* :—

न na – not; माम् mām – unto Me; दुष्कृतिनः duṣkṛtinaḥ – evildoers; मूढाः mūḍhāḥ – the foolish; प्रपद्यन्ते prapadyante – surrender; नराधमाः narādhamaḥ – the lowest among mankind; मायया māyayā – by illusion; अपहृतज्ञानाः apahṛta-jñānāḥ – whose knowledge is stolen; आसुरम् āsuram – demonic; भावम् bhāvam – nature; आश्रिताः āśritāḥ – taken refuge in.

—: *Understanding The Verse* :—

— ॐ श्रीकृष्णाय नमः ॐ —

In this profound śloka, Bhagwān Shri Krishna unveils the inner condition of those souls who, despite being endowed with human birth—the rarest of blessings—still fail to seek refuge in Him.

Krishna speaks **not of occasional falterings or transient delusions**, but of **deeply embedded tendencies** which, over lifetimes, have **distanced** these jīvas from the **very root of dharma** and from the **Divine**.

— ॐ श्रीरामाय नमः ॐ —

These beings, termed "wretches among men," are not condemned by the Lord in anger, but revealed here in clarity.

Bound by the snares of Māyā—manifesting predominantly through the guṇas of rajas, and tamas—they fall prey to a Nature that is termed āsuric—**demoniacal**—not merely in behavior but in **disposition**.

These are not seekers of truth, nor do they aspire toward the **normal goals of life—dharma, artha, kāma, and ultimately mokṣa**. Instead, they are described as those whose **discrimination (viveka) has been eclipsed**, whose discernment is lost, and whose orientation is away from the Eternal toward the ephemeral.

— ॐ योगिनां गुरवे नमः ॐ —

Thusly in this verse, Shri Krishna lays bare the tragic plight of those who do not take refuge in Him—not as a condemnation, but as a mirror, a warning, and a call to discernment.

This verse prepares us for self-reflection: to reflect deeply on **what distances us from the Divine**—and thereafter to **break those barriers** and **aspire earnestly** toward union with Him.

—: Key Sanskrit Terms :—

— ॐ तत सत ॐ —

Ah, the cadence darkens into a solemn hush. Sanskrit breathes मूढाः नराधमाः mūḍhāḥ and narādhamāḥ with a heavy, falling tone, while आसुरं भावम āsuraṃ bhavam looms like a shadowed descent. माययापहृतज्ञाना Māyayāpahṛta-jñānāḥ murmurs with quiet loss.

The verse does not condemn; it tolls with clarity. The Sanskrit feels like a deep bell rung in a cavern of forgetting, its echo carrying **both warning and sorrow** into the stillness.

Now we shall unfold the deeper resonances of this śloka by tracing the nuanced meanings of its central Sanskrit terms.

— ॐ —

दुष्कृतिनः (duṣkṛtinaḥ):
"The wicked-doers."
दुष्कृतिनः Duṣkṛtinaḥ signifies those whose actions are evil or unrighteous — those who, despite possessing human birth and opportunity, squander it in deeds that violate Dharma.
Their merits are poisoned by their own dark tendencies.

— ॐ —

मूढाः (mūḍhāḥ):
"The deluded ones."
Mūḍha points to deep confusion and misapprehension. Such souls, enveloped in ignorance, cannot discern between the transient and the eternal, the real and the unreal.
Their vision is shrouded by अविद्या avidyā.

— ॐ —

नराधमाः (narādhamāḥ):

"The lowest among men."

नराधमाः Narādhamāḥ (नर nara + अधमाः adhamāḥ) refers to those who, despite human birth — a gateway to liberation — degrade themselves by sinking into the baser instincts, living lives enslaved by passions and darkness.

— ॐ —

मायया अपहृतज्ञानाः (māyayā apahṛtajñānāḥ):

मायया by delusion अपहृत is abducted ज्ञानाः whose knowledge—"Whose knowledge is stolen by Māyā."

अपहृतज्ञानाः Apahṛta-jñāna vividly depicts the condition where even the latent spiritual knowledge inherent in beings is covered, seized away by the powerful veiling force of Māyā, leaving them unable to recognize the Divine within or without.

— ॐ —

आसुरं भावम् आश्रिताः (āsuraṁ bhāvam āśritāḥ):

आसुरम् demoniacal भावम् nature आश्रिताः taken shelter into—"Those who take recourse to demoniacal disposition."

आसुर भावम् Āsura bhāva embodies qualities such as pride, cruelty, selfishness, hypocrisy, and disdain for Dharma.

आश्रिताः Āśritāḥ (having taken refuge) indicates that these beings willingly, even joyously, adopt such darkened states as their very nature.

—: In Brief :—

— ॐ श्रीकृष्णाय नमः ॐ —

This verse reveals the fourfold category of those unfortunate souls who, despite being born as human beings, do not turn toward Shri Krishna—Lord-God Creator, the very essence of existence and the refuge of all.

The Lord identifies them as दुष्कृतिनः मूढाः नराधमाः मायया-अपहृतज्ञानाः duṣkṛtinaḥ, mūḍhāḥ, narādhamāḥ, and māyayāpahṛtajñānāḥ—each expressing a distinct yet interrelated obstruction on the spiritual path.

These are not mere labels but unveilments of deeply ingrained states of consciousness.

It is luckless souls, heavy with divine estrangement,
living inside closed doors of the mind
—proofed against tappings of reasoning and light—

by their conditioned upbringing at the hands of the enslaving system of the asuric ruling elites and the two evil men-made creeds.

The deluded, lowest of men, bereft of knowledge, godless—do not take to the Real—even if it came knocking on the door.

— ॐ श्रीरामाय नमः ॐ —

The दुष्कृतिनः duṣkṛtinaḥ are not simply those who occasionally err—rather those whose past and present karmas are **steeped in adharma**—who willfully act contrary to the śāstras, shunning righteous action and the dhārmic yajña ordained by śāstras.

The मूढाः mūḍhāḥ are veiled in inertia and ignorance—bereft not just of knowledge, but of the very need for knowledge. Their hearts remain turned toward fleeting enjoyments, and they drift through life without purpose or reverence—unknown to their own divinity.

The नराधमाः nārādhamāḥ—the lowest among men—are those who squander the sacred opportunity of human embodiment, indulging in sensuality and callousness, rejecting the call of dharma even when it stands plainly before them.

The मायया-अपहृतज्ञानाः māyayā-apahṛtajñānāḥ are those who, though perhaps intellectually equipped, are deprived of spiritual discernment due to their irreverence and inner defiance.

In them, pride masquerades as reason, and skepticism shrouds the light of śraddhā (faith).

They reject sanātana-dharma, the vedas, śāstras, deny the eternal truths handed down through the lineage of ācāryas, and thus stay severed from the roots of true knowledge—which tells man of the nature of Existence and of God and of his own divinity.

— ॐ पितृभक्ताय नमः ॐ —

At the core of all these conditions lies Māyā—not as a mere external force, but as a binding veil that deludes the jīva into identifying with the transient instead of the Eternal.

When this veil is willingly embraced—through repeated indulgence, denial, or defiance—the soul becomes ever more entrenched in his āsuric nature, where there is no reverence, no surrender, and thus no access to divine grace.

— ॐ पातालदर्पहन्त्रे नमः ॐ —

This verse serves as a solemn teaching: **that the human birth, though noble, does not guarantee spiritual vision.**

One must take the shelter of sanātana-dharma, cultivate the faculty of discernment, and turn the heart toward the Divine with humility and longing. Only then does the path of emancipation opens—leading one to the divine realm of Satt-chitt-ānanda braham, the ocean of existence-bliss-consciousness -- whose manifest form is Bhagwān Shri Krishna.

— ॐ श्रीमते नमः ॐ —

As this verse closes, a natural question arises in the heart of attentive: if such are those who do not approach the Lord, then who are they who do? In response, Shri Krishna offers a luminous answer, describing the noble souls who, driven by wisdom and yearning, surrender to Him. The next verse becomes the bright counterpart to this dark one—offering a vision of the beautiful soul who walks the path divine.

— ॐ तत सत ॐ —

Before moving on, let us once more bow in deep reverence before this sacred verse of the Bhagavad-Gītā, an eternal beacon of wisdom that ceaselessly illumines the path of seekers. Engage with its form—inscribe it with your own hand, let your heart dwell upon its meaning, and raise your voice in its chanting—for within these syllables echoes the undying proclamation delivered millennia ago on the battlefield of Kurukshetra. These words, transmitted unchanged across the unbroken chain of generations, form a living bridge, linking us to that sanctified era when Bhagwāna Shri Krishna Himself walked this earth and bestowed this divine teaching. Through the luminous vibration of these sacred Sanskrit sounds, we are drawn nearer to His timeless presence, touching the very heartbeat of the Eternal.

— ॐ —

न मां दुष्कृतिनो मूढाः प्रपद्यन्ते नराधमाः ।
na māṁ duṣkṛtino mūḍhāḥ prapadyante narādhamāḥ
माययापहृतज्ञाना आसुरं भावमाश्रिताः ॥७-१५॥
māyayāpahṛtajñānā āsuraṁ bhāvamāśritāḥ (7-15)

न मां दुष्कृतिनो मूढाः प्रपद्यन्ते नराधमाः ।
na māṁ duṣkṛtino mūḍhāḥ prapadyante narādhamāḥ
माययापहृतज्ञाना आसुरं भावमाश्रिताः ॥७-१५॥
māyayāpahṛtajñānā āsuraṁ bhāvamāśritāḥ (7-15)

ॐ तत्सदिति श्रीमद्भगवद्गीतासूपनिषत्सु ब्रह्मविद्यायां योगशास्त्रे श्रीकृष्णार्जुनसंवादे
om tatsaditi śrīmadbhagavadgītāsūpaniṣatsu brahmavidyāyāṁ yogaśāstre śrīkṛṣṇārjunasaṁvāde
ज्ञानविज्ञानयोगो नाम सप्तमोऽध्यायः श्लोकः १५
jñānavijñānayogo nāma saptamo'dhyāyaḥ ślokaḥ 15

Om-Tat-Sat—Om (Braham) is the sole Reality. In the Yogic Scripture on the Science-of-Braham, the Shrimada-Bhāgvada-Gītā Upanishad, we hereby conclude Shloka 15 of the Dialogue between Shri Krishna and Arjuna entitled Jnana-Vijnana-Yoga, Canto VII.

— ॐ श्रीकृष्णाय नमः ॐ —

<u>The Teacher They Would Not Hear</u>
I didst speak to them!
Not once—but many times. At times daily.

I once spoke through hunger.
Then—through delightful meals.
Then—through failure.
Then—through successes.
Then through great happiness.

Yes, I spoke in diverse way.
But stunned & conditioned—they would not hear Me: God.

They kept changing the station.
Truth stays boring to them.
They prefer romance, drama, comedy, action.
Ah, humans!

But worry not—for in a world bereft of godliness,
Ye do get plenty of drama & action.
And yes—it comes soon—to a city near you.
No worries!

— ॐ श्रीकृष्णाय नमः ॐ —

O Ātmā pure—the sovereign hush behind the thunders of desires,
Thou art the harbor wide as sky—open for all.
Yet some—दुष्कृतिनो मूढाः duṣkṛtino mūḍhāh—evildoers & stupes
Work mischief upon their own breath,
And प्रपद्यन्ते न prapadyante na—they surrender not—
Will not fold their wings—to rest.

They wear their weariness like a crest of iron,
Boast of fatigue—and yet fear the bed of Thine.

नराधमाः narādhamāh—lowest not by birth, but by forgetfulness,
They stay turned away from the fountain. Stay praising their thirst.

Thou callest softly through the lattice of the hour,
And still the stubborn fool refuses bread.

He starves—with a lit kitchen at his back,
He counts bones as trophies, laughs scornfully at the hallowed loaf of life.
Yet O Mercy, Thou still dost not fully close Thy doors.

ॐ गीता श्लोकः ७.१६ – Gītā Verse 7.16

ॐ श्रीमद्भगवद्गीतासूपनिषत्सु ब्रह्मविद्यायां योगशास्त्रे श्रीकृष्णार्जुनसंवादे
om śrīmadbhagavadgītāsūpaniṣatsu brahmavidyāyāṁ yogaśāstre śrīkṛṣṇārjunasaṁvāde
ज्ञानविज्ञानयोगो नाम सप्तमोऽध्यायः श्लोकः १६
jñānavijñānayogo nāma saptamo'dhyāyaḥ ślokaḥ 16

— ॐ —

चतुर्विधा भजन्ते मां जनाः सुकृतिनोऽर्जुन ।
caturvidhā bhajante māṁ janāḥ sukṛtino'rjuna
आर्तो जिज्ञासुरर्थार्थी ज्ञानी च भरतर्षभ ॥७-१६॥
ārto jijñāsurarthārthī jñānī ca bharatarṣabha (7-16)

Four kinds of people who have done virtuous deeds worship Me, O Arjuna: the afflicted, the inquisitive, the seekers after worldly possessions, and the wise.

(7.16)

—: *Word-by-Word* :—

चतुर्विधाः catur-vidhāḥ – four kinds; भजन्ते bhajante – worship; माम् mām – Me; जनाः janāḥ – people; सुकृतिनः sukṛtinaḥ – those who are virtuous; अर्जुन arjuna – O Arjuna; आर्तः ārtaḥ – the distressed; जिज्ञासुः jijñāsuḥ – the inquisitive; अर्थार्थी arthārthī – the seeker of wealth; ज्ञानी jñānī – the wise; च ca – and; भरतर्षभ bharatarṣabha – O best of the Bharatas (Arjuna).

—: *Understanding The Verse* :—

— ॐ श्रीकृष्णाय नमः ॐ —

In this exalted verse, Bhagwān Shri Krishna reveals that even among those whose hearts are yet drawn by desire or affliction, there exist noble souls who, owing mostly to past merit, seek refuge in Him.

Unlike those deluded by Māyā as described in the preceding verse, these beings—though varied in their intentions—are marked by their faith and their turning toward the Supreme.

These four—**ārtaḥ** (the distressed), **arthārthī** (the seeker of worldly gain), **jijñāsuḥ** (the seeker of truth), and **jnani** (the wise)—are all described as **sukṛtinaḥ**, men of virtuous action, whose adoration of the Lord springs from an inner refinement wrought by accumulated merit and noble association across many births.

— ॐ श्रीरामाय नमः ॐ —

Though their motives may differ—some impelled by sorrow, others by longing, still others by the hunger for truth—all of them come to look at Shri Krishna as the ultimate shelter.

The Lord—far from rejecting those of selfish or diverse driving desires—embraces them all as seekers of the Divine, each on his own path toward the Divine.

This verse thus affirms the universality of divine compassion and the sanctity of bhakti in all its forms.

It also sets the stage for a deeper discussion in the verses that follow—which distinguish the gradations among these devotees, culminating in the glorification of the jnani.

—: *Key Sanskrit Terms* :—

— ॐ तत् सत् ॐ —

Sanskrit here opens like a gentle call across a wide plain. चतुर्विधा भजन्ते मां Catur-vidhā bhajante māṃ drifts through the breath with quiet inclusiveness, while आर्तः जिज्ञासु ārtaḥ and jijñāsuḥ flicker like two different kinds of longing. भरतर्षभ अर्जुन bharatarṣabha arjuna anchor the sounds in a listening heart.

The verse does not sort or judge; it gathers.
Sanskrit becomes a welcoming field where many seekings are allowed to arrive—each carried forward by the same sacred current of sound.

Let us not seek to solve the verse, but to be stilled by it—like wind arrested by a sacred bell, or moonlight caught on a blade of grass.

The Sanskrit guides us—not by telling, but by becoming. So let us begin with the key Sanskrit terms through which the verse's intricate layers of meaning will come into sharper focus.

— ॐ —

चतुर्विधाः (caturvidhāḥ):
"चतुर् Four विधा types."
चतुर्विधाः Caturvidhāḥ indicates the categorization of devotees based on their inner motives and stages of evolution.

Though diverse in intention—these four—yet all are seen as turning towards the Divine, an act of supreme auspiciousness.

— ॐ —

भजन्ते मां (bhajante māṁ):
"भजन्ते Worship मां Me."

भजन्ते Bhajante (worship, serve with love) implies not merely external rituals, but an act of heartfelt turning, an inward devotion and surrender directed to मां Mām — unto Me, the Supreme Person, the final object of all love and aspiration.

— ॐ —

सुकृतिनः (sukṛtinaḥ):

"The virtuous ones."

सुकृतिनः Sukṛtinaḥ refers to those whose past actions (कृत kṛta) have been good (सु su), whose hearts have been sufficiently purified by righteous living, and thus who are capable of recognizing and seeking the Divine.

— ॐ —

आर्तः (ārtaḥ):

"The afflicted."

The आर्त ārta is one who, overwhelmed by suffering — physical, mental, or spiritual — cries out to the Lord for deliverance.

Suffering ends up purifying the heart, breaking the pride of self-sufficiency and opening it to the Divine.

— ॐ —

जिज्ञासुः (jijñāsuḥ):

"The inquisitive."

The जिज्ञासु jijñāsu is the seeker after knowledge, not yet fully illumined, but moved by a thirst to understand the deeper truths of existence. His devotion is born of an awakened intellect yearning for the eternal.

— ॐ —

अर्थार्थी (arthārthī):

"The seeker after wealth."

The अर्थार्थी arthārthī turns to God for the fulfillment of desires — health, prosperity, success.

Though his devotion is tinged with personal gain, it nonetheless marks a blessed movement toward the Divine, rather than toward mere worldly means.

— ॐ —

ज्ञानी (jnāni):

"The wise."

The jnāni is the highest among them—the very pinnacle!

He seeks not refuge from suffering, nor wealth, nor mere intellectual satisfaction, but yearns solely for oneness with the Supreme-Absolute—knowing God to be his very own Self.

— ॐ —

भरतर्षभ (bharatarṣabha):

O bull among the Bhāratas. This loving epithet reminds Arjuna of his noble lineage and exhorts him to rise to the heights of spiritual excellence.

—: In Brief :—

— ॐ श्रीकृष्णाय नमः ॐ —

In this verse, Bhagwān Shri Krishna, with infinite compassion, identifies four kinds of devotees who, by their past merits, are drawn toward Him—like four pilgrims upon a path.

All four—though distinct in their inner aspirations—are grouped together under the noble designation of सुकृतिनः sukṛtinaḥ.

This single word ennobles them all, for it signifies those whose karmic tendencies, forged by acts of dharma across many births, have inclined them toward the Divine.

— ॐ श्रीरामाय नमः ॐ —

The अर्थार्थी arthārthī seeks wealth, not from the world, but from Bhagwān alone—thus making his desire sacred by placing it in the hands of the Supreme.

The example of Dhruva is most luminous in this regard: a child turned away from the throne of his father, impelled by hurt and longing, yet choosing to seek the Lord rather than worldly channels.

Although his motive was tinged with ambition at first, his faith and one-pointedness drew Shri Hari to him, and later his devotion was refined into wisdom.

— ॐ यशस्विने नमः ॐ —

The आर्तः ārtaḥ, the distressed, turns to the Lord not in ambition but in agony. His cry is born not of calculation but of helplessness.

The example of Draupadī stands as a beacon for this type. Stripped of all worldly support, humiliated before the kings of the earth, it was not her cries to men that saved her, but her inner surrender to Krishna, whom she addressed not only as a Lord, but as her very own, the sole support, a selfless friend who seeks nothing in return.

Her prayer, born of utter dependence and helplessness, moved the Lord of Dvārakā to abandon all delay and rush to her side.

Such then is the glory of ārta-bhakti—when born of sincerity, it melts the heart of the Supreme.

— ॐ हरिप्रीताय नमः ॐ —

The जिज्ञासुः jijñāsuḥ, the seeker of truth, rises above both affliction and desire. Neither driven by fear nor seduced by gain, he seeks to know—to behold with inner clarity the nature of the Lord, the Self, and the Cosmos.

In this category stands Uddhava, disciple and confidant of Shri Krishna, whose inquiry into the path of final release gave rise to the sacred Uddhava Gītā. Though he sought knowledge, his pursuit was steeped in devotion, not mere intellectual curiosity. Thus, his path became a bridge between inquiry and realization.

— ॐ अग्निजन्मने नमः ॐ —

But among all, it is the ज्ञानी jnāni—the man of wisdom—who stands foremost.

The Jnāni is not drawn to the Lord because of sufferings, or gains, or even to understand. He loves the Lord because he knows the Lord to be the culmination of who he himself is: the Ocean. In his vision, the Supreme pervades all; there is none other. His love is not colored by condition or transaction; it flows naturally, as fragrance from a flower or light from a flame.

Having realized the Lord as the indwelling Self of all beings, the jnāni worships not out of need, but out of an overflowing recognition of the Divine's all-encompassing glory.

The presence of the indeclinable particle 'च ca' at the end of the verse points subtly to the distinctive excellence of the jnāni, which the Lord expounds in the succeeding verses.

While all four types are sukṛtinaḥ, and thus honored, it is the jnāni whose devotion is untainted by motive and whose worship is the highest expression of love.

— ॐ परमात्मने नमः ॐ —

Why does the ज्ञानी jnāni not seek prosperity, or stays driven by physical wants?

For his delusions stand decimated, the veils removed—and he finds nothing worthy of pursuing in this world—because now he knows his true nature—as identical with God.

Krishna is mine, and I am Krishna's—and in the end, nothing remains—just the oneness of the ocean of bliss.

The ज्ञानी jnāni knows himself to be the very heir to the sovereign of the universe: Bhagwān Shri Krishna; and so what are these little things of earth and heaven here, when he knows: I am verily one in Him, just become separated.

The jnāni would not defile his pristineness for these petty little worldly things—for to do that would be as demeaning as a sane man jumping into the pigsty and wallowing in the muck like a roach.

Ah, what a great fall that would be!

— ॐ आनन्दमूर्तिाय नमः ॐ —

Here, Shri Krishna draws a gentle but profound gradation in the inner orientation of the seeker—from the one who calls out in distress, to the one who seeks prosperity, then to the one who hungers for knowledge, and finally, to the one who has attained wisdom.

Yes, gradation perhaps, yet no degradation—He rejects none. All are His, and He is theirs.

The doors of the Divine remain ever open—not to purity alone, but to sincerity. For even when born of suffering or desire, if one turns to the Lord with श्रद्धा śraddhā, that turning itself becomes the first step on the path of liberation.

— ॐ श्रीरामभद्राय नमः ॐ —

Thus, this verse offers not only consolation to those still caught in worldly entanglement but also a vision of the progressive ascent toward divine realization.

In the verses which follow, Bhagwān Shri Krishna will extol the jnāni with words of rare reverence, declaring him as most beloved—आत्मा-एव मे मतम ātmaiva me matam—"Him I consider as My very own Self."

— ॐ तत् सत ॐ —

Before we move on, let us bow in reverence to this sacred verse—a timeless beacon of wisdom guiding seekers for ages. Write it by hand, reflect on its meaning, and chant it aloud, for these sounds alone carry the authenticity of that era. The world may have changed but the living vibration of these Sanskrit sounds still remain as original as they were when Bhagwān Shri Krishna Himself walked the earth and imparted these teachings.

— ॐ —

चतुर्विधा भजन्ते मां जनाः सुकृतिनोऽर्जुन ।
caturvidhā bhajante māṁ janāḥ sukṛtino'rjuna
आर्तो जिज्ञासुरर्थार्थी ज्ञानी च भरतर्षभ ॥७-१६॥
ārto jijñāsurarthārthī jñānī ca bharatarṣabha (7-16)

—ॐ—

चतुर्विधा भजन्ते मां जनाः सुकृतिनोऽर्जुन ।
caturvidhā bhajante māṁ janāḥ sukṛtino'rjuna
आर्तो जिज्ञासुरर्थार्थी ज्ञानी च भरतर्षभ ॥ ७-१६ ॥
ārto jijñāsurarthārthī jñānī ca bharatarṣabha (7-16)

ॐ तत्सदिति श्रीमद्भगवद्गीतासूपनिषत्सु ब्रह्मविद्यायां योगशास्त्रे श्रीकृष्णार्जुनसंवादे
om tatsaditi śrīmadbhagavadgītāsūpaniṣatsu brahmavidyāyāṁ yogaśāstre śrīkṛṣṇārjunasaṁvāde
ज्ञानविज्ञानयोगो नाम सप्तमोऽध्यायः श्लोकः १६
jñānavijñānayogo nāma saptamo'dhyāyaḥ ślokaḥ 16

**Om-Tat-Sat—Om (Braham) is the sole Reality. In the Yogic Scripture on the Science-of-Braham,
the Shrimada-Bhāgvada-Gītā Upanishad, we hereby conclude Shloka 16 of the Dialogue between
Shri Krishna and Arjuna entitled Jnana-Vijnana-Yoga, Canto VII.**

— ॐ श्रीकृष्णाय नमः ॐ —

I saw four Minds ascend to Heaven—like some rising winds:
One laden with human tears,
One dense with drudgery of books,
One dragging bags of rags to turn them into gold,
But one glowed like the Sun itself—weightless.

The first three bowed and cried out loud:
"O Lord, help me", "O Lord, teach me". "O Lord, enrich me!",

But the fourth one simply stood silent—in awe.
His eyes were aflame with recognition.
And Lo—Krishna turned to him first.

He who seeks God only for God—
Walks beyond earth, sky, stars.
This is the Gītā's inner temple,
This is a vision most esoteric—always kept hid behind veils.

Krishna Says:
*"Of the Four who came, all sought Me.
Three sought Me in outside shadows.
But one saw Me—as his own Self.*

*He who forgets even himself—in order to remember Me—
Is not a seeker any longer—but rather becomes the sought.
Aye, he's sought by Me.
That Jnāni-bhakta—even I seek."*

ॐ गीता श्लोकः ७.१७ – Gītā Verse 7.17

ॐ श्रीमद्भगवद्गीतासूपनिषत्सु ब्रह्मविद्यायां योगशास्त्रे श्रीकृष्णार्जुनसंवादे
om śrīmadbhagavadgītāsūpaniṣatsu brahmavidyāyāṁ yogaśāstre śrīkṛṣṇārjunasaṁvāde
ज्ञानविज्ञानयोगो नाम सप्तमोऽध्यायः श्लोकः १७
jñānavijñānayogo nāma saptamo'dhyāyaḥ ślokaḥ 17

— ॐ —

तेषां ज्ञानी नित्ययुक्त एकभक्तिर्विशिष्यते ।
teṣāṁ jñānī nityayukta ekabhaktirviśiṣyate
प्रियो हि ज्ञानिनोऽत्यर्थमहं स च मम प्रियः ॥७-१७॥
priyo hi jñānino'tyarthamahaṁ sa ca mama priyaḥ (7-17)

Of these the wise—who remains ever established in Me with a single-minded devotion—stands out. To that seer, I am indeed most dear—and indeed, he is most dear to me. (7.17)

—: Word-by-Word :—

तेषाम् teṣām – among them; ज्ञानी jñānī – the wise; नित्ययुक्तः nityayuktaḥ – constantly engaged; एकभक्तिः ekabhaktiḥ – with single-minded devotion; विशिष्यते viśiṣyate – is distinguished; प्रियः priyaḥ – dear; हि hi – indeed; ज्ञानिनः jñāninaḥ – to the wise; अत्यर्थम् atyartham – exceedingly; अहम् aham – I am; सः saḥ – he; च ca – and; मम mama – to Me; प्रियः priyaḥ – dear.

—: Understanding The Verse :—

— ॐ श्रीकृष्णाय नमः ॐ —

Having spoken of the four types of virtuous seekers—ārtaḥ, arthārthī, jijñāsuḥ, and jnāni—who turn to Him with faith, Bhagwān Shri Krishna now declares that among them, the jnāni, the man of wisdom, stands supreme.

This verse marks a pivotal point in the discourse, where devotion is no longer seen merely as a means to an end—be it relief, gain, or even knowledge—but as the end itself, rooted in the realization of the Lord as the all-pervading Reality.

— ॐ श्रीरामाय नमः ॐ —

Unlike others whose devotion arises out of specific circumstances or needs, the jnāni is driven by no personal desire. He has come to know the essential truth: that there is nothing in this world apart from the Lord, and thus, he offers his heart wholly and unconditionally to Him.

Jnāni's love is not transactional, but transformative; not born of need, but of recognition.

He is ever निर्ययुक्त nityayukta—unbroken in communion—and एकभक्त ekabhakta—exclusive in devotion.

Such a soul, having merged his very identity into the Lord, becomes both exceedingly dear to Him and beloved by Him.

— ॐ दशग्रीवकुलान्तकाय नमः ॐ —

This verse extols not only the greatness of the wise devotee, but also unveils the intimate reciprocity of divine love!

It is not a one-way love—but flows both ways. Receiving love from God Himself is a most-blessed state—for there's none else in existence who can reciprocate love with fidelity as can God Himself: Bhagwān Shri Krishna.

It is a love beyond duality—where the devotee and the Divine are bound not by expectation, but by the Oneness of Beingness.

This is an unbroken remembrance where the wave ever stays in remembrance of the Ocean;
and the Ocean too – in which exist a zillion waves –
stays cognizant of that particular wave **unto whom there is nothing else except the Ocean;**
and one day, when the time comes,
the wave fully merges back dissolved—
remaining thenceforth just as the vast Ocean.

—: *Key Sanskrit Terms* :—

— ॐ तत सत ॐ —

The cadence grows intimate and luminous. The Sanskrit lets ज्ञानी jñānī glow softly, and एकभक्तिः eka-bhaktiḥ moves like a single, unwavering flame. प्रियः Priyaḥ repeats itself gently, as if affection were being spoken twice to make it real.

The language feels tender without losing gravity. Here Sanskrit becomes a quiet exchange of nearness, where devotion and beloved seem to lean toward each other through the simple music of syllables.

Now let's unfold the meaning held within the verse, drawing it out from the Sanskrit terms as one would draw water from a deep well—clear, cool, and retracted in silence, without fanfare.

— ॐ —

तेषां ज्ञानी (teṣāṁ jnāni):
"तेषां Among them, ज्ञानी the wise one."
Of the four types of devotees described earlier, the jnāni — the knower — is here singled out. His devotion is not born of fear, curiosity, or desire for gain, but springs from the clear vision of the Self and the recognition of the Lord as the sole Reality.

— ॐ —

नित्ययुक्तः (nitya-yuktaḥ):
"नित्य Ever युक्तः united."
नित्ययुक्त Nitya-yukta suggests uninterrupted union; the ज्ञानि jnāni abides perpetually in the consciousness of the Divine.
His mind does not stray into worldly distractions; he remains inwardly युक्त yoked to the Supreme at all times, like a steadfast flame sheltered from the wind.

— ॐ —

एकभक्तिः (ekabhaktiḥ):
"एक Single-minded भक्ति devotion."
एकभक्ति Eka-bhakti signifies undivided love and focus, devotion directed to the Lord alone, without dispersion toward other goals or deities.
The jnāni's devotion is absolute, pure, and steadfast, not seeking fruits, but finding joy in devotion itself.

— ॐ —

विशिष्यते (viśiṣyate):
"Excels, stands out."
Among all seekers, the jnāni shines forth as the most exalted, for his devotion is illumined by knowledge and his knowledge is softened and adorned by love.

— ॐ —

प्रियः हि ज्ञानिनः अत्यर्थम् अहम् (priyaḥ hi jñāninaḥ atyartham aham):
"For the wise, I am supremely dear".
प्रियः Dear हि indeed अहम् I am, ज्ञानिनः unto the Jnāni, अत्यर्थम् exceedingly.
अत्यर्थम् Atyartham (exceedingly, beyond measure) emphasizes the intensity of the love that the jnāni bears toward the Lord — a love surpassing all worldly attachments.

— ॐ —

स च मम प्रियः (sa ca mama priyaḥ):
"And he is dear to Me."
सः he च ca too, मम to Me, is प्रियः dear.

The Lord declares a mutual love — the ज्ञानि jnāni loves the Supreme above all else, and the Supreme regards the jnāni with utmost tenderness, as His very own.

—: *In Brief* :—

— ॐ श्रीकृष्णाय नमः ॐ —

Among all seekers, Bhagwān Shri Krishna proclaims the jnāni—the man of true wisdom—as the highest.

Why? Because his love is born not from sorrow or desire, but from the realization of oneness—that I am His, and He is mine.

That is the attitude of the Bhakta-Jnāni—who loves Krishna in His with-form aspect.

But the same Jnāni—who reveres the formless, who perceives just satt-chitt-ānanda braham, the formless ocean of blissful consciousness pervading all of existence—has an attitude which takes it up a notch. He goes beyond "I am His, and He is mine" and he avers: I am He, अहं ब्रह्मास्मि aham-braham-āsmi.

Same thing, but said differently—this time from the vantage of an iconoclastic brave soul who has managed to trample over all forms.
Nothing matters to him at all—not this body, not life, not death.
Undoubtedly this is an attitude not for the fainthearted and scares most everyone away.

 That is why, although the Bhagavad-Gītā is itself an Upanishad declaring the highest truth;
and which scripture does allude to the great Mahāvākya—तत् त्वम् असि tat-tvam-asi ("Thou art That") at some places in moderated words;
and yet what the Gita more openly emphasizes is—
the other dimension of that **same Jnāna truth**:
but, by the way of Bhakti—the easier way and palatable to most.

The devotional stance of the seeker—**"I am His, and He is mine"**—is openly upheld in the Gītā, for it is accessible, natural, and digestable to most of us.
And this too leads to the same Upanishadic realization: **that all this is a just a Oneness; and all that exists is indeed Krishna and there is nothing else in existence.**

— ॐ श्रीरामाय नमः ॐ —

Remember:
The Gītā is a universal scripture,

a guiding light especially for the householder—who cannot easily assume the iconoclastic stance of the Jñānī—
for the Jnāni is that brave-heart who tramples over forms and plunges directly into the formless Absolute.

But treading in this highest state is possible only in Nivritti-Mārg, the 4th quarter of life—having entered the sanyāsa-āshram when duties are not binding any longer. Till then, one must walk in Pravritti-Mārg—as a Karma-Yogi.

Instead, the Gītā unveils the same truth, but not via the daunting yawning chasm of Vedānta but a radiant doorway: Bhakti of Krishna, the manifest form of satt-chitt-ānanda braham.

Instead of the Jnāni's mantra of अहं ब्रह्मास्मि aham-braham-āsmi, the Gītā raises to prominence the heart's cry of the bhakta—"I am Krishna's. Krishna is mine"—placing it at the very forefront.

Though both the stances are same, but this latter attitude harmonizes more intimately with most humans;
and it speaks most deeply to the life of the gṛhastha-āśrama who must stay in the Pravritti-Mārg, repaying his obligations – the rishi-rinn, pitr-rinn etc., before attempting moksha.

Such devotion rests more gently upon the heart than the austere abstraction of the Jnāni who avers: अहं ब्रह्मास्मि aham-braham-āsmi— seeking direct identity with the formless Braham, the pristine ocean of existence-bliss-consciousness.

Let it be understood: this path of devotion to God-with-form is in no sense a lesser truth.

For at its culmination—when the worshipper and the worshipped gain oneness through union—bhakti too is seen proclaiming the exact same essence as do the Jnāni's Upanishads -- that everything, seen or unseen, is none other than He: Bhagwān Shri Krishna, that all is one, that diversity is but unity in disguise.

Never forget: Satt-chitt-ānanda braham is the ocean of existence-bliss-consciousness and His manifest form is Bhagwān Shri Krishna.

— ॐ अन्जनासुतवन्दिताय नमः ॐ —

The Jnāni is **nityayuktaḥ**—ever steadfast in his inner union with the Lord—and **ekabhaktaḥ**—single-pointed in devotion, with no other object of love, attention, or worship.

The **nityayuktaḥ** is not one who merely remembers the Divine during prescribed hours—but one whose heart and mind are immersed continuously in the presence of the Lord.

Whether in solitude or society, in honor or dishonor, in activity or rest, the Jnāni's soul abides in Braham—whose manifest form is Bhagwān Shri Krishna—as his sole refuge and delight.

The world for him is not an object of enjoyment, but a reflection of the Lord's play. Every form speaks to him of the Divine, and every moment is sanctified by remembrance.

— ॐ वन्दे सूर्य शशाङ्क वह्निनयन वन्दे मुकुन्द प्रियम् ॐ —

The term **ekabhaktaḥ** denotes the rarest purity of love—untainted by distraction, unmoved by alternate aims.

Unlike others who may worship for liberation or worldly gain, the jnāni seeks not even mokṣa, **for he has no separate self left to liberate.**

His devotion is **nirhetukī** bhakti—motiveless, spontaneous, flowing from the depths of realization.

For him, Bhagwān is not a means to something higher—Bhagwān is the path, and the goal, the sole beloved, and the all.

— ॐ सर्वलोकैकनाथाय नमः ॐ —

It is this unbroken love, born of wisdom, that renders the jnāni so dear to the Lord. For what is Bhagwān if not the embodiment of Love itself—anandamayaḥ ātmā?

As Shri Krishna declares in verse 4.11 ये यथा मां प्रपद्यन्ते तांस्तथैव भजाम्यहम् ye yathā mām prapadyante tāṁstathaiva bhajāmyaham—"As one approaches Me, so do I reciprocate."

Thus, to the one who gives himself entirely to the Lord, the Lord gives Himself in return.

— ॐ नवनीतनटनाय नमः ॐ —

The mutual dearness expressed in this verse—प्रियो हि ज्ञानिनोऽत्यर्थमहं स च मम प्रियः priyo hi jñānino'tyarthamahaṁ sa ca mama priyaḥ —is not just some poetic sentiment but a spiritual truth.

When duality dissolves in knowledge, there remains not two, but One. The jnāni and the Lord abide in a union deeper than closeness—**abheda-bhāva**, the state where lover and beloved are not two.

— ॐ विजयाय नमः ॐ —

One may ask: does this high praise of the jnāni imply that the other devotees are less worthy in the eyes of the Lord?

Shri Krishna anticipates this concern and gently clarifies in the verses to follow, affirming that all who turn to Him are noble.

Yet, He honors the jnani as one who has reached the summit of the mountain—which the others have only begun to climb.

— ॐ शरणागतवत्सलाय नमः ॐ —

This verse serves both as an affirmation and an aspiration. It affirms the supreme position of realized love, and it inspires all seekers—whatever their starting point—to evolve toward that state where love of God is not prompted by fear, need, or longing, but flows naturally from the vision of God alone as the lone Reality.

In the next verse, Bhagwān Shri Krishna continues this exaltation, further describing the unique intimacy between the jnani and Himself, declaring such a soul to be "My very Self." Such then is the divine destiny which awaits the sincere seeker, when all veils fall away, and only the Lord remains.

— ॐ तत सत ॐ —

Before we move on, let us bow in reverence to this sacred verse—a timeless beacon of wisdom guiding seekers for ages. Write it by hand, reflect on its meaning, and chant it aloud, for these sounds alone carry the authenticity of that era. The world may have changed but the living vibration of these Sanskrit sounds still remain as original as they were when Bhagwān Shri Krishna Himself walked the earth and imparted these teachings.

— ॐ —

तेषां ज्ञानी नित्ययुक्त एकभक्तिर्विशिष्यते ।
teṣāṁ jñānī nityayukta ekabhaktirviśiṣyate
प्रियो हि ज्ञानिनोऽत्यर्थमहं स च मम प्रियः ॥७-१७॥
priyo hi jñānino'tyarthamahaṁ sa ca mama priyaḥ (7-17)

तेषां ज्ञानी नित्ययुक्त एकभक्तिर्विशिष्यते ।
teṣāṁ jñānī nityayukta ekabhaktirviśiṣyate
प्रियो हि ज्ञानिनोऽत्यर्थमहं स च मम प्रियः ॥७-१७॥
priyo hi jñānino'tyarthamahaṁ sa ca mama priyaḥ (7-17)

ॐ तत्सदिति श्रीमद्भगवद्गीतासूपनिषत्सु ब्रह्मविद्यायां योगशास्त्रे श्रीकृष्णार्जुनसंवादे
om tatsaditi śrīmadbhagavadgītāsūpaniṣatsu brahmavidyāyāṁ yogaśāstre śrīkṛṣṇārjunasaṁvāde
ज्ञानविज्ञानयोगो नाम सप्तमोऽध्यायः श्लोकः १७
jñānavijñānayogo nāma saptamo'dhyāyaḥ ślokaḥ 17

Om-Tat-Sat—Om (Braham) is the sole Reality. In the Yogic Scripture on the Science-of-Braham, the Shrimada-Bhāgvada-Gītā Upanishad, we hereby conclude Shloka 17 of the Dialogue between Shrī Krishna and Arjuna entitled Jnana-Vijnana-Yoga, Canto VII.

— ॐ श्रीकृष्णाय नमः ॐ —

The Jnâni, the wise-soul rare—is Krishna's most dear!
" Among the souls that call out My name,
There walks that beautiful one whose love is not for any gain.

He seeks Me—not as a prize, nor as his road to fame—
But he simply loves Me!
Innately. As naturally as rain does the sea.

Such a soul—with vision vast, and longing pure,
Does not beg or solicit; nor curses or implores.

To him, I am his inmost Self—ever abiding, always there.
He never did doubt My existence earlier—
It is just that I have become more visible to his eyes now. "

None but pure love can pass this formidable door:
It is a wonderful new Realm.
Here there are no deals, transactions, procedures, trades.
No rites, no rituals; No words, no arguments.
No give, or take. No business, or barters.
No falling down of the one before the other.
No this. No that. No duality, no another.

Here there is just only the Self facing the Supreme-Self—
Nary no barriers.
The little wave has found its oneness in the Infinite Sea.

O human, you seek the gate—
Yet the gate too is the seeker of thee.

You chase the moonlight on water,
Not knowing the moon is your own face.

To lose yourself in Krishna—is to find the Self.
To find the Self is to lose all division.

तत् त्वम् असि *tat-tvam-asi* — is the riddle that ends all riddles.
अहं ब्रह्मास्मि *aham-braham-asmi* — is that paradox fulfilled.

The nearer you approach, the farther the illusion seems.
The farther you wander, the closer the Truth really is.

Thus the moon called Krishna Chandra—opens a gate without hinges.
And you can only pass through it—**by standing still**.

O pilgrim of flickering hours,
You are not this fading lantern called the body,
Nor this trembling script of passing thoughts.
You are the steady moon behind all drifting clouds.
Rest there in the Self—where every dream has dissolved into ॐ तत् सत

ॐ गीता श्लोकः ७.१८ – Gītā Verse 7.18

ॐ श्रीमद्भगवद्गीतासूपनिषत्सु ब्रह्मविद्यायां योगशास्त्रे श्रीकृष्णार्जुनसंवादे
om śrīmadbhagavadgītāsūpaniṣatsu brahmavidyāyāṁ yogaśāstre śrīkṛṣṇārjunasaṁvāde
ज्ञानविज्ञानयोगो नाम सप्तमोऽध्यायः श्लोकः १८
jñānavijñānayogo nāma saptamo'dhyāyaḥ ślokaḥ 18

— ॐ —

उदाराः सर्व एवैते ज्ञानी त्वात्मैव मे मतम् ।
udārāḥ sarva evaite jñānī tvātmaiva me matam

आस्थितः स हि युक्तात्मा मामेवानुत्तमां गतिम् ॥७-१८॥
āsthitaḥ sa hi yuktātmā māmevānuttamāṁ gatim (7-18)

All these four seekers are indeed noble, but the man of realization I regard as my very own Self; for with his mind and intellect fixed upon Me, that devotee has taken refuge in Me alone as the supreme end. (7.18)

—: Word-by-Word :—

उदाराः udārāḥ – noble; सर्व sarve – all; एव eva – indeed; एते ete – these; ज्ञानी jñānī – the wise; तु tu – however; आत्मा-एव ātmā-eva – My very Self; मे मतम् me matam – is My opinion; आस्थितः āsthitaḥ – established; सः saḥ – he; हि hi – indeed; युक्तात्मा yukta-ātmā – one who is united in mind; माम् mām – in Me; एव eva – alone; अनुत्तमाम् anuttamām – the highest; गतिम् gatim – goal.

—: Understanding The Verse :—

— ॐ श्रीकृष्णाय नमः ॐ —

In this verse, Bhagwān Shri Krishna graciously affirms the sanctity and nobility of all four kinds of devotees who turn toward Him. He does not diminish the worth of those who seek Him to alleviate suffering, or for their longings, or for inquiry.

Indeed, all are declared udārāḥ—noble souls—because they have turned towards the Eternal—the source.

Yet, even while honoring them all, the Lord singles out the jnāni, the realized sage, as His very Self.

— ॐ शाश्वताय नमः ॐ —

Why this distinction?
Well the Jnāni is not merely a seeker—he is one who has arrived.
A Jnāni's devotion is not born of need, but of vision.
He has known Krishna not merely as the fulfiller of desires or the remover of sorrow, but as the Supreme Reality, the Self of all.

With unwavering intellect (buddhi) and mind (manas), he has taken full refuge in Shri Krishna—the manifest form of satt-chitt-ānanda braham—seeking nothing else, worshiping none else, depending on none else.

The Jnāni sees no separation between himself and the Divine—and in turn, Krishna sees no separation between such a devotee and Himself.

— ॐ भरताग्रजाय नमः ॐ —

This verse ends up establishing the profound identity between the knower and the Known, between the jnani and the Lord, forming the philosophical climax of the earlier gradation of devotion.

It also prepares the way for the next teaching, where Krishna emphasizes the rarity of such realized souls.

—: Key Sanskrit Terms :—

— ॐ तत सत ॐ —

The Sanskrit here breathes उदाराः सर्व एवैते udārāḥ sarva evaite with broad, generous warmth, while ज्ञानी त्वात्मैव मे मतम् jñānī tv ātmaiva me matam settles like a sacred identification. गतिम् आस्थितः Gatim āsthitaḥ glimmers as a steady inward turning.

The verse has deepened from longing into belonging.
Nothing is claimed; everything is recognized. The Sanskrit feels like a seal of intimacy, quietly declaring that oneness which needs no explanation.

Let us hear the words as with rain watering every field, touching every parched ground—soft, steady, allowing the Sanskrit to sink in where it must, in places we hadn't known were dry. "Noble are all these, but the wise is as My very Self,"—Each word an embrace of devotion of various types.

— ॐ —

उदाराः सर्व एव एते (udārāḥ sarva eva ete):
All these indeed are noble.
उदाराः Udāra means noble, generous, and high-minded.
Krishna affirms that whether approaching out of suffering, curiosity, desire, or wisdom, all who turn toward the Divine are magnanimous souls, possessed of sacred merit and blessed tendencies.

— ॐ —

ज्ञानी तु आत्मैव मे मतम् (jñāni tu ātmaiva me matam):

But the wise one is, in My view, My very Self.

The word तु tu (but) marks a distinction: although all are noble, the ज्ञानी jnāni — endowed with direct knowledge of the Supreme — is considered by the Lord as आत्मैव ātmaiva (My very own Self), for he has realized the essential non-duality between himself and the Divine.

— ॐ —

आस्थितः स हि युक्तात्मा (āsthitaḥ sa hi yuktātmā):
For he, having a mind ever united (with Me), stands firm.
आस्थितः Āsthitaḥ means "firmly established";
and युक्तात्मा yuktātmā describes one whose entire being — mind, intellect, and will — is harmonized and yoked to the Lord, without deviation or distraction.

— ॐ —

माम् एव अनुत्तमां गतिम् (mām eva anuttamāṁ gatim):
Me alone as the unsurpassable goal.
अनुत्तमां गतिम् Anuttamā gatim refers to the highest and supreme destination, beyond which there is no further attainment.

The ज्ञानी jnāni recognizes that the Lord is not a step toward some other fulfillment, but the ultimate aim and consummation of all existence.

—: In Brief :—

— ॐ श्रीकृष्णाय नमः ॐ —

Bhagwān Shri Krishna, having already spoken of the various devotees who seek Him through differing motives, now proclaims a supreme truth: "All of them are noble (udārāḥ), but the jnāni—he is My very Self."

The word udāra does not merely imply generosity, but spiritual magnanimity, an expansive inner purity that qualifies one for divine grace.

Thus, even those who come seeking relief or blessings are graced with divine honor, for they have turned from apara-prakṛti (the lower nature) to para-prakṛti—the supreme.

Still, among these noble ones, the jnāni shines like the sun amidst stars. His mind (manas) and intellect (buddhi) are wholly absorbed in the Lord, unmoved by the tremors of worldly longing.

— ॐ अग्निजन्मने नमः ॐ —

The Jnāni-bhakta seeks not deliverance from misery nor attainment of heaven, but union with the Supreme.

For him, Bhagwān is not a refuge away from the world—but rather reaching its most pristine manifest state in the shape of Krishna – for although the entire world itself is a manifestation of Bhagwān, but mostly it stays sullied and defiled, and only as the Avatar Bhagwān Shri Krishna does He become manifest at His best.

This total identification, born of knowledge (jñāna), blossoms naturally into unsurpassed love (bhakti)—for He is the ocean of bliss.

There is no duality in his worship—no 'I' and 'Thou', no supplicant and master. There is only one reality, fully known, fully loved, and fully surrendered to.

— ॐ कृष्णाय वासुदेवाय नमः ॐ —

The Lord declares such a sage as "My very Self" (ātmā eva me matam), for in that being, the distinction between devotee and Divinity has vanished.
This is not mere metaphor but metaphysical identity.
It is the culmination of the spiritual path—the full realization of advaya-jñāna—non-dual knowledge.

Just as a wave merges into the ocean and becomes the ocean, so too the jnāni, through knowledge and love, merges into the Lord—not to lose his identity, but to transcend limitation.

— ॐ जनकप्रियाय नमः ॐ —

This identity is affirmed by the Lord out of the fullness of His love and truth.
For the Lord is not distant; He is not a deity apart, seated in a remote heaven.
He is the indwelling Self of all beings (sarvabhūtānām ātmā),
   and the jnāni alone knows this not in theory but in lived realization.
Hence, such a devotee does not merely worship Krishna—he abides in Krishna; and Krishna abides in him.

The phrase "sthitaḥ sa hi mayi paramaṁ gatim" points to the highest state of being: the devotee who is firmly established in Me as the Supreme Goal.

This is parā-bhakti, a state beyond even liberation, where love and knowledge fuse into oneness. The jnāni no longer seeks anything, not even union—for he knows that he has never been separate from the Lord.

— ॐ श्रीवत्साङ्काय नमः ॐ —

Such a soul is most rare.

As Shri Krishna will say in the next verse: "Out of thousands, scarcely one strives for perfection; and among those, hardly one truly knows Me."

Thus, in preparing to speak of that rarity, this verse honors the realized devotee not only as an object of divine love but as the very embodiment of the Divine.

In essence, this verse stands as a crown upon the Lord's teaching on the paths of devotion. It invites all of us—whether drawn by sorrow, desire, or curiosity—to eventually evolve toward wisdom, and in wisdom, to discover the Lord not as a distant goal but as our very own Self -- ever present, ever beloved.

— ॐ तत् सत् ॐ —

Before we move on, let us bow in reverence to this sacred verse. Write it by hand, reflect on its meaning, chant it aloud, make it your own.

— ॐ —

उदाराः सर्व एवैते ज्ञानी त्वात्मैव मे मतम्।
udārāḥ sarva evaite jñānī tvātmaiva me matam
आस्थितः स हि युक्तात्मा मामेवानुत्तमां गतिम् ॥७-१८॥
āsthitaḥ sa hi yuktātmā māmevānuttamāṁ gatim (7-18)

उदाराः सर्व एवैते ज्ञानी त्वात्मैव मे मतम्।
udārāḥ sarva evaite jñānī tvātmaiva me matam
आस्थितः स हि युक्तात्मा मामेवानुत्तमां गतिम् ॥७-१८॥
āsthitaḥ sa hi yuktātmā māmevānuttamāṁ gatim (7-18)

ॐ तत्सदिति श्रीमद्भगवद्गीतासूपनिषत्सु ब्रह्मविद्यायां योगशास्त्रे श्रीकृष्णार्जुनसंवादे
om tatsaditi śrīmadbhagavadgītāsūpaniṣatsu brahmavidyāyāṁ yogaśāstre śrīkṛṣṇārjunasaṁvāde
ज्ञानविज्ञानयोगो नाम सप्तमोऽध्यायः श्लोकः १८
jñānavijñānayogo nāma saptamo'dhyāyaḥ ślokaḥ 18

Om-Tat-Sat—Om (Braham) is the sole Reality. In the Yogic Scripture on the Science-of-Braham, the Shrimada-Bhāgvada-Gītā Upanishad, we hereby conclude Shloka 18 of the Dialogue between Shrī Krishna and Arjuna entitled Jnana-Vijnana-Yoga, Canto VII.

— ॐ श्रीकृष्णाय नमः ॐ —

"The man of realization—who lives only within My oneness—
Him I regard as My very own Self."—says Bhagwân Krishna.

I so wish I too could be like him—the Jnâni wise.
But I wasted away my life.
Always willing to settle—for less than the Complete!

Aye, I did go to Krishna—but never really for Him,
And it was only occasionally—just for strength & for peace—
When my days became grim, when my heart grew dim.

Answers, blessings, boons—endless things I prayed for,
I went to Him for coin & skin, sometimes for cure—
And yet I thought—my love for Krishna was pure and for sure!

I never did ask for more than fruits & things.
I never sought Krishna—for the sake of Krishna—purely for grace.
'Twas too bold, I thought—for a sinner to seek His face.

All life long I was content just only to bow,
Never didst burn for union—as I must do now—
With the body just about ready to fall off.

I didst call Him Lord, But Kept my Own Lordship, Will
And though my lips would speak, "त्वमेव माता च पिता त्वमेव—
tvameva mātā ca pitā tvameva—O Krishna, Thou alone are the One,"
Yet I chose my own tasks, my own paths, my own Sun.
I clung to my own plans, my own self, my applause, my loved ones.

O yes, I did sprinkle Krishna into my daily routines of life—
As one, upon the food, would sprinkle a little spice.

Sometimes I did serve Him—as an ostensible fan,
But I made sure I looked good, while doing exactly that—
Kept me looking spick & span before anyone watching.

Aye, it was just only a partial pact,
I did **not** color me with Krishna—I kept me fully intact.

Krishna was in my life—but only in parts and bits.
My devotion did flow—but was never really complete.

I knelt in prayers, but made sure to stay on my own feet—
When in fact—I should have surrendered in defeat.

The world is enough—is what I thought.
Ah, it was so beautiful—and so I never let go of it.
But the world is just the outer bark—the real deal is the root:
Of which essence—Krishna—I totally forgot.

From upon His face, my gaze never should have wavered
—Not scattered by noise. Not shaken by grief. Not drawn by glint—
Aye, I should have just held on to Krishna—the Ocean of Bliss.

ॐ गीता श्लोकः ७.१९ – GĪTĀ VERSE 7.19

ॐ श्रीमद्भगवद्गीतासूपनिषत्सु ब्रह्मविद्यायां योगशास्त्रे श्रीकृष्णार्जुनसंवादे
om śrīmadbhagavadgītāsūpaniṣatsu brahmavidyāyāṁ yogaśāstre śrīkṛṣṇārjunasaṁvāde
ज्ञानविज्ञानयोगो नाम सप्तमोऽध्यायः श्लोकः १९
jñānavijñānayogo nāma saptamo'dhyāyaḥ ślokaḥ 19

— ॐ —

बहूनां जन्मनामन्ते ज्ञानवान्मां प्रपद्यते ।
bahūnāṁ janmanāmante jñānavānmāṁ prapadyate

वासुदेवः सर्वमिति स महात्मा सुदुर्लभः ॥७-१९॥
vāsudevaḥ sarvamiti sa mahātmā sudurlabhaḥ (7-19)

In the very last of all births, O Arjuna, the man of realization takes direct refuge in Me: when he comes by the knowledge that all which exists in existence is just only Me: Vāsudeva. Aye, such a saint is exceedingly rare.
(7.19)

—: *Word-by-Word* :—

बहूनाम् bahūnām – of many; जन्मनाम् janmanām – births; अन्ते ante – at the end; ज्ञानवान् jñānavān – one with knowledge; माम् mām – unto Me; प्रपद्यते prapadyate – surrenders; वासुदेवः Vāsudevaḥ – Vāsudeva (Krishna); सर्वम् sarvam – all; इति iti – thus; सः saḥ – that; महात्मा mahātmā – great soul; सुदुर्लभः sudurlabhaḥ – very rare.

—: *Understanding The Verse* :—

— ॐ श्रीकृष्णाय नमः ॐ —

In this verse, Bhagwān Shri Krishna brings into sharp focus the supreme culmination of the soul's journey through countless lifetimes: the realization that Vāsudevaḥ sarvam iti—"All this is indeed Vāsudeva."

This is no mere intellectual assent, nor an emotional sentiment, but the direct vision of the highest truth: that there exists nothing apart from the Lord-God.

— ॐ गोविन्दाय नमः ॐ —

This realization is not casually attained. It is described as the fruit of many births (bahūnāṁ janmanām ante), implying not only the passage of time but the ripening of merit, devotion, and understanding.

Only after repeated births steeped in sat-karma, devotion, renunciation, and spiritual effort does the soul attain this final insight. And when it does, the seeker ceases to be a seeker—he becomes a jñānavān—a true knower -- and a lover of God.

— ॐ धीरोद्दात्तगुणोत्तमाय नमः ॐ —

Such a being is not merely a devotee, but a mahātmā, a great soul, exceedingly rare in this world.

He no longer sees multiplicity or separation, but beholds all beings, all forms, all actions, all elements, as manifestations of Shri Krishna Himself.

His surrender is total, and his individuality wholly merged in the all-pervading presence of the Divine.

This verse stands as one of the most exalted affirmations of the non-dual essence of Bhakti and Jñāna fused into one.

—: Key Sanskrit Terms :—

— ॐ तत सत ॐ —

The verse feels like a culmination sung softly. We see the cadence widening into a vast, slow horizon. The Sanskrit lets बहूनां जन्मनामन्ते bahūnām janmanām ante drift like countless lifetimes folding into one. वासुदेवः सर्वमिति Vāsudevaḥ sarvam iti shines with rare, concentrated brilliance. महात्मा सुदुर्लभः Mahātmā su-durlabhaḥ lingers like a final, reverent hush.

The Sanskrit has been carried this way across time: not brittle, but alive. Let us hold each word as we might hold a smooth stone from a riverbed—cool, weathered, shaped not by force but by flow.

And so we linger with the Sanskrit as with a river reaching sea after long journey. "After many births, the wise comes to Me, realizing all is Vāsudeva." Each syllable is arrival, completion, homecoming. It becomes the voice of long ripening—where realization arrives not with noise, but with an almost unbearable simplicity.

— ॐ —

बहूनां जन्मनाम् अन्ते (bahūnāṁ janmanām ante):
"At the end of many births."

बहूनां जन्मनाम् Bahūnām janmanām signifies countless cycles of birth and rebirth, wherein the soul, through joys and sorrows, through striving and error, slowly ripens.

अन्ते Ante (at the end) points to the culmination of this long pilgrimage of the Jīva toward the Light.

— ॐ —

ज्ञानवान् मां प्रपद्यते (jñānavān māṁ prapadyate):

"The one possessed of knowledge surrenders unto Me."

ज्ञानवान् Jñānavān is not a mere scholar, but one endowed with अपरोक्ष ज्ञान aparokṣa-jñāna — direct, experiential knowledge of the Supreme Reality.

Such a one, abandoning all separate egohood, ज्ञानवान् prapadyate (surrenders) completely unto the Lord.

— ॐ —

वासुदेवः सर्वम् इति (vāsudevaḥ sarvam iti):

"Vāsudeva is all."

This sublime realization — that Vāsudeva, the indwelling Supreme Being, alone pervades and constitutes the entire universe — marks the pinnacle of wisdom.

There remains no second thing, no separate existence apart from the Divine.

— ॐ —

सः महात्मा सुदुर्लभः (saḥ mahātmā sudurlabhaḥ):

"Such a great soul is exceedingly rare."

The term महात्मा mahātmā denotes one whose mind and heart have expanded to embrace the All, who lives in constant communion with the Infinite.

सुदुर्लभः Sudurlabhaḥ (extremely rare) underscores the profound difficulty of reaching such realization — it is the fruit not of mere effort, but of countless births purified by virtue, tapas, and divine grace.

—: In Brief :—

— ॐ श्रीकृष्णाय नमः ॐ —

बहूनां जन्मनामन्ते ज्ञानवान्मां प्रपद्यते । वासुदेवः सर्वमिति स महात्मा सुदुर्लभः ॥

Bhagwān Shri Krishna has lifted the veil on the inner mystery of the soul's long journey through samsāra.

He affirms that the birth in which a soul awakens to the supreme truth is the final one—for what need remains for rebirth, once the veil of ignorance has been rent and the Self known?

— ॐ श्रीरामाय नमः ॐ —

The term ज्ञानवान् jñānavān does not refer to one who merely reads or philosophizes, but to one who has realized—jñāta-tattvaḥ.

He is not concerned with arguments about form and formlessness, about names or doctrines.

He knows by direct experience that the essence of all names and forms is वासुदेव Vāsudeva—the all-pervading Supreme Lord.

His knowledge is not fragmented; it is samyag-darśana—integral vision.

— ॐ पुण्यश्रवणकीर्तनाय नमः ॐ —

To such a one, Shri Krishna is not only the object of worship, but the substratum of all existence, the Self of all beings, the goal of all striving.

The universe ceases to be a place of dualities and becomes a field of Divine expression.

His perception is not colored by ahaṅkāra (ego) or mamkāra (mine-ness).

For him, Vāsudeva is not only the supreme being **but all that is.**

— ॐ योगमायाधराय नमः ॐ —

The phrase "वासुदेवः सर्वमिति vāsudevaḥ sarvam iti" is the crown of this verse. It proclaims the culmination of jñāna and the purest flowering of bhakti.

It is the realization of unity amidst apparent multiplicity, the awakening to the truth that nothing exists apart from the Lord—not the body, not the mind, not even the ego.

This is the heart of the Gītā's teaching: that the Supreme is both immanent and transcendent, manifest in all forms, and yet beyond all forms.

— ॐ आत्मारामाय नमः ॐ —

Such a sage, Bhagwān says, is a mahātmā, a great soul. And then comes the quiet, majestic utterance: "स महात्मा सुदुर्लभः sa mahātmā su-durlabhaḥ".

This rare soul is exceedingly hard to find—not because the path is concealed, but because few persist with unwavering faith and one-pointed devotion through the storms of desire, doubt, and distraction.

Many begin the path, few complete it. Even fewer arrive at this state of non-dual realization where all is seen as the One Divine.

— ॐ जितवाराशये नमः ॐ —

And yet, the grace of the Lord is not bounded by the number of births.

Though He speaks of many births here, elsewhere—He affirms that even in a single life, one may attain Him, if devotion and surrender are complete.

Thus, time is not the deciding factor—niṣṭhā (steadfastness), śraddhā (faith), and ananya-bhakti (exclusive devotion) are.

— ॐ हृषीकेशाय नमः ॐ —

Finally, this verse prepares the ground for the next unfolding: why, despite the clarity of this supreme truth, the majority of beings remain caught in the web of lower desires, running after transient deities and partial manifestations.

But the jñānavān—the rare one—sees only the Whole. His worship is not confined to a form or image, but embraces the Infinite through unbroken vision.

Thus, the Lord, in this verse, exalts such a soul—not only as dear to Him, but as one with Him, one who lives in truth, who sees all beings in Me, and Me in all beings.

Such is the splendor of jñāna-yukta-bhakti—devotion illumined by wisdom, culminating in liberation.

— ॐ तत् सत ॐ —

Before we move on, let us bow in reverence to this sacred verse—a timeless beacon of wisdom guiding seekers for ages. Write it by hand, reflect on its meaning, and chant it aloud, for these sounds alone carry the authenticity of that era. The world may have changed but the living vibration of these Sanskrit sounds still remain as original as they were when Bhagwān Shri Krishna Himself walked the earth and imparted these teachings.

— ॐ —

बहूनां जन्मनामन्ते ज्ञानवान्मां प्रपद्यते ।
bahūnāṁ janmanāmante jñānavānmāṁ prapadyate
वासुदेवः सर्वमिति स महात्मा सुदुर्लभः ॥७-१९॥
vāsudevaḥ sarvamiti sa mahātmā sudurlabhaḥ (7-19)

ॐ

बहूनां जन्मनामन्ते ज्ञानवान्मां प्रपद्यते ।
bahūnāṁ janmanāmante jñānavānmāṁ prapadyate
वासुदेवः सर्वमिति स महात्मा सुदुर्लभः ॥७-१९॥
vāsudevaḥ sarvamiti sa mahātmā sudurlabhaḥ (7-19)

ॐ तत्सदिति श्रीमद्भगवद्गीतासूपनिषत्सु ब्रह्मविद्यायां योगशास्त्रे श्रीकृष्णार्जुनसंवादे
om tatsaditi śrīmadbhagavadgītāsūpaniṣatsu brahmavidyāyāṁ yogaśāstre śrīkṛṣṇārjunasaṁvāde
ज्ञानविज्ञानयोगो नाम सप्तमोऽध्यायः श्लोकः १९
jñānavijñānayogo nāma saptamo'dhyāyaḥ ślokaḥ 19

Om-Tat-Sat—Om (Braham) is the sole Reality. In the Yogic Scripture on the Science-of-Braham, the Shrimada-Bhāgvada-Gītā Upanishad, we hereby conclude Shloka 19 of the Dialogue between Shri Krishna and Arjuna entitled Jnana-Vijnana-Yoga, Canto VII.

In the very last of his long series of births,
The ज्ञानवान् Jnânavân's ज्ञान Jnâna finally fully awakens—
When he comes by the realization,
That all that exists Is just only He—Vāsudeva Krishna:
The Manifest-Form of the Formless Satt-chitt-ânanda Braham.

No longer stirred by restless winds. No longer, driven blind—
The Jnânavân rises sure and calm—full stillness in his mind.

He builds no worlds—on these fleeting "realities",
He does not clutch—at the shifting sand,
For he has seen the One silent source,
Which alone permeates—through all the manifest realms.

No longer he stands, as a questioner benumbed—
He who once probed—every trench unplumbed.
Now he himself becomes the Tree—whose roots—
Descend in silence to the great abyssal Deeps—
Where highest eternal truths of Sanâtana-Dharma stay held, upheld.
This magic happens—by the grace of Krishna & His Song-Divine.

Bhagavad-Gitâ—the Fount of Wisdom

Hear O world: Deep beneath the soil of eras, lies this radiant root—
Bhagavad-Gitâ its name—fed by a fiery blaze called Krishna.

On the surface of Life—frothy activity, waves of grief, chaos of words.
And deep below? Full silence. Crushing calm.
The deep-sea pressure of Gita—collapses all shallow worldly drama to naught.
God Himself speaks here—from unfathomable depths profound.

Up above—empires will stay sprouting and withering,
Ideologies will bloom and rot—
Just only the Gitâ Root endures eternal,
Ever will—even if humans were to disappear from earth.

Carriers stay changing—Sanâtana-Dharma always abides unceasing.
And the sutra-grantha of Sanâtana-Dharma is the Bhagavad-Gitâ
Fierce, lucid, unyielding—Bhagwân Shri Krishna its Sap.

Come soul, stop drifting in the world as a fallen leaf.
Stand tall as the mighty trunk of Dharma itself.
But ye first have to connect to Krishna and His Gitâ—
The living fiery current of Sanâtana-Dharma.

ॐ गीता श्लोकः ७.२० – Gītā Verse 7.20

ॐ श्रीमद्भगवद्गीतासूपनिषत्सु ब्रह्मविद्यायां योगशास्त्रे श्रीकृष्णार्जुनसंवादे
om śrīmadbhagavadgītāsūpaniṣatsu brahmavidyāyāṁ yogaśāstre śrīkṛṣṇārjunasaṁvāde
ज्ञानविज्ञानयोगो नाम सप्तमोऽध्यायः श्लोकः २०
jñānavijñānayogo nāma saptamo'dhyāyaḥ ślokaḥ 20

— ॐ —

कामैस्तैस्तैर्हृतज्ञानाः प्रपद्यन्तेऽन्यदेवताः ।
kāmaistaistairhṛtajñānāḥ prapadyante'nyadevatāḥ
तं तं नियममास्थाय प्रकृत्या नियताः स्वया ॥७-२०॥
taṁ taṁ niyamamāsthāya prakṛtyā niyatāḥ svayā (7-20)

Deprived of discrimination, owing to their diverse desires, people get drawn to various gods—in accordance with their inner nature—and they worship them adopting the norms peculiar to that deity. (7.20)

—: *Word-by-Word* :—

कामैः kāmaiḥ – by desires; तैस्तैः taiḥ taiḥ – various; हृतज्ञानाः hṛta-jñānāḥ – whose knowledge is stolen; प्रपद्यन्ते prapadyante – surrender; अन्यदेवताः anya-devatāḥ – to other deities; तम् tam – that; तम् tam – each; नियमम् niyamam – rule or discipline; आस्थाय āsthāya – following; प्रकृत्या prakṛtyā – by their nature; नियताः niyatāḥ – controlled; स्वया svayā – by their own.

—: *Understanding The Verse* :—

— ॐ श्रीकृष्णाय नमः ॐ —

In this verse, Bhagwān Shri Krishna compassionately reveals the inner dynamics behind the diverse patterns of worship observed amongst humans.

Krishna explains that those whose understanding has been eclipsed by manifold desires are drawn by their inherent nature to worship various deities.

Such worship is not born of an integrated vision of the Supreme, but out of sense of fragmentation—an awareness defiled -- caused by nescience and attachment to finite objectives.

— ॐ श्रीरामाय नमः ॐ —

Rather than seeking union with the Supreme Being—the all-pervading Vāsudeva—people are seen approaching partial manifestations of the Divine, often with specific and limited aims. Their faith, although mixed with desire, is not entirely dismissed—for their sincerity is real.

However their vision stays veiled and their spiritual journey stays hunched, curved, incomplete;

they are driven not by knowledge of the One Reality, but by the momentum of their own prakṛti—their inborn tendencies shaped over many births.

Hence, their worship—even though regulated by scriptural forms and ritual disciplines of Sanātana-Dharma—still remains within the domain of the transient and the conditioned.

This verse marks a shift in the discourse, transitioning from the glorification of the wise knower of Vāsudeva to a compassionate exposition of **why most beings fall short of that realization, despite their faith and devotion.**

—: Key Sanskrit Terms :—

— ॐ तत् सत् ॐ —

The tone turns subtly complex. The Sanskrit breathes कामैस्तैस्तैर्हृतज्ञानाः kāmais tais tair hṛta-jñānāḥ like a soft scattering of attention, while अन्यदेवताः anya-devatāḥ glimmers with many directions at once.

The words do not condemn; they glide by. Here Sanskrit feels like a many-channeled river, where desire carries beings into different currents, each moving according to its own inner gravity.

Now let us explore the verse. The verses of the Bhagavad-Gītā are not a monologue—but a conversation. The Sanskrit does not speak to us; it **speaks with us, and within us.**

It does ask something in return: stillness, listening, an open mind, willingness, a change towards better.

— ॐ —

कामैः तैः तैः हृतज्ञानाः (kāmaiḥ taiḥ taiḥ hṛtajñānāḥ):
"Their knowledge stolen by those very various desires."
कामैः Kāmaiḥ (by desires),
तैः तैः taiḥ taiḥ (of various kinds) suggests the multitude of cravings that cloud human consciousness.
हृतज्ञानाः Hṛta-jñānāḥ (those whose knowledge is stolen) describes souls whose innate discernment has been eclipsed, whose vision is veiled by restless wanting.

— ॐ —

प्रपद्यन्ते अन्यदेवताः (prapadyante anyadevatāḥ):
"They surrender to other deities."

Rather than seeking the Supreme directly, such individuals, driven by particular desires, प्रपद्यन्ते prapadyante (take refuge in) अन्यदेवताः anya-devatāḥ — other gods — deities representing specific powers or fulfillments within the cosmic manifestation.

— ॐ —

तं तं नियमम् आस्थाय (taṁ taṁ niyamam āsthāya):
"Adopting those particular regulations and disciplines."
नियम Niyama signifies specific rules, observances, or rites appropriate to the worship of particular deities.

Each form of worship follows its own आस्था ritualistic discipline, shaped according to the devotee's aim and the nature of the deity.

— ॐ —

प्रकृत्या नियताः स्वया (prakṛtyā niyatāḥ svayā):
"Compelled by their own nature."
प्रकृत्या स्वया Prakṛtyā svayā indicates that beings are driven by their inherent tendencies — their स्वभाव sva-bhāva — accumulated over countless lifetimes.

Thus, their choices are not arbitrary but governed by deep-seated inclinations springing from their essential nature.

—: In Brief :—

— ॐ श्रीकृष्णाय नमः ॐ —

कामैस्तैस्तैर्हृतज्ञानाः प्रपद्यन्तेऽन्यदेवताः । तं तं नियममास्थाय प्रकृत्या नियताः स्वया ॥

Bhagwān Shri Krishna, in this verse, speaks with clarity and gentleness about the many who, though religiously inclined, fall short of realizing the One Supreme Reality.

"Those whose wisdom is stolen by desire worship other gods, following various rites"—each word flickers with devotion yet stays scattered, dispersed -- like candles lit to many deities.

The key phrase, "कामैस्तैस्तैर्हृतज्ञानाः kāmais tais tair hṛta-jñānāḥ"—"those whose wisdom is carried away by various desires"—reveals the essential obstruction: the dispersal of inner clarity caused by longing for ephemeral goals.

— ॐ श्रीरामाय नमः ॐ —

Here कामैः desire in itself is not condemned.
Rather understandingly, it is shown to be a powerful force that determines the orientation of one's spiritual path –
albeit now—become whelmed by desires—

it remain no more the direct efficient path to emancipation – to godliness itself.

When jñāna
—the innate capacity to discern the Eternal from the transient—
is overpowered by shifting varied desires,
the mind no longer seeks the Truth, the Infinite, the Real –
but settles for its fragmented reflections.

No condemnation here—by Lord-God Krishna,
no hell, fire, sin damnation against काम kāma, desires,
but simply a fault shown for what it is—and its consequences --
so that we humans can make our choice wisely.

Souls who are not driven towards the highest, are drawn
—by their innate nature (prakṛtyā niyatāḥ)—
to various deities who fulfill desires—each representing particular powers or aspects of the Supreme Being Himself.

— ॐ श्रीकृष्णाय परमात्मने नमः ॐ —

The Lord here refers to those who worship devas—gods such as Sūrya, Chandra, Agni, Vāyu, Varuṇa, Indra, and others—out of specific intentions: health, wealth, progeny, success, celestial enjoyments etc.

These deities are indeed luminous manifestations of the Lord, and the worship directed to them, when performed in accordance with the rules and mantras proper to each, is not invalid.

Yet, it remains within the sphere of saguṇa-upāsanā—worship of limited forms for limited results.

— ॐ श्रीगोपजनप्रियाय नमः ॐ —

Importantly, this verse distinguishes such devotees from those described earlier in verse 7.15—where what was being showcased were the utterly deluded and demoniacal.

The worshippers here possess faith, and their nature is said to be predominantly sāttvic—although touched by rajas.

They are still following the śāstric path which are designated for fulfilling worldly desires,
but these desires have a binding effect;
they keep them stay revolving in this transmigratory cycle—
and their journey of birth-death-sorrows continues unabated.

They are not condemned, but the shortcoming of their path is pointed out:
- they seek the part rather than the Whole;

- they chase the gift rather than the Giver;
- they go after the transient fruit rather than the imperishable Self
-- which quest in fact takes them fully out of the transmigratory
cycle of sorrows altogether.

— ॐ व्रतधराय नमः ॐ —

The repetition of "तं तं नियममास्थाय tam tam niyamam āsthāya"—
"adopting the norms appropriate to each"—emphasizes that these
forms of worship are orderly and scripturally sanctioned.

But the motivation behind them remains colored by desire, and
thus the realization they yield is correspondingly limited.

Yet, a subtle teaching is woven into the Lord's words: if one were
to worship these very deities while recognizing them as forms of the
One Supreme Vāsudeva, and if the worship is offered with surrender,
faith, and renunciation of desire, then even such worship becomes a
ladder to the Supreme—eventually.

— ॐ अर्जुनप्रियाय नमः ॐ —

In essence, Shri Krishna is gently guiding the aspirant to move
beyond the diversity of worship, toward the unity of vision.

Until desires are exhausted and the intellect is anchored in the
Infinite, the soul will continue to revolve among lesser goals.

But when, through devotion and clarity, one comes to see वासुदेवः
सर्वमिति Vāsudevaḥ sarvam iti—"All this is Vāsudeva"—then all worship
finds its fulfillment in the Supreme.

— ॐ जानकीवल्लभाय नमः ॐ —

In the verses that follow, Bhagwān will explain how the desires of
such worshippers are indeed granted—but granted by Him alone,
and bound by the limitations of time and space.

These verses further deepen the understanding of the distinction
between transient attainments and eternal realization.

In the final analysis—It is Lord-God Bhagwān Shri Krishna Himself
who responds to men's varied forms of faith, sustaining them.

Unto Bhagwān Shri Krishna, it matters not who worships whom—
whether people worship Him directly or not;
for everyone and everything is just He;
and all this is merely His sport;
and sometimes the crazier it gets, the more this show entertains
Him.

— ॐ तत् सत ॐ —

Before we move on, let us bow in reverence to this sacred verse—a timeless beacon of wisdom guiding seekers for ages. Write it by hand, reflect on its meaning, and chant it aloud, for these sounds alone carry the authenticity of that era. The world may have changed but the living vibration of these Sanskrit sounds still remain as original as they were when Bhagwān Shri Krishna Himself walked the earth and imparted these teachings.

— ॐ —

कामैस्तैस्तैर्हृतज्ञानाः प्रपद्यन्तेऽन्यदेवताः ।
kāmaistaistairhṛtajñānāḥ prapadyante'nyadevatāḥ
तं तं नियममास्थाय प्रकृत्या नियताः स्वया ॥७-२०॥
taṁ taṁ niyamamāsthāya prakṛtyā niyatāḥ svayā (7-20)

— ॐ —

कामैस्तैस्तैर्हृतज्ञानाः प्रपद्यन्तेऽन्यदेवताः ।
kāmaistaistairhṛtajñānāḥ prapadyante'nyadevatāḥ
तं तं नियममास्थाय प्रकृत्या नियताः स्वया ॥७-२०॥
taṁ taṁ niyamamāsthāya prakṛtyā niyatāḥ svayā (7-20)

ॐ तत्सदिति श्रीमद्भगवद्गीतासूपनिषत्सु ब्रह्मविद्यायां योगशास्त्रे श्रीकृष्णार्जुनसंवादे
om tatsaditi śrīmadbhagavadgītāsūpaniṣatsu brahmavidyāyāṁ yogaśāstre śrīkṛṣṇārjunasaṁvāde
ज्ञानविज्ञानयोगो नाम सप्तमोऽध्यायः श्लोकः २०
jñānavijñānayogo nāma saptamo'dhyāyaḥ ślokaḥ 20

Om-Tat-Sat—Om (Braham) is the sole Reality. In the Yogic Scripture on the Science-of-Braham, the Shrimada-Bhāgvada-Gītā Upanishad, we hereby conclude Shloka 20 of the Dialogue between Shrī Krishna and Arjuna entitled Jnana-Vijnana-Yoga, Canto VII.

— ॐ श्रीकृष्णाय नमः ॐ —

O thee seeker of felicity, what stirs thy prayerful call to God?
Is it fleeting gain? Gold?—or glimpse of Him who pervades it all?

Verse 7-7 said: "Besides and beyond Me—there exists naught.
Like beads threaded on string, upon Me the universe stays wrought."

But do thou yearn for Krishna—the all-pervading ocean of bliss?
Or is it desires that wrap thy soul in silk—
Which silken threads, alas, end up veiling the-One, the Supreme—
He Krishna—the single shining string?

O mortal, awaken—for when worldly longings sit pressing thy eyes,
True vision never comes—falls dead by the side.

Full of loaded heavenly carts, gods are many—each selling his ware,
There are plentiful heavenly rides—ye just needs pay the fare.

Go worship them for fruits—if ye like,
But worship born of hunger's cry,

Eventually ends up breaking the inner heart.

Beware: Kāma—subtle thief of peace—first steals the Lamp: thy Mind.
Then, alas, where else could you turn within—
But to that which has now been defiled, reset, redefined?

And that Mind, which ere was tranquil bliss—
Now lies mauled, befouled by the Kali's conditioning of this age.

Yet even here, the Lord's grace stays near,
He still calls ye from beyond the veils—
"O child, seek not this glittering clutter—come return to Me.
And I promise: the Love of Me—shall never betray thee".

Light as air, sharp as Revelation—
Krishna's teachings drift like feathers of Clarity.
Heed O human—do not brush them aside,

Seek not any heavy illusions to cling to.
Do not allow your mind—to prefer weight over the Gitā's Truths.

Do not let your mind to spiral in worldly circles, O seeker—
Round and down, round and down spins the world—
While Krishna Himself stands as the **Still Center**—
Right besides everything—watching without judgment.

"You mistook this whirlpool for the Ocean,
And thus never reached Me—Who am **its waveless Depth**", states Krishna.

— ॐ श्रीकृष्णाय नमः ॐ —

Awaken, O pilgrim, you already stand before the temple gate—
Carved with symbols of gods and galaxies.
You hesitate, thinking yourself unworthy.
You stay bowing to stones and sculpted flames.
But the threshold glows with the quiet laughter of Krishna.
"तत् त्वम् असि tat-tvam-asi" — He smiles and states.

O mortal, The sanctum you seek is in your **own** awareness.
The lamp within the shrine is your own seeing.
Come, step forward without any fears!

The door was never locked.
You were never outside.
Enter by recognizing you are one in That.
"तत् त्वम् असि tat-tvam-asi" — Krishna says again.

ॐ गीता श्लोकः ७.२१ – Gītā Verse 7.21

ॐ श्रीमद्भगवद्गीतासूपनिषत्सु ब्रह्मविद्यायां योगशास्त्रे श्रीकृष्णार्जुनसंवादे
om śrīmadbhagavadgītāsūpaniṣatsu brahmavidyāyāṁ yogaśāstre śrīkṛṣṇārjunasaṁvāde
ज्ञानविज्ञानयोगो नाम सप्तमोऽध्यायः श्लोकः २१
jñānavijñānayogo nāma saptamo'dhyāyah ślokah 21

— ॐ —

यो यो यां यां तनुं भक्तः श्रद्धयार्चितुमिच्छति ।
yo yo yāṁ yāṁ tanuṁ bhaktaḥ śraddhayārcitumicchati
तस्य तस्याचलां श्रद्धां तामेव विदधाम्यहम् ॥७-२१॥
tasya tasyācalāṁ śraddhāṁ tāmeva vidadhāmyaham (7-21)

And whichever particular divinity a devotee chooses to worship with faith—I stabilize his belief in that very form. (7.21)

—: Word-by-Word :—

यः यः yaḥ yaḥ – whichever; यां यां yām yām – whichever; तनुं tanum – form; भक्तः bhaktaḥ – a devotee; श्रद्धया śraddhayā – with faith; अर्चितुम् arcitum – to worship; इच्छति icchati – desires; तस्य तस्य tasya tasya – for that (devotee); अचलाम् acalām – steady; श्रद्धाम् śraddhām – faith; ताम् एव tām eva – that very; विदधामि vidadhāmi – I grant; अहम् aham – I.

—: Understanding The Verse :—

— ॐ श्रीकृष्णाय नमः ॐ —

In this verse, Bhagwān Shri Krishna affirms His universal and impartial nature, revealing how He sustains and strengthens the faith of every sincere worshipper—regardless of the deity they approach.

Here, the Lord does not condemn the diverse sanātani paths of devotion, nor diminish the varied forms of divine adoration that exist within the broad spiritual landscape of sanātana-dharma.

Instead, He declares that wherever a devotee turns with unwavering faith—even if driven by worldly desire—it is Krishna Himself who sustains that faith and makes it fructify.

— ॐ महादेवादिपूजिताय नमः ॐ —

This teaching reflects the sacred pluralism of Sanātana Dharma: that the Divine, being infinite and compassionate, allows each soul to approach Him in accordance with their nature (svabhāva), tendencies (saṁskāra), and desires (kāma).

While the wise devotee recognizes the One in all forms, others—still entangled in worldly dualities—perceive the Divine through particular manifestations. **And Shri Krishna, ever-gracious, nourishes their faith, guiding them along the path they have chosen.**

This verse gently transitions from the prior analysis of desire-led devotion toward a deeper insight into how even such devotion, when filled with sincerity, is not outside the Lord's grace.

—: Key Sanskrit Terms :—

— ॐ तत सत ॐ —

Let us wander through the tapestry of this śloka, pausing at its woven Sanskrit strands, where hidden lights shimmer beneath the warp and weft of its poetic expressions.

The cadence becomes quietly stabilizing. Sanskrit lets श्रद्धां तामेव विदधाम्यहम् śraddhāṃ tam eva vidadhāmy aham rest like a steady hand placed beneath belief. तामेव Tām eva glows with gentle precision. Nothing is imposed; everything is upheld. Here Sanskrit feels like a hidden support beneath devotion, silently holding each chosen form in place.

— ॐ —

यो यो यां यां तनुं भक्तः (yo yo yāṃ yāṃ tanuṃ bhaktaḥ):
"Whatever form a devotee seeks to worship."
तनुं Tanuṃ (form) suggests a particular manifestation — a deity's specific form or embodiment.

The devotee (भक्तः bhaktaḥ) is drawn to a chosen manifestation through personal affinity, संस्कार samskāras, or specific desires.

The poetic repetition "यो यो यां यां yo yo, yāṃ yāṃ" emphasizes the manifold diversity of worship across the landscape of Sanātana-Dharma.

— ॐ —

श्रद्धया अर्चितुम् इच्छति (śraddhayā arcitum icchati):
"Desiring to worship with faith."
Here, श्रद्धा śraddhā (faith) is not mere external belief, but deep, inner conviction and sincerity of heart.

अर्चितुम् इच्छति Arcitum icchati shows the natural longing of the soul to offer homage and devotion to a beloved form.

— ॐ —

तस्य तस्य अचलां श्रद्धां (tasya tasya acalāṃ śraddhāṃ):
"His unwavering faith."

अचल Acala (unmoving, firm) indicates that the Lord does not allow the devotee's faith to remain fickle or transient.

He grants stability and steadfastness (अचलता) to the faith, fostering its growth and endurance.

— ॐ —

ताम् एव विदधामि अहम् (tām eva vidadhāmi aham):

"That very faith I indeed bestow."

Krishna declares Himself as the inner upholder of devotion, nurturing and strengthening the devotee's inclination towards the form he cherishes.

Even the faith directed toward other forms is ultimately bestowed and sustained by the Supreme Himself.

—: *In Brief* :—

— ॐ श्रीकृष्णाय नमः ॐ —

Here, the repetition of यो यो यां यां yo yo and yām yām points to the vast diversity of individual inclinations and the equally vast manifestations of the Divine to accommodate them.

Mind it these are not the false deities of men-made sects, rather these are the approved forms per the Sanātani śāstras—for all indeed is Braham, but not all can be placed on the worship altar—especially not the tamasic deities that have become prevalent in these present times -- and which pursuit has brought the world to such dire straits where humanity stands on the brink of destruction.

The gods worshipped—be they Sūrya, Agni, Soma, Varuṇa, Indra, or others—are not independent powers but partial expressions of the One Supreme Being. Yet to the devotee, they appear distinct, each embodying specific qualities and capacities, suited to fulfill particular desires.

— ॐ अज्ञनसुतरक्षणाय नमः ॐ —

The key term śraddhā in this verse is significant—it denotes not mere belief, but a deep-rooted conviction, an inner sincerity, and reverent confidence in the path and the deity chosen.

Such śraddhā may be driven by desire, as described in the previous verse, but once it ripens, it becomes a channel for divine connection. The Lord does not shatter such nascent faith. Rather, He supports it, making it अचला acalā—firm and unwavering.

— ॐ सर्वदेवास्तुताय नमः ॐ —

This is the glory of Bhagwān's compassion. He does not impose a singular path, nor does He demand philosophical precision before extending His grace. Rather, He meets each soul where he stands.

If one approaches a Sanātani devatā with reverence, in accordance with scriptural prescriptions, that devotion becomes sanctified. The rituals, the mantras, the offerings—all find their legitimacy because the inner current of faith is upheld by the Supreme Himself.

— ॐ योगीश्वराय नमः ॐ —

However, it must also be understood that the fruit of such worship is determined by the motive behind it. When a soul worships for finite results, even if with great faith, the result is finite. Yet, the very path of sincere worship, even if desire-bound at first, can gradually purify the heart, leading the devotee from partial vision to total surrender.

The तनु tanum (form) mentioned in this verse may be a मूर्ति mūrti, an idol crafted from stone, metal, or wood, or even a mental image sanctified by scriptural tradition.

In any case, the worship becomes efficacious not by the form itself, but by the śraddhā with which it is offered, and the inner presence of the Supreme that gives it life.

— ॐ व्रजेश्वराय नमः ॐ —

Ultimately, this verse illumines a vital truth of Sanātana Dharma: all sincere paths, though diverse in appearance, are sustained by the One Reality, and all worship, if deepened and purified, can lead to the Supreme.

Shri Krishna, who is the heart of all deities and the end of all devotion, works behind every altar, upholds every act of sincere adoration, and guides every soul gradually toward Himself.

— ॐ विभीषणशरणागतवत्सलाय नमः ॐ —

In the following verse, Bhagwān will explain how the fruits of such faith—though granted—remain limited, for they are bound to time and desire.

This further sharpens the contrast between temporal attainments and eternal realization, urging the seeker to move beyond the worship of parts, toward the realization of the Whole.

The desires of such worshippers are no doubt fulfilled—but only temporarily—according to the limitations of the form they worship—for what they seek is the impermanent, worldly or ethereal pleasures and joys.

The only abiding happiness is in the formless, in complete emancipation—and which comes only from seeking Bhagwān Shri Krishna directly Himself.

— ॐ तत् सत् ॐ —

Before moving on, let us once more bow in deep reverence before this sacred verse of the Bhagavad-Gītā, an eternal beacon of wisdom that ceaselessly illumines the path of seekers. Engage with its form—inscribe it with your own hand, let your heart dwell upon its meaning, and raise your voice in its chanting—for within these syllables echoes the undying proclamation delivered millennia ago on the battlefield of Kurukshetra. These words, transmitted unchanged across the unbroken chain of generations, form a living bridge, linking us to that sanctified era when Bhagwāna Shri Krishna Himself walked this earth and bestowed this divine teaching. Through the luminous vibration of these sacred Sanskrit sounds, we are drawn nearer to His timeless presence, touching the very heartbeat of the Eternal.

— ॐ —

यो यो यां यां तनुं भक्तः श्रद्धयार्चितुमिच्छति ।
yo yo yāṁ yāṁ tanuṁ bhaktaḥ śraddhayārcitumicchati
तस्य तस्याचलां श्रद्धां तामेव विदधाम्यहम् ॥७-२१॥
tasya tasyācalāṁ śraddhāṁ tāmeva vidadhāmyaham (7-21)

यो यो यां यां तनुं भक्तः श्रद्धयार्चितुमिच्छति ।
yo yo yāṁ yāṁ tanuṁ bhaktaḥ śraddhayārcitumicchati
तस्य तस्याचलां श्रद्धां तामेव विदधाम्यहम् ॥७-२१॥
tasya tasyācalāṁ śraddhāṁ tāmeva vidadhāmyaham (7-21)

ॐ तत्सदिति श्रीमद्भगवद्गीतासूपनिषत्सु ब्रह्मविद्यायां योगशास्त्रे श्रीकृष्णार्जुनसंवादे
om tatsaditi śrīmadbhagavadgītāsūpaniṣatsu brahmavidyāyāṁ yogaśāstre śrīkṛṣṇārjunasaṁvāde
ज्ञानविज्ञानयोगो नाम सप्तमोऽध्यायः श्लोकः २१
jñānavijñānayogo nāma saptamo'dhyāyaḥ ślokaḥ 21

Om-Tat-Sat—Om (Braham) is the sole Reality. In the Yogic Scripture on the Science-of-Braham, the Shrimada-Bhāgvada-Gītā Upanishad, we hereby conclude Shloka 21 of the Dialogue between Shri Krishna and Arjuna entitled Jnana-Vijnana-Yoga, Canto VII.

— ॐ श्रीकृष्णाय नमः ॐ —

Appreciate this O mortal:
the God of **Ekam-Sanātana-Dharma**,
—the one true religion, the only and only—
is not a selfish, possessive, vindictive God,
who insists on beating ye on the head if ye do not come directly to Him following the advice of an alleged "prophet-son-messenger" holding on to "my-book"—
—aye, that little book of inanities and tales and whispering angels,
with which the flock stays getting hit on head right from birth, till they become fully numb, dumb, stuporous, ready to believe in any irrational nonsense thrown their way.

Awaken even now, O human.

Wakeup to the true religion

—Sanātana-Dharma, the breathed word of God—

—which was painstakingly instituted into our ancient, ancient way of life and human history by the great rishis of yore—

and of which true religion, these two men-made vicious sects, are but shoddy copy-pastes jobs—slapped together from distorted idea floating in foreign lands in non-Sanskrit at that time.

— ॐ श्रीरामाय नमः ॐ —

The God of sanātana-dharma declares:

"All this is a Oneness—an ocean of blissful consciousness—

and ye may be a little wave for now, O human, but ye too abide in oneness with Me."

Though a wave held within the ocean, but following the paths laid out in Sanātana-Dharma, thou can one day gain the supreme realization:

अहं ब्रह्मास्मि aham-braham-āsmi—I too am He, the Ocean.

— ॐ —

O wakeup human.

Wakeup to the True-God: who does not control thee with carrots and sticks—but shows the blessed paths forward;

following which paths, thou too reach the supreme state of Godliness thyself—becoming eternal, one who never dies—

becoming the ocean of bliss itself.

O wakeup world to this beautiful Dharma:

completely emancipating, which does not control thee for exploitation—at the hands of men,

—but verily reaches thee one day to the supreme state of godhood itself—

if only thou would embrace Ekam-Sanātana-Dharma,

of which, the sutra-grantha is: the Bhagavad-Gītā,

and then diligently follow, the paths laid out.

— ॐ श्रीकृष्णाय नमः ॐ —

Sanātana-Dharma is the Cosmic-Code—breathed by God as Vedas
But the wretches, the wicked, the luckless—
Cannot take refuge in Sanātana-Dharma—perhaps it's their fate;

Not all—though born in human form—seek the Deathless way—
The supreme path to Godliness itself.

They turn away—entranced by ego, dominance, dark, war, riches—
Staying blind—ravished by lust, pride, fear, guile, hatred, stupidities.

And yet wonders! They call their asinine belief to be "Religion"—
- They who never understood God,
- The stunted little-minds who cling to my-prophet, my-savior,
my kosherness, my-book of copy-paste fairy-tales,
- Fools who never understood Ātmā and Consciousness,
- Who never even acknowledge that creatures have soul,
- Whose religion is comprised in how they slaughter animals to eat,
-Who brought untold mayhem, death, destruction, misery, pain on earth,
—Those barbarians talk so slickly of god, kindness. mercy, love—
Even while gorging on meats of creatures just like them.
Ah, What deadly virus must have gnawed out their brains!

Men are born to rise, but these malich asuras fall instead—
They cast their beautiful life into the gutter of two men-made creeds.
Hit daily on head by their little book—they live stunned & bedazed,
In stuporous sleep, they can't see what fetters rob their freedom, life,
Alas, the godliness for which humans birth is given—
Stays unclaimed by them.

Veiled by plays of Rajas/Tamas, they stay far away from Sattva's light.
They worship not Truth—nor yearn to scale their true heights.

O wakeup world, to the redeeming song—the Gītā Divine,
Which deathless light alone reveals the path—to who you truly are.

— ॐ तत सत ॐ —

Come arise, O pilgrim

Let the light of Gītā wisdom shine upon your beautiful path,
Let the shadows of ignorance dissolve before thy awakened sight.
Let your heart abide in fearlessness & serenity & peace.

Awaken to the Knowing: Om Tat Sat ॐ तत सत — That-One alone is Real.
Aye, **That-One: satt-chitt-ānanda braham,**
Whose manifest form is **Bhagwān Shrī Krishna,**
The ocean of existence-bliss-consciousness,
Of which Ocean, you are perhaps a sullied **wave** for now—
But could become fully **pristine**—following the Gītā-Way
And who knows?
Thou could verily become the **Ocean itself** in some life, some day.

— ॐ तत् सत् ॐ —

Remember: before Time's beginning, **you are**.
Beyond Time's ending, **you remain**.

Birth and death are but fleeting echoes of Māyā's illusion.
The Self stands untouched by their passing appearance.

Rest in the infinite embrace of thy own **Beingness**.
Let Realization blossom into unending freedom.
Abide in the changeless ground of Truth.
Know: you too are He— तत् त्वम् असि tat-tvam-asi.

— ॐ श्रीकृष्णाय नमः ॐ —

Come arise, O Pilgrim—ever radiant, ever serene
let the Mountains tremble before thy awakened recognition,
Let all false identities upon thee—crumble like dust in storm.

Know: I am That which no tempests can destroy,
Stand unshaken in the unveiled clarity of Krishna—
And His Song-Divine, the Bhagavad-Gītā.

Let the Truths of Gītā resound through all chambers of your being.
Awaken to who ye are: beyond sorrow, beyond fear.
Know thyself to be the undying Ātmā—which endures eternal.

I am the Self that never dies. Always abides—
Which remains unslain, stays untouched, ever unbreakable.

Let your own life prove that—to yourself—unconcerned of the world.
Come, be the bearer of the immortal blaze—the Bhagavad-Gītā.

— ॐ श्रीकृष्णाय नमः ॐ —

O Pilgrim, Be a Prayer carved in Granite—
This is the devotion Krishna looks forward to, accepts with love:
Solid, unwavering, everlasting, flame-backed, deathless.

Be not the same soppy sentimentalities; Not merely those stale petitions;
Not just frayed folklore that have stayed softening Krishna—
For a change be a Diamond of substance. Be worthy of Krishna.
Krishna abides and speaks as the Infinite Deathless Ocean Eternal.
If thou wouldst pray—pray as Deathless Self unto that Supreme-Self.

Realize who ye are—O pilgrim. And perhaps one day ye can say:
अहं ब्रह्मास्मि aham-braham-āsmi—I am one in Thee, O Krishna,
And that would please Krishna no end.

ॐ गीता श्लोकः ७.२२ – Gītā Verse 7.22

— ॐ —

स तया श्रद्धया युक्तस्तस्याराधनमीहते ।
sa tayā śraddhayā yuktastasyārādhanamīhate
लभते च ततः कामान्मयैव विहितान्हि तान् ॥ ७-२२॥
labhate ca tataḥ kāmānmayaiva vihitānhi tān (7-22)

Endowed with that faith he worships that very specific deity; and he obtains through that deity all the objectives of his desires—which have indeed been granted only by Me. (7.22)

—: *Word-by-Word* :—

सः saḥ – he; तया tayā – with that; श्रद्धया śraddhayā – faith; युक्तः yuktaḥ – endowed; तस्य tasya – of that (deity); आराधनम् ārādhanam – worship; ईहते īhate – endeavors; लभते labhate – obtains; च ca – and; ततः tataḥ – from that; कामान् kāmān – desires; मया एव mayā eva – by Me alone; विहितान् vihitān – bestowed; हि hi – indeed; तान् tān – those.

—: *Understanding The Verse* :—

— ॐ श्रीकृष्णाय नमः ॐ —

In this verse, Bhagwān Shri Krishna clarifies the underlying divine order that governs all acts of worship and their corresponding results.

Though a devotee may turn to various deities, impelled by specific desires and bound by individual temperament, and though the worship may be directed toward a particular form of the Divine, it is ultimately Krishna Himself—the Supreme Puruṣa, the controller of all—that bestows the fruit of such devotion.

— ॐ श्रीरामाय नमः ॐ —

The gods, or devas, are not independent bestowers of boons, but functionaries within the cosmic order established by the Lord.

Like ministers in a divine kingdom, they may administer the workings of specific domains—health, wealth, progeny, rain, fire, or death—but the final authority behind all such dispensation is the Supreme Being: our Lord-God Bhagwān Shri Krishna.

Shri Krishna thus upholds both the sincerity of the devotee and the dignity of the deities while making it clear that all power flows from Him alone.

The results obtained—though seemingly granted by the deity—are but manifestations of God's will, proportionate to the devotee's faith and karma.

—: *Key Sanskrit Terms* :—

— ॐ तत सत ॐ —

Let us now continue with reverence, not for the verse alone, but for the Sanskrit that anchors it. The cadence flows onward with soft inevitability. The Sanskrit offers लभते च ततः कामान् labhate ca tataḥ kāmān as though desire itself were being gently answered, while मया एव विहितान् हि तान् mayā eva vihitān hi tān hums beneath like an unseen source.

The verse does not interrupt the movement of seeking; it quietly reveals its deeper rhythm. Sanskrit becomes a subtle echo, reminding the ear that every gift has already passed through a greater hand.

The Sanskrit words of the Bhagavad-Gītā are not just words—they are roots. Let us tend to them, for in doing so, the whole tree of understanding begins to bloom.

— ॐ —

स तया श्रद्धया युक्तः (sa tayā śraddhayā yuktaḥ):
"Endowed with that very faith."
The devotee, युक्तः yuktaḥ (imbued, united) with the श्रद्धा śraddhā that the Lord Himself has stabilized, becomes firm in his worship.
His mind, energized and sustained by unwavering faith, is wholly directed towards the deity of his devotion.

— ॐ —

तस्य आराधनम् ईहते (tasya ārādhanam īhate):
"He strives to worship that specific deity."
आराधनम् Ārādhanam refers to intense worship or adoration — not a mere mechanical ritual, but a heartfelt effort to propitiate and please the chosen form.
ईहते Īhate (strives for) denotes that the devotee actively engages with sincerity and devotion.

— ॐ —

लभते च ततः कामान् (labhate ca tataḥ kāmān):
"And from that worship, he attains the objects of his desires."

कामान् Kāmān (desires, wishes) are the fruits sought by the devotee — prosperity, progeny, health, or other worldly attainments — which, through his worship, he लभते obtains.

— ॐ —

मया एव विहितान् हि तान् (mayā eva vihitān hi tān):
"For those very fruits have indeed been dispensed by Me alone."
विहितान् Vihitān (ordained, granted) signifies that although the devotee worships a specific deity, but हि तान् indeed the ultimate bestowal of those fruits flows मया एव only from Me — the Supreme Lord — who acts through all forms and deities as the singular sovereign power.

—: *In Brief* :—

— ॐ श्रीकृष्णाय नमः ॐ —

स तया श्रद्धया युक्तस्तस्याराधनमीहते । लभते च ततः कामान्मयैव विहितान्हि तान् ॥

Here, Bhagwān Shri Krishna is stating: "Endowed with that faith, he worships that very deity and obtains from it his desired enjoyments—though in truth, they are granted by Me alone."

In this verse, the Divine once again has revealed the unity behind the multiplicity of worship.

A devotee, endowed with faith (śraddhā)—which, as established in the previous verse, is itself stabilized by the Lord—approaches a chosen deity, performing rituals in accordance with scriptural rules, driven by some particular desire (kāma).

The deity, acting within the cosmic order, grants the fruit of this worship. It appears to come from the deity; but here the Lord lifts the veil very poetically मया एव विहितान् हि तान् Māyā-eva vihitān hi tān—"It is I alone who have sanctioned these results."

— ॐ श्रीरामाय नमः ॐ —

Just as ministers in a king's court may appear to reward or punish, yet all their authority stems from the king himself, so too the devas, though luminous and powerful, act only as empowered agents of the Supreme.

They cannot grant anything outside the bounds of what the Lord has ordained—na adhikaṁ na ūnaṁ—not more, not less.

— ॐ सर्वयज्ञाधिपाय नमः ॐ —

This verse also subtly challenges a naïve interpretation of hita (good or beneficial).

Some may argue that since the kāmān (objects of enjoyment) are received through divine sanction, they must be inherently beneficial; but Shri Krishna does not say they are hita, only that they are vihita—appointed, permitted, allotted according to the devotee's desire and karmic eligibility.

Enjoyments, even if divinely granted, remain within the realm of the perishable. They are not in themselves conducive to ultimate welfare—śreyas—unless eventually they mature into renunciation and yearning for the Infinite.

— ॐ अर्जुनप्रियाय नमः ॐ —

Therefore, the Lord does not reject such worship but gently reveals its limitation.

The fruits obtained—however pleasing—remain bound to the world of saṁsāra, and in their enjoyment lies the seed of future bondage.

One may obtain wealth, progeny, honor, or even celestial pleasures in heavenly realms—but these do not lead to final liberation unless the heart is purified and turns exclusively toward the Lord.

And yet, there is divine compassion in this arrangement. The Lord, though unmanifest and complete in Himself, lovingly sustains the multitude of forms through which seekers approach Him.

He responds even to desire-laden worship, gradually guiding the soul toward higher understanding.

This underscores His impartiality and accessibility. He does not insist upon a singular path but stands behind all sincere seeking, gently drawing all toward Himself.

— ॐ सर्वपुण्याधिक फलाय नमः ॐ —

Do stay cognizant of this O pilgrim: What is being talked about throughout is **śāstric worship in the context of sanātana-dharma**—
and **not** the "worship/faith" in the context of **adharma**—the disease in the shape of the two ferocious men-made sects promulgated by the malich asuras—and which alleged "worship" of theirs
—and do read their gory histories first before remonstrating—
has wrought endless suffering on earth over the last 2000 years, especially these past 1400—
and which outspread of evil viciousness **continues unabated,**
—although far subtler methods are employed today—since they already have over half the world in their grip now—and so with their

numbers hugely up, they find that outright carnage is no longer necessary.

But make no mistakes as to their viciousness and intent—which remains unchanged: a complete annihilation of Sanātana-Dharma;
and even behind their outer "calm", their gory sword,
—stained with the blood of billions of innocents—
has **not** been laid down—
it has merely been replaced with tiny blades that keep slashing, keep delivering their little vicious daily cuts—to bleed away all goodness in the shape of sanātana-dharma that still remains standing midst some humans on earth.

Death with a thousand daily cuts is their new strategy; and Sanātana-Dharma is now almost on the verge of collapse.

— ॐ त्रिलोकात्मने नमः ॐ —

In the next verse, Bhagwān will deepen His teaching by showing the limitation of the finite attainments entailing worship of gods— declaring them as perishable and contrasting them with the result of exclusive devotion to the eternal – which alone can emancipate us, get us out of this birth-death cycle of sorrows.

Shri Krishna explicitly contrasts the temporary results of demigod worship with the eternal nature of devotion directed solely toward Him. Beyond partial worship and transient gains, we are led toward the fullness of surrender and to the full bliss of satt-chitt-ānanda braham—whose manifest form is Bhagwān Shri Krishna.

— ॐ तत् सत् ॐ —

Before we move on, let us bow in reverence to this sacred verse. Write it by hand, reflect on its meaning, chant it aloud, make it your own.

— ॐ —

स तया श्रद्धया युक्तस्तस्याराधनमीहते ।
sa tayā śraddhayā yuktastasyārādhanamīhate
लभते च ततः कामान्मयैव विहितान्हि तान् ॥७-२२॥
labhate ca tataḥ kāmānmayaiva vihitānhi tān (7-22)

स तया श्रद्धया युक्तस्तस्याराधनमीहते ।
sa tayā śraddhayā yuktastasyārādhanamīhate
लभते च ततः कामान्मयैव विहितान्हि तान् ॥७-२२॥
labhate ca tataḥ kāmānmayaiva vihitānhi tān (7-22)

ॐ तत्सदिति श्रीमद्भगवद्गीतासूपनिषत्सु ब्रह्मविद्यायां योगशास्त्रे श्रीकृष्णार्जुनसंवादे
om tatsaditi śrīmadbhagavadgītāsūpaniṣatsu brahmavidyāyāṁ yogaśāstre śrīkṛṣṇārjunasaṁvāde
ज्ञानविज्ञानयोगो नाम सप्तमोऽध्यायः श्लोकः २२
jñānavijñānayogo nāma saptamo'dhyāyaḥ ślokaḥ 22

Om-Tat-Sat—Om (Braham) is the sole Reality. In the Yogic Scripture on the Science-of-Braham, the Shrimada-Bhāgvada-Gītā Upanishad, we hereby conclude Shloka 22 of the Dialogue between Shrī Krishna and Arjuna entitled Jnana-Vijnana-Yoga, Canto VII.

— ॐ श्रीकृष्णाय नमः ॐ —

A man lights a lamp—before a figure, a form—
And he whispers a prayer to the god of his choice,
His faith too is like that tiny flickering flame—aspiring after Little.

He asks. He prays. He pleads before his chosen deity.
Then one day the image glints. Wishes are answered—the gift arrives.
But behind the statue's stillness,
There was another One—who actually made the miracle transpire.

Unseen, He lifts the boon. Unheard, He delivers the answer.
Even dreams of atheists come true—through the touch of His grace.

This is Krishna, the Silent Responder. Unnoticed. Invisible.
This is the hush that lurks behind the Gita's chant.

Chanting before lesser thrones, men stay boasting:
"See how our rites bear fruit! See how our god provides!"

But the Real-One—concealed behind the veils—
—He, who is the Real Giver, silent & unseen—
Who is satt-chitt-ânanda Braham—Krishna, His manifest form—
He merely yawns. Or sometimes He smiles.

Yes Krishna simply smiles. Or sometimes He laughs and tells:
"The Faith Was True, his longing pure; Did not doubt, did not cheat.
So I answered back—even though he was praying to My shadows.

Had he prayed directly to Me, and for Me—
He would have received the most precious treasure: I **Myself**—
And he would have also gotten his **godhood back**."

Aye, godhood—as in अहं ब्रह्मास्मि aham-braham-âsmi.
O mortal, when Krishna speaks—illusions thin.
So let Gita strike—and straighten thy spine.

O come, burn the timid self. Why fear magnitude—thy true scale?
Lower your doubt into the well—draw up some real Fire.
The Bhagavad-Gītā is that Well. And Krishna its blazing depth.
Come, stop playing small—**Drink of the Self.**

Unvanish O mortal—emerge incandescent & transcendent!
Let the Gita fuel thy rebirth—without frenzy, or smallness!

ॐ गीता श्लोकः ७.२३ – GĪTĀ VERSE 7.23

ॐ श्रीमद्भगवद्गीतासूपनिषत्सु ब्रह्मविद्यायां योगशास्त्रे श्रीकृष्णार्जुनसंवादे
om śrīmadbhagavadgītāsūpaniṣatsu brahmavidyāyāṁ yogaśāstre śrīkṛṣṇārjunasaṁvāde
ज्ञानविज्ञानयोगो नाम सप्तमोऽध्यायः श्लोकः २३
jñānavijñānayogo nāma saptamo'dhyāyaḥ ślokaḥ 23

— ॐ —

अन्तवत्तु फलं तेषां तद्भवत्यल्पमेधसाम् ।
antavattu phalaṁ teṣāṁ tadbhavatyalpamedhasām
देवान्देवयजो यान्ति मद्भक्ता यान्ति मामपि ॥७-२३॥
devāndevayajo yānti madbhaktā yānti māmapi (7-23)

However this fruit—gained by these people of limited understanding—is found to be perishable; the worshippers of gods go to the gods—whereas my devotees come directly to Me. (7.23)

—: *Word-by-Word* :—

अन्तवत् antavat – perishable; तु tu – but; फलम् phalam – the result; तेषाम् teṣām – of those; तत् tat – that; भवति bhavati – becomes; अल्पमेधसाम् alpamedhasām – of those with little intelligence; देवान् devān – to the gods; देवयजः devayajaḥ – worshipers of the gods; यान्ति yānti – go; मद्भक्ताः madbhaktāḥ – My devotees; यान्ति yānti – go; माम् mām – to Me; अपि api – also.

—: *Understanding The Verse* :—

In this profound verse, Bhagwān Shri Krishna contrasts the transient fruits of worship offered to the various deities with the eternal outcome of devotion directed toward Himself.

Krishna does not deny the efficacy of such worship, nor does He disparage its ritual integrity; rather, He unveils its limitation.

The worship of devas—though sincere and regulated—yields perishable results, bound by the finitude of the gods themselves, who exist within the temporal framework of creation.

— ॐ सर्वदेवस्तुताय नमः ॐ —

By contrast, those who turn to Krishna with devotion—however simple, however initially motivated—are lifted beyond the cycles of karma, rebirth, and decay.

For the Lord, being Avināśī (imperishable), bestows not only the object of the seeker's yearning but ultimately draws the soul toward Himself, granting liberation and eternal union.

— ॐ राघवाय नमः ॐ —

This verse thus stands as a clear affirmation of the superiority of exclusive devotion to the Supreme Lord over fragmentary worship rooted in desire and limited vision.

It deepens the teaching of the preceding verses by bringing us seeker's attention from external forms to the inner Reality from which all divinities derive their power.

—: Key Sanskrit Terms :—

— ॐ तत सत ॐ —

Now let us embark on an exploration of the verse—drawing out its subtle depths. By dwelling upon the core Sanskrit expressions of the śloka, we begin to perceive the hidden tides of meaning that move beneath its tranquil surface.

Here the tone shifts into a sober stillness. The Sanskrit lets अन्तवत्तु फलं तेषां *antavat tu phalaṁ teṣāṁ* fall with a faint sense of passing, while देवान् यान्ति *devān yānti* drifts away like fading light. मद्भक्ता यान्ति मामपि *Mad-bhaktā yānti mām api* glows with a quieter, enduring pull.

The verse does not argue; it contrasts through sound alone. Here Sanskrit feels like a path that does not flicker, guiding the listener beyond what withers into what remains.

— ॐ —

अन्तवत् तु फलं तेषाम् (antavat tu phalaṁ teṣām):
"But their fruit is perishable."
अन्तवत् Antavat (having an end) signifies that the फलं results attained through the worship of lesser deities are bound by time, destined to decay and dissolve.
तु Tu (however) contrasts the limited results of such worship with the eternal fruits of surrender to the Supreme.

— ॐ —

तत् भवति अल्पमेधसाम् (tat bhavati alpa-medhasām):
"This occurs for those of limited intelligence."
अल्पमेधसाम् Alpa-medhasaḥ (those with little wisdom) refers to those whose vision does not extend beyond transient achievements, who seek fruits within the realm of माया Māyā, unable to discern the imperishable Truth.

— ॐ —

देवान् देवयजः यान्ति (devān devayajaḥ yānti):
"The worshippers of the gods go to the gods."

देवयजः Devayajaḥ (worshippers of the devas) attain the देवान् - realms presided over by their chosen deities - enjoying pleasures commensurate with their merits, but remaining within the cycle of birth and death.

— ॐ —

मद्भक्ताः यान्ति माम् अपि (madbhaktāḥ yānti mām api):

"My devotees come unto Me alone."

मद्भक्ताः Madbhaktaḥ — the devotee of the Supreme, not seeking anything but the Lord Himself (माम् अपि Me alone)— transcends the worlds of merit and यान्ति reaches the Supreme Being, the state of मोक्ष Mokṣa, final freedom and union with the eternal.

—: *In Brief* :—

— ॐ श्रीकृष्णाय नमः॰ॐ —

अन्तवत्तु फलं तेषां तद्भवत्यल्पमेधसाम् । देवान्देवयजो यान्ति मद्भक्ता यान्ति मामपि ॥

Here, the Lord speaks not with condemnation but with compassionate precision. Those who, due to alpamedhasāḥ—limited understanding or short-sighted intellect—worship the devas with desire for worldly or celestial rewards, attain what they seek.

But what they attain is antavat—having an ending, subject to decay, bounded by time. The devatās, being functionaries of the manifest universe, reside in realms that are themselves impermanent, and thus the pleasures they bestow are likewise transient.

Even if the seeker reaches the world of the deity, enjoying celestial happiness in their company, that abode too is kṣara—perishable.

And after the exhaustion of the accrued merit, the soul returns once again to the realm of mortality. This is the cycle of punarāvṛtti—return and rebirth.

— ॐ श्रीरामाय नमः॰ॐ —

By contrast, मद्भक्ता यान्ति मामपि madbhaktā yānti mām api—"My devotees come to Me." The Lord does not say they "attain My world" or receive a certain result; He says they come to Me, to His own essential being.

This signifies the realization of mama tattvaṁ—the inner essence of Bhagwān. The fruit here is not an abode or an object, but union with the Supreme Self ब्रह्म —final and eternal, the supreme state which the Rishis have hinted at when they proclaimed: अहं ब्रह्मास्मि aham-braham-āsmi—अहं I am ब्रह्म Braham—He.

The above para is stated from the perspective of the jnāni, the worshipper of formless Braham, but from the perspective of the bhakta, this path of devotion (bhakti-yoga) transcends even the need for liberation as an abstract goal—for that devotee seeks not freedom from suffering, nor even divine reward, not even emancipation (mergence within the ocean) but the loving embrace of the Lord Himself—in form.

The bhakta—who venerates Braham in His manifest form as Bhagwān Shri Krishna—desires the Darśana of the Lord with form, to live in His remembrance, to serve Him in joy and sorrow alike. Such bhakti is not rooted in bargaining, but in surrender.

— ॐ जनकप्रियाय नमः ॐ —

A deeper mystery stands revealed here. Though even desire-driven worship may eventually lead to God, it is the pure-hearted devotee who recognizes all deities as aspects of the One Supreme ब्रह्म and offers his love solely at the feet of the Lord.

This recognition—that all devatās are empowered only by the Supreme Vāsudeva—is the sign of a mature intellect, freed from the delusion of plurality.

— ॐ जरामरणवर्जिताय नमः ॐ —

Importantly, the Lord is not dismissing the sincerity or sanctity of devatā worship, which is an integral part of Vedic religion.

He merely points out that those who do not recognize the unity behind the many are limited in their vision, and thus, the results they reap are similarly limited;

whereas the direct devotee of Bhagwān, regardless of his initial motive—be it inquiry, wisdom, desire or alleviating of suffering —is gradually refined by grace.

Even if the bhakta comes with a worldly aim, once the connection is forged with the Supreme, that connection does not dissolve.

The Lord, being the well-wisher of all souls, leads every sincere devotee, step by step, toward Himself.

— ॐ श्रीगर्भाय नमः ॐ —

The use of api—"even" or "also"—at the close of the verse underscores the certainty and graciousness of this path.

Howsoever we approach, whatever the stage of our seeking—if our heart is offered to the Supreme, we shall ultimately reach Him.

In the next verse, Shri Krishna will further contrast the nature of His own worship with that of others, making clear that His own essential nature is difficult to perceive for those whose hearts remain entangled in worldliness.

Thus now, Shri Krishna prepares the ground for deeper philosophical inquiry into the nature of the Divine and the veiling power of Māyā.

— ॐ तत् सत ॐ —

Before we move on, let us bow in reverence to this sacred verse. Write it by hand, reflect on its meaning, chant it aloud, make it your own.

— ॐ —

अन्तवत्तु फलं तेषां तद्भवत्यल्पमेधसाम् ।
antavattu phalaṁ teṣāṁ tadbhavatyalpamedhasām
देवान्देवयजो यान्ति मद्भक्ता यान्ति मामपि ॥७-२३॥
devāndevayajo yānti madbhaktā yānti māmapi (7-23)

अन्तवत्तु फलं तेषां तद्भवत्यल्पमेधसाम् ।
antavattu phalaṁ teṣāṁ tadbhavatyalpamedhasām
देवान्देवयजो यान्ति मद्भक्ता यान्ति मामपि ॥७-२३॥
devāndevayajo yānti madbhaktā yānti māmapi (7-23)

ॐ तत्सदिति श्रीमद्भगवद्गीतासूपनिषत्सु ब्रह्मविद्यायां योगशास्त्रे श्रीकृष्णार्जुनसंवादे
om tatsaditi śrīmadbhagavadgītāsūpaniṣatsu brahmavidyāyāṁ yogaśāstre śrīkṛṣṇārjunasaṁvāde
ज्ञानविज्ञानयोगो नाम सप्तमोऽध्यायः श्लोकः २३
jñānavijñānayogo nāma saptamo'dhyāyaḥ ślokaḥ 23

Om-Tat-Sat—Om (Braham) is the sole Reality. In the Yogic Scripture on the Science-of-Braham, the Shrimada-Bhāgvada-Gītā Upanishad, we hereby conclude Shloka 23 of the Dialogue between Shri Krishna and Arjuna entitled Jnana-Vijnana-Yoga, Canto VII.

— ॐ श्रीकृष्णाय नमः ॐ —

They beg for forms—such as gold—
And they do receive that sparking dust from God.

They kneel to names,
And they are carried to realms of high names—such as Heavens.

But the Wise sees beyond forms & names
He wants not power, or paradise—but **Presence—the-Being Himself.**

The gods give what they have: Celestial-Wares.
But Krishna gives what He Himself is—
He turns the soul back into God.

One path ends in hall-of-mirrors—the other in the Real.
Such is Gītā's thunderous split:
The fleeting things from gods—versus godliness itself—
A godliness reaching which one gets to proclaim:
अहं ब्रह्मास्मि *aham-braham-asmi*—I am He.

ॐ गीता श्लोकः ७.२४ – Gītā Verse 7.24

ॐ श्रीमद्भगवद्गीतासूपनिषत्सु ब्रह्मविद्यायां योगशास्त्रे श्रीकृष्णार्जुनसंवादे
om śrīmadbhagavadgītāsūpaniṣatsu brahmavidyāyāṁ yogaśāstre śrīkṛṣṇārjunasaṁvāde
ज्ञानविज्ञानयोगो नाम सप्तमोऽध्यायः श्लोकः २४
jñānavijñānayogo nāma saptamo'dhyāyaḥ ślokaḥ 24

— ॐ —

अव्यक्तं व्यक्तिमापन्नं मन्यन्ते मामबुद्धयः ।
avyaktaṁ vyaktimāpannaṁ manyante māmabuddhayaḥ
परं भावमजानन्तो ममाव्ययमनुत्तमम् ॥७-२४॥
paraṁ bhāvamajānanto mamāvyayamanuttamam (7-24)

Not knowing of my unsurpassable, immutable, undecaying nature, the ignorant regard Me—the Lord-God, the embodiment of Existence, Knowledge and Bliss, the Supreme Spirit beyond the reach of the mind and senses—to have come into being as an ordinary mortal. (7.24)

—: *Word-by-Word* :—

अव्यक्तम् avyaktaṁ – the unmanifest; व्यक्तिम् vyaktim – having assumed a manifest form; आपन्नम् āpannam – appeared as; मन्यन्ते manyante – think; माम् mām – Me; अबुद्धयः abuddhayaḥ – the ignorant; परम् param – supreme; भावम् bhāvam – nature; अजानन्तः ajānantaḥ – not knowing; मम mama – My; अव्ययम् avyayam – immutable; अनुत्तमम् anuttamam – unsurpassed.

—: *Understanding The Verse* :—

— ॐ श्रीकृष्णाय नमः ॐ —

In this profound śloka, Bhagwān Shri Krishna addresses a core misunderstanding that arises in the hearts of those bound by limited intellect: the failure to recognize the Lord's eternal, immutable, and all-transcendent nature.

Ignorant of His true essence, such individuals perceive the appearance of the अवतार avatāra in human-form to be merely Shri Krishna—a king, warrior, philosopher, guide, adept in many arts, expert even as a charioteer on battlefield—as just another human being. Aye an extraordinary man—but nevertheless a mortal still.

The fools know not of Krishna to be the self-willed descent of the supreme-absolute: saccidānanda-rūpa!

This mistaken view is born of spiritual blindness.

Unable to grasp that the Lord who assumes form is none other than the eternal, unmanifest, all-pervading Reality itself—

saccidānanda-braham, the ocean of existence-bliss-consciousness; and the fools regard Him as subject to the dualities of birth and death, like any finite being.

Such is the delusion born of Māyā—wherein the eye sees the form but not the Essence.

— ॐ श्रीरामाय नमः ॐ —

The Lord clarifies here: that while He may appear within space-time, yet He is not bound by causality, space, time; and that while He may seem to assume a form, He is not delimited by form.

Bhagwān Shri Krishna is Purushottam, the supreme absolute. And His descents in manifested existence are His Avatāras—
- divine self-manifestations, undertaken for the protection of Sanātana-Dharma
—and for the upliftment of beings of earth,
—and for the destruction of adharma on earth.

— ॐ सत्यपराक्रमाय नमः ॐ —

Should the Lord-God choose to descend at this juncture—all these false men-made sects will forever disappear from earth—
and just the goodness of Ekam-Sanātana-Dharma shall prevail.
But then again.
Aye, then again, for who can really say—even though Bhagwān Shri Krishna Himself has promised in Verses 4.7-8:

यदा यदा हि धर्मस्य ग्लानिर्भवति भारत । अभ्युत्थानमधर्मस्य तदात्मानं सृजाम्यहम् ॥४-७॥
परित्राणाय साधूनां विनाशाय च दुष्कृताम् । धर्मसंस्थापनार्थाय सम्भवामि युगे युगे ॥४-८॥

"Whenever Dharma is on a decline, O Bhārata, and whenever Adharma (unrighteousness) is on an ascent, then I body myself forth in this world. For the protection of the righteous, and for the destruction of the evil, and for the establishment of Dharma upon earth, I take advent from age to age."

But then again, God may find that there are no more any Pāndavas and Arjunas remaining—not even in semblance—that need saving!

God may decide that humans have not proven worthy—
and He may simply do away with this cruel creature altogether—
and establish Sanātana-Dharma through a species more worthy.

For ye see, He—that great-God before whom we humans are ants
—has infinite time at hand and infinite creativity;
And unlike we—He has no human-centric view on existence.
And yes the sport will still continue on earth—but through other better forms;

and Sanātana-Dharma--will make a return again—for it is the one thing that never dies. Only its carriers change.

Sanātana-Dharma—breathed through His words, the Vedas, at the beginning of Creation—persists eternal throughout the cosmos, on endless realms, through some carrier or another.

Only those with unwavering śraddhā, or those of purified intellect—those who have directly experienced that Reality, the formless realm—they alone can perceive this sublime truth.

On the other hand, most humans here remain just the glorified animals which they are—and they can never fathom the truth of satt-chitt-ānanda braham, and His manifest form in the shape of Bhagwān Shri Krishna.

—: Key Sanskrit Terms :—

— ॐ तत सत ॐ —

The Sanskrit of the verse moves with a veiled, luminous gravity, as though something vast were gently cloaked in human sound. अव्यक्तम् व्यक्तिम् avyaktaṁ vyaktim glimmers behind the breath; while मामबुद्धयः mām mūḍhāḥ passes like a soft mishearing; and अव्ययम् अनुत्तमम् avyayam anuttamam, the immutable absolute, the satt-chitt-ānanda braham hums with a quiet fullness which the tongue can barely hold.

The verse feels like a hidden jewel spoken aloud yet still half concealed. Sanskrit becomes a shimmering veil, letting the mystery of presence be felt without ever being fully seen.

Now let us gaze into the mirror of this verse, where its Sanskrit terms shimmer with layered beauty and secret depth. Let us cradle these words like fragile lotus petals fallen from the heavens — each holding the fragrance of realms where language ever stays in prayer.

— ॐ —

अव्यक्तं व्यक्तिम् आपन्नं (avyaktaṁ vyaktim āpannam):
"The Unmanifest assumed a manifest form."

अव्यक्तं Avyaktam refers to that which is beyond sense-perception — the formless, the infinite, the subtle Essence.

व्यक्तिम् आपन्नं Vyaktim āpannam means "having taken on a visible, manifest form," such as a human body.

The Lord speaks of His own descent into a perceivable form while remaining in essence the unmanifest Reality.

— ॐ —

मन्यन्ते माम् अबुद्धयः (manyante mām abuddhayaḥ):

"The ignorant think of Me thus."

अबुद्धयः Abuddhayaḥ (those without true understanding) regard the Lord's manifest form as conditioned like an ordinary being, unaware of His transcendental nature.

Their perception, clouded by ignorance, sees only the external, missing the Infinite within.

— ॐ —

परं भावम् अजानन्तः (param bhāvam ajānantaḥ):

"Not knowing My supreme state."

परं भावम् Param bhāvam refers to the Supreme Nature — the absolute, changeless, and all-pervading Reality of the Lord.

अजानन्तः Ajānantaḥ (not knowing) points to their inability to recognize the true nature hidden behind the manifest appearance.

— ॐ —

मम अव्ययम् अनुत्तमम् (mama avyayam anuttamam):

"My imperishable, unsurpassable Being."

अव्ययम् Avyayam denotes that which is undecaying, imperishable, eternal.

अनुत्तमम् Anuttamam means the highest, beyond which there is none greater.

The Lord is pointing to His true, ineffable nature — untouched by birth, decay, or limitation.

—: In Brief :—

— ॐ श्रीकृष्णाय नमः ॐ —

अव्यक्तं व्यक्तिमापन्नं मन्यन्ते मामबुद्धयः । परं भावमजानन्तो ममाव्ययमनुत्तमम् ॥

The term अबुद्धयः abuddhayaḥ refers to those whose intellects remain unillumined—not necessarily devoid of learning or ritual observance, but lacking in spiritual insight.

The learned fools, if you will.

Enmeshed in worldly notions and dualistic thinking, they cannot discern the truth that the Divine, though appearing in a visible form, remains untouched by finitude.

Mistaking the व्यक्त Vyakta (manifest form) as the totality of the Lord, they fail to recognize the अव्यक्त Avyakta (unmanifest, eternal essence) that underlies it.

— ॐ श्रीरामाय नमः ॐ —

This delusion arises from an inability to comprehend the mystery of अवतार Avatāra—the descent of the Infinite into the finite without undergoing any diminution.

The Lord, in His own will and with perfect freedom, assumes forms appropriate to time, place, and need—while ever remaining the immutable Paramātmā, beyond the reach of indriyas (senses) and manas (mind).

The Lord's परं भावम param bhāvam—His supreme nature—is ajānantaḥ (unknown) to such people, not due to the absence of revelation, but due to their inner incapacity to see beyond appearances.

They do not realize that this param bhāva is avyaya (imperishable) and anuttama (unsurpassed)—the very foundation of all existence, untouched by change, and resplendent beyond all attributes.

— ॐ राधाकान्ताय नमः ॐ —

Some philosophical schools err by asserting that the Divine can never manifest, insisting on an abstract, formless Absolute.

Others err in the opposite direction, limiting the Lord entirely to His visible incarnate forms.

The Gītā harmonizes these views: the Lord is both—formless and with form, manifest and unmanifest.

Satt-chitt-ānanda braham pervades throughout existence as the unmanifest Reality (अव्यक्त avyakta); and yet He reveals Himself out of love and grace as व्यक्त vyakta—embodied, accessible, near.

To regard Shri Krishna as merely a historical figure, or a mortal sage, is to miss the grandeur of His svarūpa.

This is not a rejection of His embodied presence, but a failure to see through it to the pūrṇatā—the completeness—that is veiled. Hence, the Lord reveals: "Such persons are unable to grasp My higher nature."

— ॐ रणप्रियाय नमः ॐ —

This verse also indirectly calls the devotee to a higher vision. Even those who may initially approach the Lord out of desire or confusion must grow to see Him as He truly is—not merely the giver of finite boons, but as the Eternal Self of all.

When this insight dawns, all delusions fall away, and the devotee sees that the one who walked on earth as Krishna—and exists still in that very form—is the unbounded, ever-blissful Supreme Absolute.

This teaching prepares us for the next verse, where Bhagwān further reveals why He remains hidden from the eyes of most— shielded by His own Yogamāyā—and how only those with purified hearts can behold Him in truth. Krishna speaks of His self-veiling through Yogamāyā, and how that concealment hides Him from the deluded but not from the sincere.

— ॐ तत् सत् ॐ —

Before we move on, let us bow in reverence to this sacred verse. Write it by hand, reflect on its meaning, chant it aloud, make it your own.

— ॐ —

अव्यक्तं व्यक्तिमापन्नं मन्यन्ते मामबुद्धयः ।
avyaktaṁ vyaktimāpannaṁ manyante māmabuddhayaḥ
परं भावमजानन्तो ममाव्ययमनुत्तमम् ॥ ७-२४ ॥
paraṁ bhāvamajānanto mamāvyayamanuttamam (7-24)

— ॐ —

अव्यक्तं व्यक्तिमापन्नं मन्यन्ते मामबुद्धयः ।
avyaktaṁ vyaktimāpannaṁ manyante māmabuddhayaḥ
परं भावमजानन्तो ममाव्ययमनुत्तमम् ॥ ७-२४ ॥
paraṁ bhāvamajānanto mamāvyayamanuttamam (7-24)

ॐ तत्सदिति श्रीमद्भगवद्गीतासूपनिषत्सु ब्रह्मविद्यायां योगशास्त्रे श्रीकृष्णार्जुनसंवादे
om tatsaditi śrīmadbhagavadgītāsūpaniṣatsu brahmavidyāyāṁ yogaśāstre śrīkṛṣṇārjunasaṁvāde
ज्ञानविज्ञानयोगो नाम सप्तमोऽध्यायः श्लोकः २४
jñānavijñānayogo nāma saptamo'dhyāyaḥ ślokaḥ 24

Om-Tat-Sat—Om (Braham) is the sole Reality. In the Yogic Scripture on the Science-of-Braham, the Shrimada-Bhāgvada-Gītā Upanishad, we hereby conclude Shloka 24 of the Dialogue between Shrī Krishna and Arjuna entitled Jnana-Vijnana-Yoga, Canto VII.

— ॐ श्रीकृष्णाय नमः ॐ —

<u>The God Who Walked Midst Us.</u>
Lo, Krishna chose to walk among us
No roar. No thunder. No emblem. No crown. No flag.
God chose to be born as the simplest of us: a Cowherd—
So that the simplest of us can feel blessed.

The hallowed earth of Âryâvarta, got to kiss His feet.
Watching amazed—space-time, stars, galaxies—withheld their speech.

Bhagwân Krishna bore no marks—or mighty little
—Except one mark: That Infinity had somehow become Embodied—
And that, O sir, alone was the Indication:
That the Ocean had chosen to become confined into Perfection.

ॐ गीता श्लोकः ७.२५ – Gītā Verse 7.25

ॐ श्रीमद्भगवद्गीतासूपनिषत्सु ब्रह्मविद्यायां योगशास्त्रे श्रीकृष्णार्जुनसंवादे
om śrīmadbhagavadgītāsūpaniṣatsu brahmavidyāyāṁ yogaśāstre śrīkṛṣṇārjunasaṁvāde
ज्ञानविज्ञानयोगो नाम सप्तमोऽध्यायः श्लोकः २५
jñānavijñānayogo nāma saptamo'dhyāyaḥ ślokaḥ 25

— ॐ —

नाहं प्रकाशः सर्वस्य योगमायासमावृतः ।
nāhaṁ prakāśaḥ sarvasya yogamāyāsamāvṛtaḥ
मूढोऽयं नाभिजानाति लोको मामजमव्ययम् ॥७-२५॥
mūḍho'yaṁ nābhijānāti loko māmajamavyayam (7-25)

Veiled by my Yoga-Māyā—my divine potency—I do not become apparent to all; the ignorant world does not know Me—who am the unborn, immutable Absolute. (7.25)

—: Word-by-Word :—

न aham – I am not; प्रकाशः prakāśaḥ – visible; सर्वस्य sarvasya – to everyone; योगमाया yogamāyā – by My divine illusion; समावृतः samāvṛtaḥ – covered; मूढः mūḍhaḥ – the deluded; अयम् ayam – this; न नाभिजानाति nābhijānāti – does not recognize; लोकः lokaḥ – the world; माम् mām – Me; अजम् ajam – unborn; अव्ययम् avyayam – immutable.

—: Understanding The Verse :—

— ॐ श्रीकृष्णाय नमः ॐ —

In this verse, Bhagwān Shri Krishna reveals why His supreme nature remains concealed from the majority of people, despite His eternal presence pervaded throughout. He declares that He is veiled by योग-माया Yoga-Māyā, His own divine power of concealment and projection.

As a result, the world, deluded by appearances and confined to sense-bound thinking, fails to recognize Him as the unborn, eternal, and immutable Reality—अजम् Ajam (unborn) and अव्ययात्मा Avyayātmā (imperishable Self).

— ॐ श्रीरामाय नमः ॐ —

This veil of Yoga-Māyā is not mere illusion, but a divine potency (शक्ति śakti) that operates under the Lord's will. It is the very force through which He manifests creation, sustains the play of duality, and veils His divinity—from those not yet inwardly prepared.

Only those whose hearts have been purified through devotion, surrender and scriptural wisdom are granted the grace to perceive Him beyond form, beyond name—as the eternal essence behind all that is manifest.

— ॐ यमलार्जुनभञ्जनाय नमः ॐ —

The Lord's concealment is not a denial of truth, but a compassionate means of allowing beings to approach Him gradually, according to their own evolution.

This verse also continues the response to the question:
Why do people—although born into this sacred human form—and provided with the blessed opportunity to realize who they are, through the worship of the Supreme Reality, fail to do so?

The answer lies here: **in the self-veiling nature of the Divine and Māyā**—the ignorance that binds the vision of ordinary minds.

—: *Key Sanskrit Terms* :—

— ॐ तत् सत् ॐ —

The cadence crosses over into sacred concealment. The Sanskrit lets योगमायासमावृतः yoga-māyā-samāvṛtaḥ drift like a luminous mist, with नाभिजानाति लोको nābhijānāti loko sounding as though the world itself were softly turning away, and yet अजम् अव्ययम् ajam avyayam glows faintly behind the veil as the all pervading presence. The language does not lament the hiding—it sanctifies it.

The Sanskrit feels like a curtain of light, through which the Absolute chooses how and when to be glimpsed.

Now let us hear again the verse, but let's not rush.

The essence behind the words of the Gītā is most ancient—older than any human voice.

We are reminded of the cosmic breath that first breathed out—with the advent of manifest existence billions of years ago—that is how primal Sanātana-Dharma is;

and the Bhagavad-Gītā—the sutra-grantha of Sanātana-Dharma—is only the most recent breathing of that essence—and even that is many millennium ancient.

Rejoice O pilgrims! Feel blessed that thou get to participate in the sounds of these ancient voices!

Now let the Sanskrit speak in its own time—and we'll simply listen—the way one would listen to the sounds of God breathing existence into creation eons ago.

— ॐ —

नाहं प्रकाशः सर्वस्य (nāhaṁ prakāśaḥ sarvasya):
"I do not become revealed to all."

प्रकाशः Prakāśaḥ (manifest, revealed) here means fully evident, self-revealed.

The Lord, though all-pervading, does not disclose His true nature to every being.

His presence remains ever hidden to those whose hearts stay clouded.

— ॐ —

योगमायासमावृतः (yogamāyā-samāvṛtaḥ):
"Being covered by Yoga-Māyā."

योगमाया Yogamāyā is the divine power of the Lord — distinct from अविद्या-माया Avidyā-Māyā — and which purposefully conceals the Supreme's true nature.

समावृतः Samāvṛtaḥ (enveloped) indicates that this veiling is complete, preventing unprepared souls from perceiving the Divine essence.

— ॐ —

मूढः अयम् न अभिजानाति (mūḍho'yaṁ na abhijānāti):
"The deluded do not recognize Me."

मूढः Mūḍhaḥ — the bewildered, the deluded — refers to beings whose understanding is clouded by माया Māyā.

न अभिजानाति Na abhijānāti means they fail to know or realize the true nature of the Lord, mistaking the superficial for the real.

— ॐ —

लोकः माम् अजम् अव्ययम् (lokaḥ mām ajam avyayam):
"The world does not know Me as the unborn and immutable."

अजम् Ajam (unborn) and अव्ययम् avyayam (imperishable) describe the true nature of the Lord: untouched by birth, death, change, or decay.

Yet the लोकः lokaḥ — the worldly-minded — perceive only the external, failing to see the eternal Reality.

—: *In Brief* :—

— ॐ श्रीकृष्णाय नमः ॐ —

Here, Bhagwān Shri Krishna has proclaimed a truth of great profundity: the Supreme Lord, though pervading all, and remaining nearer than the nearest—still remains unseen by the deluded.

Yoga-Māyā is the Lord's inscrutable divine energy—which serves also as the self-imposed veil through which He conceals His boundless glory from those immersed in संसार saṁsāra, staying bound in ego, desire, ignorance.

— ॐ श्रीरामाय नमः॥ॐ —

It is not that the Lord's form is hidden in darkness, but rather, that the inner eyes of the world remains closed—and thus God stays veiled!

The ignorant (मूढः mūḍhaḥ) mistake the Lord's embodiment—in the form of Shri Krishna—to be the ordinary birth of a finite being, not realizing that the one who appears in human form is in truth Ajā, the Unborn, and Avyayātmā, the Unchanging Self of all beings.

— ॐ जितवाराशये नमः ॐ —

The analogy often given is that of the sun hidden by clouds.
The sun is never actually obscured; it shines always in its full brilliance;
yet, for those beneath the clouds, its light seems lost/dimmed.
Similarly, the Lord remains ever manifest to those with purified hearts; but to others—He appears absent or limited.
The concealment lies not in the Lord, but in the perceiver.

— ॐ द्वारकानाथाय नमः ॐ —

The use of "नाहं प्रकाशः सर्वस्य nāhaṁ prakāśaḥ sarvasya"—"I am not manifest to all"—is significant.
The Divine makes Himself known selectively, not through favoritism, but according to receptivity.
To the bhakta who surrenders with love and unwavering faith, He becomes fully manifest;
to the egoic and sense-bound, He remains hidden.

— ॐ पुण्यश्रवणकीर्तनाय नमः ॐ —

The word योगमाया yogamāyā too is crucial. It does not denote ordinary māyā—the illusory power that deludes—but a higher, divine expression of it.

This Yoga-Māyā is the Lord's own power, used to reveal or conceal as He wills, not subject to the play of karma or limitation.

By this very power, He takes on form while remaining formless—enters into the world while remaining transcendental.

— ॐ नवनीतनटनाय नमः ॐ —

The world (अयम् ayam लोकः lokaḥ), referred to here, includes not only the sinful or wicked, but even the morally upright who are yet spiritually unawakened.

It includes all who, despite intelligence or ritual piety, fail to recognize the Lord's infinite essence behind His incarnate form.

Lacking devotion and philosophical clarity, they see only the outer man—Shri Krishna, the cowherd, the charioteer, the king, the mighty warrior, the sage, the philosopher, the counselor —while missing the Supreme Puruṣa veiled within.

— ॐ चित्रकूट समाश्रयाय नमः ॐ —

Yet, this veil of concealment is not the final word. It is a veil that can be pierced—not by force, but by bhakti, by humility, by longing.

The Lord remains hidden only **until** the seeker, exhausted by external pursuits, turns inward in love.

And then, as Bhagwān Shri Krishna Himself declares in verse 10.10: "To such a devotee, I give the light of knowledge by which he comes to Me."

तेषां सततयुक्तानां भजतां प्रीतिपूर्वकम् । ददामि बुद्धियोगं तं येन मामुपयान्ति ते ॥१०-१०॥

teṣāṁ satatayuktānāṁ bhajatāṁ prītipūrvakam,
dadāmi buddhiyogaṁ taṁ yena māmupayānti te (10-10).

To such who are thus devoted to Me and worship Me with love, I confer upon them that very Yoga of understanding by which they are able to reach Me. (10.10)

— ॐ सत्यवाचे नमः ॐ —

This verse thus serves both as explanation and invitation. It explains the spiritual blindness of the world, while at the same time inviting us to transcend it.

For those who, through śraddhā, tapas, and bhakti, purify their inner being, the veil is lifted—and the Avyayātmā is known not as a theory, but as the living Reality pervaded throughout the world and within the heart.

In the verse that follows, Bhagwān Shri Krishna deepens this teaching by showing how the bonds of karma and the dualities of delusion (dvandva-mohaḥ) prevent even the virtuous from turning toward Him until the right moment of inner maturity arrives.

— ॐ तत सत ॐ —

Before we move on, let us bow in reverence to this sacred verse—a timeless beacon of wisdom guiding seekers for ages. Write it by hand, reflect on its meaning, and chant it aloud, for these sounds alone carry the authenticity of that era. The world may have changed but the living vibration of these Sanskrit sounds still remain as original as they were when Bhagwān Shri Krishna Himself walked the earth and imparted these teachings.

— ॐ —

नाहं प्रकाशः सर्वस्य योगमायासमावृतः ।
nāhaṁ prakāśaḥ sarvasya yogamāyāsamāvṛtaḥ
मूढोऽयं नाभिजानाति लोको मामजमव्ययम् ॥७-२५॥
mūḍho'yaṁ nābhijānāti loko māmajamavyayam (7-25)

नाहं प्रकाशः सर्वस्य योगमायासमावृतः ।
nāhaṁ prakāśaḥ sarvasya yogamāyāsamāvṛtaḥ
मूढोऽयं नाभिजानाति लोको मामजमव्ययम् ॥७-२५॥
mūḍho'yaṁ nābhijānāti loko māmajamavyayam (7-25)

ॐ तत्सदिति श्रीमद्भगवद्गीतासूपनिषत्सु ब्रह्मविद्यायां योगशास्त्रे श्रीकृष्णार्जुनसंवादे
om tatsaditi śrīmadbhagavadgītāsūpaniṣatsu brahmavidyāyāṁ yogaśāstre śrīkṛṣṇārjunasaṁvāde
ज्ञानविज्ञानयोगो नाम सप्तमोऽध्यायः श्लोकः २५
jñānavijñānayogo nāma saptamo'dhyāyaḥ ślokaḥ 25

Om-Tat-Sat—Om (Braham) is the sole Reality. In the Yogic Scripture on the Science-of-Braham,
the Shrimada-Bhāgvada-Gītā Upanishad, we hereby conclude Shloka 25 of the Dialogue between
Shrī Krishna and Arjuna entitled Jnana-Vijnana-Yoga, Canto VII.

— ॐ श्रीकृष्णाय नमः ॐ —

A Fiery-Blaze all around. And still I missed that hidden Light
I wandered in broad daylight,
Yet I continued stumbling—as though it were gloom and night.

I kept asking—"Where's God?"
Even though He is in all breaths and heartbeats of Existence.

He stood beside me in silence—yet I heard Him not.
His eyes were right on me—but my own gaze stayed fully outwards.
He was the light of my eyes—and still I asked: "Where's the Sun?"

नाहं प्रकाशः Naham prakashah—I do not become manifest to the deluded."
Wrapt in pride and worldly sights, I failed to read His words.

Veiled by my own mind—shrouded in dense fog of my thoughts,
I mistook the absence of His vision—as the absence of His.

A fool I was—who perceived just the outer forms—
I never saw the within Flame—that pervades throughout existence.

Then a Turnaround!
Lo, with the Gītā came an Invitation to Stillness.
And in fractured quietness—the veils started to part.

In the hush, Krishna even whispers to people's heart, sometimes.
Though not seen with eyes—that, alas, stay roaming place to place—
But in silent depths within—man does feel His presence—at times.

Despair not. Take heart.
To those who will not simply stop at the outward-anchored pleas,
That Unseen God, will one day emerge—to set us free.

ॐ गीता श्लोकः ७.२६ – GĪTĀ VERSE 7.26

ॐ श्रीमद्भगवद्गीतासूपनिषत्सु ब्रह्मविद्यायां योगशास्त्रे श्रीकृष्णार्जुनसंवादे
oṁ śrīmadbhagavadgītāsūpaniṣatsu brahmavidyāyāṁ yogaśāstre śrīkṛṣṇārjunasaṁvāde
ज्ञानविज्ञानयोगो नाम सप्तमोऽध्यायः श्लोकः २६
jñānavijñānayogo nāma saptamo'dhyāyaḥ ślokaḥ 26

— ॐ —

वेदाहं समतीतानि वर्तमानानि चार्जुन ।
vedāhaṁ samatītāni vartamānāni cārjuna
भविष्याणि च भूतानि मां तु वेद न कश्चन ॥७-२६॥
bhaviṣyāṇi ca bhūtāni māṁ tu veda na kaścana (7-26)

O Arjuna, I know all beings—from past and present and those yet to come—but no one knows Me for who I truly am. (7.26)

—: Word-by-Word :—

वेद vedā – I know; अहम् aham – I; समतीतानि samatītāni – past; वर्तमानानि vartamānāni – present; च ca – and; अर्जुन arjuna – O Arjuna; भविष्याणि bhaviṣyāṇi – future; च ca – and; भूतानि bhūtāni – all beings; माम् mām – Me; तु tu – but; वेद veda – knows; न na – not; कश्चन kaścana – anyone.

—: Understanding The Verse :—

— ॐ श्रीकृष्णाय नमः ॐ —

In this verse, Bhagwān Shri Krishna declares His complete and timeless omniscience, affirming that He knows all beings—those who have lived in the past, those living in the present, and those yet to come.

This knowledge, boundless and eternal, stems from His nature as Kāla-svarūpa, the Supreme Being who transcends the flow of time and yet sustains it.

While He fully knows all jīvas, their past births, present inclinations, and future trajectories, they, bound by the limitations of body, mind, and ego, fail to recognize Bhagwān Shri Krishna in His true essence.

This ignorance is not merely a cognitive deficiency, but a spiritual blindness arising from lack of bhakti, śraddhā, and inner purity.

— ॐ खरध्वंसिने नमः ॐ —

This verse draws a clear contrast between the Lord's perfect knowledge of all beings and the jīva's inability to know Him, unless guided by devotion and illumined by His grace.

The Lord's omniscience is not mechanical knowledge, but a luminous awareness inherent to His very being as the Avyayātma— the changeless Self of all.

—: Key Sanskrit Terms :—

— ॐ तत् सत् ॐ —

The verse here becomes strangely expansive. Sanskrit carries भूतानि वर्तमानानि भविष्याणि bhūtāni vartamānāni bhaviṣyāṇi ca like a slow procession of time itself, while मां तु वेद न कश्चन mām tu veda na kaścana settles with quiet, impenetrable dignity.

The words feel like an infinite gaze meeting a finite one. Sanskrit here becomes the voice of knowing that does not need to be known—holding past, present, and future in a single, still breath.

We shall open the door of this verse through its syllables—each a step deeper into the stillness of its inner light. Come, let's lean in a little closer—as if the verse were about to share a secret, softly, through its Sanskrit, where each word feels less like something said and more like something of yore become remembered.

— ॐ —

वेदाहं समतीतानि (vedāhaṁ samatītāni):
"I know all that has passed."
वेदाहं Veda aham — "I know" — spoken by the Lord, expresses omniscience.
समतीतानि Samatītāni refers to all beings and events that have occurred in the past, without exception.
The Lord's knowledge encompasses all prior manifestations of existence.

— ॐ —

वर्तमानानि च अर्जुन (vartamānāni ca arjuna):
"And the beings present, O Arjuna."
वर्तमानानि Vartamānāni — the beings presently existing — are also fully known to the Lord.
His awareness is immediate and all-pervasive, unbounded by the limitations of space or time.

— ॐ —

भविष्याणि च भूतानि (bhaviṣyāṇi ca bhūtāni):

"And the beings yet to come."

Not only past and present, but also future beings and their destinies lie within the Lord's perfect knowledge.

Time's unfolding is transparent before His infinite vision.

— ॐ —

मां तु वेद न कश्चन (māṁ tu veda na kaścana):

"Yet none knows Me truly."

न कश्चन Kaścana (none whatsoever) signifies the universal limitation among embodied beings.

Though the Lord knows all, none — bound by Māyā and limited intellect — can comprehend Him fully in His essential, infinite nature.

—: In Brief :—

— ॐ श्रीकृष्णाय नमः ॐ —

Here, Bhagwān speaks not from a position of remoteness but as the indwelling Self, the Kṣetrajña who resides in all beings yet is untouched by their limitations.

He sees the jīvas moving through countless births, driven by karma, desire, and ignorance.

He witnesses the entirety of their journey—not sequentially, as in human perception—but simultaneously, in the eternal present of His being.

Unto God—Time is not a progression but a transparent field of manifestation.

— ॐ श्रीरामाय नमः ॐ —

The word 'भूतानि bhūtāni' encompasses all living beings, sentient and insentient, from the devas to the blades of grass.

The Lord knows each soul's karmic origins, tendencies, desires, and destinies.

Yet 'मां तु वेद न कश्चन māṁ tu veda na kaścana'—no one, He says, truly knows Me.

Not because He is unwilling to be known, but because the ordinary intellect, veiled by ego and moha, is incapable of beholding the Divine in His fullness.

— ॐ कुरुक्षेत्रधनञ्जयस्य सारथये नमः ॐ —

Here, the use of '**तु** tu' (indeed, however) introduces a profound contrast: while the Lord knows all, the jīva, by default, knows nothing of the Lord's true nature unless blessed by insight.

This points to the radical asymmetry between Divine and human consciousness.

Whereas the jīva's knowledge is limited by mind, senses, and temporal conditioning, the Lord's awareness is pūrṇa—complete, eternal, undivided.

— ॐ उपेन्द्राय नमः ॐ —

Though revealing of the Jiva's piteous state, yet this verse is not one of despair. It is a quiet call to acceptance, humility, surrender—and then striving through the strength of God.

For those who, recognizing their ignorance, approach the Lord with devotion—and lo, the darkness starts to part.

Thunder—with the might of God Himself within ye.
Demand: let there be light. And there *will* be light.

— ॐ द्वारकाधीशाय नमः ॐ —

In earlier verses, Shri Krishna has stated that the wise one who sees "Vāsudevaḥ sarvam iti" comes to Him after many births.

In verse 11.54 He will again affirm: "भक्त्या त्वनन्यया शक्य bhaktyā tv ananyayā śakyaḥ"—"By exclusive devotion alone can I be known in truth."

Therefore, the inability to know the Lord is not a permanent barrier, but a condition to be transcended by bhakti, viveka, and śaraṇāgati.

When the Lord is pleased, He reveals Himself—not through logic, nor sense perception, but in the purified heart of the devotee.

— ॐ अच्युताय नमः ॐ —

A subtle philosophical point is also implied: even the past, present, and future do not exist independently of the Lord.

He is not merely a knower of time—He is the very source of time (Mahākāla).

To know Bhagwān Krishna is not merely to know about Him, but to transcend the illusion of separation and to awaken into oneness with the Eternal.

— ॐ अन्जनासुतवन्दिताय नमः ॐ —

Thus, while He knows all beings perfectly, the soul knows Him only when the veils fall away.

In the next verse, Shri Krishna begins to explain why this knowledge remains hidden: the deluding influence of the dualities of rāga-dveṣa—attachment and aversion—rooted in moha (delusion), which obscure the inner light of truth.

All beings, deluded by duality from birth, are kept from knowing Him due to moha born of rāga and dveṣa.

— ॐ तत सत ॐ —

Before we move on, let us bow in reverence to this sacred verse—a timeless beacon of wisdom guiding seekers for ages. Write it by hand, reflect on its meaning, and chant it aloud, for these sounds alone carry the authenticity of that era. The world may have changed but the living vibration of these Sanskrit sounds still remain as original as they were when Bhagwān Shri Krishna Himself walked the earth and imparted these teachings.

— ॐ —

वेदाहं समतीतानि वर्तमानानि चार्जुन ।
vedāhaṁ samatītāni vartamānāni cārjuna
भविष्याणि च भूतानि मां तु वेद न कश्चन ॥७-२६॥
bhaviṣyāṇi ca bhūtāni māṁ tu veda na kaścana (7-26)

वेदाहं समतीतानि वर्तमानानि चार्जुन ।
vedāhaṁ samatītāni vartamānāni cārjuna
भविष्याणि च भूतानि मां तु वेद न कश्चन ॥७-२६॥
bhaviṣyāṇi ca bhūtāni māṁ tu veda na kaścana (7-26)

ॐ तत्सदिति श्रीमद्भगवद्गीतासूपनिषत्सु ब्रह्मविद्यायां योगशास्त्रे श्रीकृष्णार्जुनसंवादे
om tatsaditi śrīmadbhagavadgītāsūpaniṣatsu brahmavidyāyāṁ yogaśāstre śrīkṛṣṇārjunasaṁvāde
ज्ञानविज्ञानयोगो नाम सप्तमोऽध्यायः श्लोकः २६
jñānavijñānayogo nāma saptamo'dhyāyaḥ ślokaḥ 26

Om-Tat-Sat—Om (Braham) is the sole Reality. In the Yogic Scripture on the Science-of-Braham, the Shrimada-Bhāgvada-Gītā Upanishad, we hereby conclude Shloka 26 of the Dialogue between Shri Krishna and Arjuna entitled Jnana-Vijnana-Yoga, Canto VII.

— ॐ श्रीकृष्णाय नमः ॐ —

<u>Krishna is All. He knows All.</u>
" I stay silent and unseen—yet I hold all threads.
I know all souls. Know them inside out. Aye, I know them *All*.

Yes all. Saint & sinner. Each and everyone. Each cry. Each little turn.
All souls born. Souls unborn. Those gone. Those yet to come.

I know the soul's propensity for forgetting.
I do forgive—**even though they forget Me**. For this is merely a sport.
All this? This is just My play. My Lila. **No Purpose. No agenda.** "

— ॐ श्रीकृष्णाय नमः ॐ —

We know not Him—but Nature knows Krishna so well!

The breeze knows Him. The rivers still remember.
Even the birds sing His name without syllables.

But man?
Man painted Krishna in soft colors—
So he would not have to face his own potential.

Krishna says in the gentle tone of devastating truth:
" Men know Me not—for who I truly am
Nature recognizes Me directly. Only humans require stories."

— ॐ श्रीकृष्णाय नमः ॐ —

Stone in river, river around stone—
So was Krishna among mortals—
The unmoved anchor. The unmistakable rock.

Yet men, like water, flowed past Him
Without absorbing His spirit, His fire.
Do ye, O human, hear Krishna voice carved out in space-time?
"I, thy anchor, stay firm for thee; and yet ye stay ever drifting!"
Whatever happened to thee—humans?

— ॐ श्रीकृष्णाय नमः ॐ —

O mortal, enter the canyon of the Inward Mind—
Where Krishna once placed the compass of pure insight.

But, humans stay ignoring the compass and its needle,
They trust their own trembling guesses—over the cosmic calibration.

And the echoing voice from the cave declares:
"I oriented you to infinity—तत् त्वम् असि tat-tvam-asi
And yet ye chose the nearest distraction!"

Alas, alas, O humans, alas.

O humans, follow the trails of thy ruin & ashes across the centuries—
Each fleck a memory of those who twisted, warped, perverted Krishna.

Krishna's steps left blazing fire. Thy faltering decrepit steps left ugly soot.
And from the dirty sooty ashes, a tragic truth stands revealed:
"You preserved Krishna's festivals and tales. But, not His Flame."

Alas, alas, O humans of Āryāvarta, alas—and Shame on Ye!

ॐ गीता श्लोकः ७.२७ – Gītā Verse 7.27

ॐ श्रीमद्भगवद्गीतासूपनिषत्सु ब्रह्मविद्यायां योगशास्त्रे श्रीकृष्णार्जुनसंवादे
om śrīmadbhagavadgītāsūpaniṣatsu brahmavidyāyāṁ yogaśāstre śrīkṛṣṇārjunasaṁvāde
ज्ञानविज्ञानयोगो नाम सप्तमोऽध्यायः श्लोकः २७
jñānavijñānayogo nāma saptamo'dhyāyaḥ ślokaḥ 27

— ॐ —

इच्छाद्वेषसमुत्थेन द्वन्द्वमोहेन भारत ।
icchādveṣasamutthena dvandvamohena bhārata
सर्वभूतानि सम्मोहं सर्गे यान्ति परन्तप ॥७-२७॥
sarvabhūtāni sammohaṁ sarge yānti parantapa (7-27)

O valiant one, through delusion—in the form of pairs of opposites that are born of desire and aversion—all beings are held prey to my Māyā from their very births. (7.27)

—: *Word-by-Word* :—

इच्छा icchā – desire; द्वेष dveṣa – aversion; समुत्थेन samutthena – arising from; द्वन्द्व dvandva – pairs of opposites; मोहेन mohena – by delusion; भारत bhārata – O descendant of Bharata (Arjuna); सर्वभूतानि sarva-bhūtāni – all beings; सम्मोहम् sammohaṁ – complete delusion; सर्गे sarge – at birth; यान्ति yānti – go into; परन्तप parantapa – O conqueror of enemies (Arjuna).

—: *Understanding The Verse* :—

— ॐ श्रीकृष्णाय नमः ॐ —

In this verse, Bhagwān Shri Krishna reveals the fundamental cause of delusion that veils the truth of His divine nature from beings.

From the moment of birth, all beings are subject to the dualities of rāga (attachment) and dveṣa (aversion), which give rise to the ceaseless pairs of opposites—pleasure and pain, joy and sorrow, success and failure.

These opposites are not merely external conditions but are deeply internalized, shaping perception, desire, and action.

— ॐ मिथिलेशप्रियाय नमः ॐ —

Rooted in kāma and krodha, these polarities bind the mind to the world of transient experience and obscure the eternal Reality.

This delusion, born of Māyā, causes beings to remain entangled in saṁsāra, mistaking the fleeting for the permanent, the shadow for the substance.

However, this verse also implicitly teaches that liberation is possible. For those who, through discrimination (viveka), devotion (bhakti), and discipline (sādhana), rise above the tyranny of these dualities, the veil begins to lift. The truth of the Self—and of the Supreme Lord—can then be directly known.

—: *Key Sanskrit Terms* :—

— ॐ तत सत ॐ —

The tone shifts into a soft, entrancing entanglement. Sanskrit whispers इच्छाद्वेषसमुत्थेन icchā-dveṣa-samutthena like a subtle tug of opposites, while मोह moha spreads its gentle haze. सर्वभूतानि Sarva-bhūtāni drifts within it like figures moving through a dream.

The verse does not accuse; it drapes. Sanskrit becomes a twilight field of sound where duality weaves its spell over every birth.

Let us begin our journey through the verse by pausing at its essential Sanskrit terms—each a quiet lantern casting light upon the path of deeper meaning.

— ॐ —

इच्छा द्वेष समुत्थेन (icchā-dveṣa-samutthena):
"Arising from desire and aversion."
इच्छा Icchā (desire) and द्वेष dveṣa (aversion) are the two fundamental forces that agitate the mind and entangle the soul in संसार saṁsāra.
समुत्थेन Samutthena (arising from) shows that these forces are born simultaneously with the embodied existence, deeply rooted in the very experience of individuality.

— ॐ —

द्वन्द्व मोहेन (dvandva-mohena):
"Through the delusion caused by the pairs of opposites."
द्वन्द्व Dvandva refers to dualities — pleasure and pain, gain and loss, honor and dishonor.
मोह Moha (delusion) arises when beings, caught between these fluctuating pairs, lose sight of the unchanging Self and become enmeshed in external conditions.

— ॐ —

भारत (bhārata):
O descendant of Bhārata!
Krishna addresses Arjuna with this noble epithet, reminding him of his dharmic heritage and innate capacity to rise above delusion.

— ॐ —

सर्वभूतानि सम्मोहं सर्गे यान्ति (sarvabhūtāni sammoham sarge yānti):

"All beings fall into delusion at the time of birth."

सम्मोहं Sammoham — bewitched, hypnotized as it were, the great bewilderment which overtakes them — and which ends up in the loss of true knowledge.

सर्गे Sarge (at creation or at the beginning of embodiment) signifies that from the very commencement of life, सर्वभूतानि all beings are plunged into ignorance — captivated, enamored, bewitched (सम्मोहित) by माया Māyā.

— ॐ —

परन्तप (parantapa):

O scorcher of foes!

Another name for Arjuna, parantapa evokes his inner strength and valor, a subtle call to transcend the inner enemies of ignorance and attachment.

—: In Brief :—

— ॐ श्रीकृष्णाय नमः ॐ —

इच्छाद्वेषसमुत्थेन द्वन्द्वमोहेन भारत । सर्वभूतानि सम्मोहं सर्गे यान्ति परन्तप ॥

This verse strikes at the root of saṁsāric bondage. The delusion (moha) that clouds the vision of beings arises from the tension between इच्छा icchā (craving) and द्वेष dveṣa (aversion).

These twin impulses form the basic polarity of the conditioned mind.

Whatever appears pleasurable, the mind clings to; whatever appears painful, it rejects.

From these reactions are born endless dvandvas—pairs of opposites—that churn the heart and obscure the gaze from truth.

— ॐ श्रीरामाय नमः ॐ —

The word समुत्थेन samutthena ("arising from") reveals that dualities are not inherent to Reality but arise from within the conditioned psyche.

The द्वन्द्वमोह dvandva-moha—the delusion of opposites—is a product of saṅkalpa (mental projection) driven by ego-centered desire.

Thus, the world is not binding in itself; it becomes binding only when filtered through the lens of attachment and aversion.

— ॐ योगीश्वराय नमः ॐ —

The phrase सर्वभूतानि sarva-bhūtāni ("all beings") may seem to indicate universal entrapment, yet the context—flowing from the previous verses—makes it clear that this applies to all ordinary souls, not to the realized sages or the bhaktas whose hearts are fixed in the Lord.

Those who are ananya-bhaktāḥ—exclusively devoted to the Lord—are not swayed by these dualities. Rather, they are nirdvandvāḥ—free from the pull of opposites, as declared elsewhere in the Gītā as well (for instance see verses 2.45, 5.3).

— ॐ श्रीकान्ताय नमः ॐ —

The designation Parantapa ("scorcher of foes") is not incidental here. It reminds Arjuna—and through him all spiritual seekers—that the real enemy lies not outside but within: desire, hatred etc., ungoverned emotions, which manifest as attachment to pleasures etc.

These are the inner foes to be conquered if one wishes to perceive the eternal and birthless Lord who dwells within all.

— ॐ सीताशरण्याय नमः ॐ —

Importantly, the delusion begins "सर्गे sarge"—at the very moment of embodiment.

This indicates that as soon as the soul takes birth, its consciousness is veiled by Māyā, and the pull of likes and dislikes begins to govern it.

Hence, liberation is not a natural outcome of birth but must be consciously pursued through self-inquiry, viveka, vairāgya—and above all, bhakti.

— ॐ समुद्रसेतुबंधकर्त्रे नमः ॐ —

Yet even within this veiling darkness, the Lord's grace quietly abides.

This dvandva-moha—the spell of duality—is woven by Māyā, the subtle power that moves at His behest.

But when the heart turns toward Him in refuge, a deeper strength awakens—and through that light, all illusions gently fall away.

In later verses, Shri Krishna will teach that those who, by devotion and right vision, rise above rāga-dveṣa, become fit to attain Him.

Thus, this verse prepares the ground for the next teaching, where the Lord reveals the character of those rare souls whose puṇyakarma (meritorious deeds) and freedom from delusion enable them to worship Him with unwavering hearts; and freed from the bonds of duality, are able to seek Him with firm resolve.

— ॐ तत् सत् ॐ —

Before we move on, let us bow in reverence to this sacred verse. Write it by hand, reflect on its meaning, chant it aloud, make it your own.

— ॐ —

इच्छाद्वेषसमुत्थेन द्वन्द्वमोहेन भारत ।
icchādveṣasamutthena dvandvamohena bhārata
सर्वभूतानि सम्मोहं सर्गे यान्ति परन्तप ॥७-२७॥
sarvabhūtāni sammohaṁ sarge yānti parantapa (7-27)

इच्छाद्वेषसमुत्थेन द्वन्द्वमोहेन भारत ।
icchādveṣasamutthena dvandvamohena bhārata

सर्वभूतानि सम्मोहं सर्गे यान्ति परन्तप ॥७-२७॥
sarvabhūtāni sammohaṁ sarge yānti parantapa (7-27)

ॐ तत्सदिति श्रीमद्भगवद्गीतासूपनिषत्सु ब्रह्मविद्यायां योगशास्त्रे श्रीकृष्णार्जुनसंवादे
om tatsaditi śrīmadbhagavadgītāsūpaniṣatsu brahmavidyāyāṁ yogaśāstre śrīkṛṣṇārjunasaṁvāde
ज्ञानविज्ञानयोगो नाम सप्तमोऽध्यायः श्लोकः २७
jñānavijñānayogo nāma saptamo'dhyāyaḥ ślokaḥ 27

Om-Tat-Sat—Om (Braham) is the sole Reality. In the Yogic Scripture on the Science-of-Braham, the Shrimada-Bhāgvada-Gītā Upanishad, we hereby conclude Shloka 27 of the Dialogue between Shrī Krishna and Arjuna entitled Jnana-Vijnana-Yoga, Canto VII.

— ॐ श्रीकृष्णाय नमः ॐ —

These Chains come With the Body
Ah me, how deep the-Sleep that begins with Birth!
It is an old, old malady—many, many lifetimes ancient!

No sooner did I wake up in this earthy flesh—
Forthwith I forgot the Realm whence I came!

सर्गे यान्ति Sarge yanti — it was at Creation's very first breath that I fell,
Fell into a dream where joys-sorrows reign as king-queen pair. Conjoined.

Now I know not who I am—nor whence I came.
No longer clothed in my innate light,
I stay draped thick—in my otiose inane longings.

I became snared, entrapped, laid down—
Not by fate but by my own becoming!

O enchantress Maya, Thou spinnest a world of endless portrayals,
And I keep chasing reflections—mistaking this Reel for Truth & Real.

Alas, O soul, thy very first cry on earth—Mā—
Is not for mother, father, air —
It is a cry for Māyā—to clutch at her illusions!

ॐ गीता श्लोकः ७.२८ – Gītā Verse 7.28

ॐ श्रीमद्भगवद्गीतासूपनिषत्सु ब्रह्मविद्यायां योगशास्त्रे श्रीकृष्णार्जुनसंवादे
om śrīmadbhagavadgītāsūpaniṣatsu brahmavidyāyāṁ yogaśāstre śrīkṛṣṇārjunasaṁvāde
ज्ञानविज्ञानयोगो नाम सप्तमोऽध्यायः श्लोकः २८
jñānavijñānayogo nāma saptamo'dhyāyaḥ ślokaḥ 28

— ॐ —

येषां त्वन्तगतं पापं जनानां पुण्यकर्मणाम् ।
yeṣāṁ tvantagataṁ pāpaṁ janānāṁ puṇyakarmaṇām
ते द्वन्द्वमोहनिर्मुक्ता भजन्ते मां दृढव्रताः ॥७-२८॥
te dvandvamohanirmuktā bhajante māṁ dṛḍhavratāḥ (7-28)

But those of virtuous deeds, whose sins past and present have come to an end, they are freed from this delusion of dualities—and they go on to worship Me with a firmness of vow. (7.28)

—: *Word-by-Word* :—

येषाम् yeṣām – whose; तु tu – but; अन्तगतम् antagatam – completely destroyed; पापम् pāpam – sins; जनानाम् janānām – of the people; पुण्यकर्मणाम् puṇya-karmaṇām – of those engaged in pious deeds; ते te – they; द्वन्द्वमोहनिर्मुक्ताः dvandva-moha-nirmuktāḥ – freed from the delusion of dualities; भजन्ते bhajante – worship; माम् mām – Me; दृढव्रताः dṛḍha-vratāḥ – with firm resolve.

—: *Understanding The Verse* :—

— ॐ श्रीकृष्णाय नमः ॐ —

In this verse, Bhagwān Shri Krishna introduces the class of exalted souls who, through sustained virtue and inner purification, rise above the delusion of dualities—such as pleasure and pain, gain and loss, attachment and aversion.

Unlike the deluded beings bound by desire and hatred described in the previous verse, these rare ones have exhausted the momentum of their sins, both past and present, and thus attained clarity of heart (śuddha-citta).

— ॐ रामभद्राय नमः ॐ —

Freed from the pull of the opposites (dvandva-moha), they turn their minds and lives wholly toward the Divine.

Their devotion is not impulsive or circumstantial but grounded in firm resolve (dṛḍha-vrataḥ), reflecting a deeply rooted commitment to the path of Truth.

These are not seekers shaken by joy or sorrow, nor distracted by worldly allurements; rather, they have recognized the Supreme as the true aim of human life.

Their worship is not mechanical ritual or mere sentiment—it is total, pervading all aspects of their being.

And now thought, word, and deed are harmonized in single-pointed remembrance of, and surrender, **unto the Supreme.**

—: Key Sanskrit Terms :—

— ॐ तत सत ॐ —

And now a clearer light enters the cadence. Sanskrit lets पुण्यकर्मणाम् puṇyakarmaṇām glimmer with quiet purification, while द्वन्द्वमोहनिर्मुक्ता dvandva-moha-nirmuktāḥ feels like a loosening of invisible knots. भजन्ते मां Bhajante māṁ sounds steady and resolved.

The verse does not necessarily celebrate—it stays steadfast in calm. The Sanskrit feels like a calm, upright flame, burning away confusion without noise, leaving only a firm, simple devotion behind.

Let us sit beside these phrases as we would beside a stream— watching, listening, not forcing meaning but letting the meaning rise unseen, like mist in water.

— ॐ —

येषां तु अन्तगतं पापं (yeṣāṁ tu antagataṁ pāpam):
"But for those whose sins have come to an end."
अन्तगतं पापं Antagatam pāpam signifies that the accumulated sins (pāpa), the stains of ignorance and wrong action, have been exhausted.
तु Tu (but) signals a contrast: unlike those bound in delusion, these souls are purified and thus prepared for higher realization.

— ॐ —

जनानां पुण्यकर्मणाम् (janānāṁ puṇyakarmaṇām):
"Among the men of meritorious deeds."
पुण्यकर्मणाम् Puṇyakarmaṇaḥ are those beings जना who, across many births, have performed actions in accordance with Dharma — righteous, selfless, and pure deeds — which purify the heart and prepare the soil for the flowering of wisdom.

— ॐ —

ते द्वन्द्वमोहनिर्मुक्ताः (te dvandvamohanirmuktāḥ):
"They, freed from the delusion of dualities."

द्वन्द्वमोह Dvandva-moha — the bewilderment caused by the pairs of opposites (pleasure and pain, success and failure) — once the heart is purified, no longer binds these souls.

They stand निर्मुक्ताः nirmuktāḥ — free, established in equipoise.

— ॐ —

भजन्ते मां दृढव्रताः (bhajante māṁ dṛḍhavratāḥ):
"They worship Me with firm resolve."

दृढव्रताः Dṛḍha-vratāḥ — those of firm, unwavering vow — approach the Lord with steadfastness, with a heart that neither wavers in faith nor is distracted by fleeting desires.

Their भजन devotion is strong, single-pointed, and unbreakable.

—: In Brief :—

— ॐ श्रीकृष्णाय नमः ॐ —

येषां त्वन्तगतं पापं जनानां पुण्यकर्मणाम् । ते द्वन्द्वमोहनिर्मुक्ता भजन्ते मां दृढव्रताः ॥

"But those of virtuous deeds, free from sin, worship Me with firm vows"— each word is sunlight breaking cloud, or like a path cleared after storm.

A contrast is painted between the deluded multitude and the rare, purified souls.

These are not ordinary people swept away by the tides of fate.

They are those janāḥ of पुण्यकर्मणाम् puṇya-karmaṇām—beings who have accumulated puṇya (merit) through acts of selfless virtue across many lifetimes.

Their meritorious actions—yajña, dāna, tapas, sat-saṅga, and most of all bhakti—have steadily cleansed the mirror of their consciousness.

— ॐ श्रीरामाय नमः ॐ —

More importantly, अन्तगतम् पापम् anta-gataṁ pāpaṁ—their sins have come to an end.

This does not merely refer to outer wrongdoing but to the subtle vāsanās and saṁskāras—deep-rooted tendencies that bind the soul to ignorance.

Only when both gross and subtle impurities have been removed can the light of the Self shine forth unobstructed.

— ॐ योगिनां पतये नमः ॐ —

Such souls are द्वन्द्वमोहनिर्मुक्ताः dvandva-moha-nirmuktāḥ—liberated from the delusion caused by the pairs of opposites.

These dvandvas—joy and sorrow, honor and dishonor, heat and cold—are the tests of life, and the unprepared mind is tossed about by them. But the devotee who has transcended these, through wisdom and surrender, walks the earth in peace.

A true seer sees both pleasant and unpleasant with equanimity, knowing them to be fleeting reflections of prakṛti.

— ॐ यज्ञप्रियाय नमः ॐ —

Then comes the heart of the verse: भजन्ते मां दृढव्रताः bhajante māṁ dṛdha-vratāḥ—"they worship Me with firm resolve."

This worship is not occasional prayer or ritual formality.

It is an unbroken current of remembrance, rooted in deep understanding.

Their vrata—their vow—is दृढ dṛdha—firm, unwavering, untouched by circumstance.

Their mind, intellect, heart, and senses are harmonized in the service and contemplation of the Lord.

— ॐ स्मितवक्त्राय नमः ॐ —

Such all-encompassing bhajana spans the entirety of life.
It means to engage:
- the body and our wealth, resources etc., in service of Him and His Sanātana-Dharma,
  - the speech in His praise,
  - the mind reflecting upon Him,
  - the intellect in discrimination between dualities such as real-unreal, good-bad, dharma-adharma etc.,
  - our every breath in loving remembrance of the Supreme.

This verse illumines the pathway from bondage to liberation.

While the previous verses show the root of delusion, this one shows the means of release: virtuous action, purification of sin, transcendence of duality, and firm devotion to the Lord.

This is the journey of the soul from the restless sea of saṁsāra to an unshakable refuge within the Divine.

— ॐ दशरथात्मजाय नमः ॐ —

In the verses that follow, Bhagwān Shri Krishna will reveal the fruit of such devotion—the vision of His integral transcendent nature—and the final movement of the soul toward Him.

There are the deluded fools of the world—and then there are those who, knowing Him as the source of all bliss, completeness, and the origin of our own beingness—strive for emancipation and take refuge exclusively in Him!

And so, which side are we on, O pilgrim?

— ॐ तत् सत ॐ —

Before we move on, let us bow in reverence to this sacred verse. Write it by hand, reflect on its meaning, chant it aloud, make it your own.

— ॐ —

येषां त्वन्तगतं पापं जनानां पुण्यकर्मणाम् ।

yeṣāṁ tvantagataṁ pāpaṁ janānāṁ puṇyakarmaṇām

ते द्वन्द्वमोहनिर्मुक्ता भजन्ते मां दृढव्रताः ॥७-२८॥

te dvandvamohanirmuktā bhajante māṁ dṛḍhavratāḥ (7-28)

— ॐ —

येषां त्वन्तगतं पापं जनानां पुण्यकर्मणाम् ।

yeṣāṁ tvantagataṁ pāpaṁ janānāṁ puṇyakarmaṇām

ते द्वन्द्वमोहनिर्मुक्ता भजन्ते मां दृढव्रताः ॥७-२८॥

te dvandvamohanirmuktā bhajante māṁ dṛḍhavratāḥ (7-28)

ॐ तत्सदिति श्रीमद्भगवद्गीतासूपनिषत्सु ब्रह्मविद्यायां योगशास्त्रे श्रीकृष्णार्जुनसंवादे

om tatsaditi śrīmadbhagavadgītāsūpaniṣatsu brahmavidyāyāṁ yogaśāstre śrīkṛṣṇārjunasaṁvāde

ज्ञानविज्ञानयोगो नाम सप्तमोऽध्यायः श्लोकः २८

jñānavijñānayogo nāma saptamo'dhyāyaḥ ślokaḥ 28

Om-Tat-Sat—Om (Braham) is the sole Reality. In the Yogic Scripture on the Science-of-Braham, the Shrimada-Bhāgvada-Gītā Upanishad, we hereby conclude Shloka 28 of the Dialogue between Shrī Krishna and Arjuna entitled Jnana-Vijnana-Yoga, Canto VII.

— ॐ श्रीकृष्णाय नमः ॐ —

" O Arjuna, some do manage to come very near to Me
—Not those still confused, not those still mired—
But those whose stains have been washed away in tears & fire. "

Minds pure; gaze steady; their karmas dissipated—
They are no longer torn by the dualities of opposites.

Not seeking joy, nor fleeing sorrows—they face what just came.
And with one-pointed hearts they stay in worship—
" To return to Me—with Me alone as their Center. "

And yes. When you come in as light —
You do end up rebecoming the Flame,

This is the jewel at Gītā's core:
When delusion dies, true devotion is born.

Yes True Devotion.

Real Devotion. For the **Real** Krishna—the **Krishna** of the **Gītā**.
Yes alas—for we fools have turned the Infinite into a Caricature.

— ॐ श्रीकृष्णाय नमः ॐ —

O seeker—know this bitter truth:
Humanity did not merely misunderstand Krishna;
It betrayed Him.

The Infinite who gave to us the blazing Gītā,
Was reduced by us foolish humans into:
- a soft legend; - a festival mascot; - a sentimental toy.

He Who took human form and even fought our battles—
That Great Infinite walked among us—not for drama—
But to realign the age back to Dharma.

Yet humans shrank Bhagwān Krishna into petty stories
Because His true fire terrified them.

Humans have mocked and blasphemed Krishna—
By ignoring His teachings, and allowing Dharma to be spat on,

The fools have glorified ignorance and cowardice—
All while claiming "devotion" to the very Krishna they
Refuse to acknowledge, or follow, or understand.

Today Sanātana-Dharma is on the verge of extinction,
And the verdict therefore stands:
The failure is not His—it is the species that made Him small.

Yes, Bhagwān Krishna—the Absolute, verily God—didst declare:
"When Dharma falls, I restore it"
But He never foretold—if He will do it **with** humans, or **without** them!

O humans, if ye refuse awakening,
Then Krishna leaves thee to thy own destruction!

And yes, Sanātana-Dharma will still be restored and prevail—
But through another people more capable.
Or even another species—if thy entire human lot is found rotten.

Yet, God grants thee one final opening:
Mend thyself. Return to the principles of Sanātana-Dharma.
Prove thyself worthy of Gītā & Krishna—whom ye have reduced to tales.
Till then, no gods shall intervene to save thee—
Until ye choose True Krishna—over the caricature ye crafted of Him.

ॐ गीता श्लोकः ७.२९ – GĪTĀ VERSE 7.29

ॐ श्रीमद्भगवद्गीतासूपनिषत्सु ब्रह्मविद्यायां योगशास्त्रे श्रीकृष्णार्जुनसंवादे
om śrīmadbhagavadgītāsūpaniṣatsu brahmavidyāyāṃ yogaśāstre śrīkṛṣṇārjunasaṃvāde
ज्ञानविज्ञानयोगो नाम सप्तमोऽध्यायः श्लोकः २९
jñānavijñānayogo nāma saptamo'dhyāyaḥ ślokaḥ 29

— ॐ —

जरामरणमोक्षाय मामाश्रित्य यतन्ति ये ।
jarāmaraṇamokṣāya mamāśritya yatanti ye
ते ब्रह्म तद्विदुः कृत्स्नमध्यात्मं कर्म चाखिलम् ॥७-२९॥
te brahma tadviduḥ kṛtsnamadhyātmaṃ karma cākhilam (7-29)

Those who strive for deliverance from the cycle of death and decay, they take refuge in Me, and they find of Brahama, and of the embodied soul, and of this entire bailiwick of Karma. (7.29)

—: Word-by-Word :—

जरा jarā – old age; मरण maraṇ – death; मोक्षाय mokṣāya – for liberation; माम् mām – Me; आश्रित्य āśritya – taking refuge in; यतन्ति ye – those who strive; ते te – they; ब्रह्म brahma – Braham; तद् tad – that; विदुः viduḥ – know; कृत्स्नम् kṛtsnam – in entirety; अध्यात्मम् adhyātmaṃ – the self; कर्म karma – action; च ca – and; अखिलम् akhilam – all.

—: Understanding The Verse :—

— ॐ श्रीकृष्णाय नमः ॐ —

In this verse, Bhagwān Shri Krishna reveals the state and aspirations of the highest class of spiritual seekers—those who, weary of the impermanence of worldly existence, yearn for release from the cycle of जरा jarā (old age) and मरण (death).

These are not seekers of pleasure or power, but of mokṣa—liberation from the bondage of saṃsāra.

With resolute hearts, they take exclusive refuge in the Supreme, directing their energy and devotion toward the Eternal.

— ॐ श्रीरामाय नमः ॐ —

To such seekers, the Lord bestows knowledge of three profound realities:
Braham, the eternal, formless Absolute;
the Adhyātma, the true nature of the individual Self;
and Karma, the principle of karmas and its deep, deep plays.

Thus, this verse marks a pivotal turning point in the Gītā's discourse—linking bhakti (devotion) with jñāna (knowledge), and showing that the path of wholehearted surrender to the Lord leads not only to liberation, but also to the highest wisdom.

—: Key Sanskrit Terms :—

— ॐ तत सत ॐ —

Let us study the verse and its key Sanskrit terms.

The language grows deep and inward. Sanskrit breathes जरामरणमोक्षाय jarā-maraṇa-mokṣāya with grave tenderness, while मामाश्रिय mām āśritya feels like a soft resting of the soul. ब्रह्म कर्म Brahma and karma hover like vast, quiet chambers.

The verse does not chart the path; it simply opens infinite space near us. The Sanskrit becomes a sanctuary of resonance—where liberation is felt as a hushed nearness rather than a distant goal.

Each term is both precise and porous. It says what it says, and yet it gestures beyond itself—toward nuance, toward resonance, toward something just beyond the reach of plain speech. Let us follow those gestures—shall we?

— ॐ —

जरामरणमोक्षाय (jarāmaraṇa-mokṣāya):
"For the sake of liberation from old age and death."
जरा Jarā (old age) and मरण maraṇa (death) are seen in Sanātana-Dharma as inevitable consequences of embodiment within saṁsāra.
मोक्षाय Mokṣāya signifies the striving for release from them — not merely from physical death of this life but altogether -- from the endless cycle of births and deaths.

— ॐ —

माम् आश्रिय यतन्ति ये (mām āśritya yatanti ye):
"Those who, taking refuge in Me, strive."
आश्रिय Āśritya (having taken shelter) implies not a casual acknowledgment but a profound, complete surrender.
यतन्ति Yatanti (they strive) points to earnest spiritual endeavor, undertaken under the Lord's protection and guidance.

— ॐ —

ते ब्रह्म तद् विदुः (te brahma tad viduḥ):
"They come to know Braham."

ते They, such seekers, purified by surrender and effort, attain विदुः direct knowledge of ब्रह्म Braham — the infinite, indivisible, eternal Reality that underlies all appearances.

—: ॐ :—

कृत्स्नम् अध्यात्मं (kṛtsnam adhyātmam):
"The entire nature of the Self."

अध्यात्म Adhyātma refers to the essential principle of the individual self — the nature of Ātmā —

and कृत्स्नम् kṛtsnam emphasizes completeness: they realize the total truth of the Self, free of partial understanding.

—: ॐ :—

कर्म च अखिलम् (karma ca akhilam):
"And the entire field of action."

अखिलम् Akhilam कर्म karma points to a full understanding of the cosmic law of action — the entire framework of karma: how karma binds the soul, how it operates through cause and effect, and how it is ultimately transcended through knowledge and devotion.

—: In Brief :—

— ॐ श्रीकृष्णाय नमः ॐ —

जरामरणमोक्षाय मामाश्रित्य यतन्ति ये । ते ब्रह्म तद्विदुः कृत्स्नमध्यात्मं कर्म चाखिलम् ॥

Here, Bhagwān Shri Krishna speaks of the most earnest aspirants—those who are no longer captivated by the glitter of the world, but who long for release from the prison of transience.

जरामरणमोक्षाय Jarā-maraṇa-mokṣāya—"for the sake of freedom from old age and death"—does not merely imply a fear of bodily decline, but the deep, existential weariness of the jīva who has wandered through countless births, seeking permanence in the impermanent.

Such a soul turns away from external supports and mām āśritya—"takes refuge in Me"—as the sole shelter, guide, and goal.

— ॐ सत्यव्रताय नमः ॐ —

To such a seeker, knowledge unfolds as a natural fruit of devotion. He comes to know Braham—the unmanifest, formless Absolute that is beyond mind, beyond speech, and untouched by change.

And this knowledge is not an abstract philosophy. It is a lived insight, ripened through surrender.

It is an actual experience experienced.

Simultaneously, the seeker realizes Adhyātma—the Self within— the individual jīva as not separate, but one in essence with Braham.

He experiences that he is the Ātmā; and that the Ātmā is neither born nor does it die; it is unbound, luminous, and of the nature of pure consciousness.

— ॐ श्रीसुधाकराय नमः ॐ —

The seeker comes to understand कर्म चाखिलम् karma cākhilam—"the entire bailiwick of karma." Not merely the mechanics of cause and effect, but the deeper truth: that all action, when performed with awareness of the Divine and without attachment to fruit, becomes karma-yoga—a path to liberation.

The purified soul sees that true action is not for personal gain, but a sacrificial offering (yajña) to the Supreme.

— ॐ कोदण्डधारिणे नमः ॐ —

In this verse, Bhagwān subtly unifies the three great domains of Vedāntic inquiry: Braham (the Absolute), Ātmā (the individual self), and Karma (action)—and shows that all three are rightly understood only through surrender to Him.

This is the hallmark of the bhakta-jnāni—one who worships the Lord not only with love, but also with wisdom; not only through emotion, but through insight into Reality.

— ॐ आत्मरूपाय नमः ॐ —

This verse shows that true liberation is not mere escape from suffering, but the attainment of comprehensive knowledge of existence—तद्विदुः कृत्स्नम tad viduḥ kṛtsnam—"they know all this in its entirety."

These rare souls reach the culmination of all śāstra, all tapas, all devotion, not by their effort alone, but by the transforming grace that comes through taking refuge in the Supreme.

— ॐ विजयाय नमः ॐ —

In the following verse, Shri Krishna will continue this exalted teaching by describing those who, having known this truth, attain the Divine at the very moment of death—those who, steadfast in their devotion, do not wander again but merge into the Eternal.

Krishna will elucidate the state of those who, understanding Him in His threefold manifestation (Adhibhūta, Adhidaiva, and Adhiyajña), remember Him right up to the final hour, and thus attain the supreme-state beyond return.

— ॐ तत् सत ॐ —

Before we move on, let us bow in reverence to this sacred verse. Write it by hand, reflect on its meaning, chant it aloud, make it your own.

gītā-mūlam 07

— ॐ —

जरामरणमोक्षाय मामाश्रित्य यतन्ति ये ।
jarāmaraṇamokṣāya māmāśritya yatanti ye
ते ब्रह्म तद्विदुः कृत्स्नमध्यात्मं कर्म चाखिलम् ॥७-२९॥
te brahma tadviduḥ kṛtsnamadhyātmaṁ karma cākhilam (7-29)

ॐ तत्सदिति श्रीमद्भगवद्गीतासूपनिषत्सु ब्रह्मविद्यायां योगशास्त्रे श्रीकृष्णार्जुनसंवादे
om tatsaditi śrīmadbhagavadgītāsūpaniṣatsu brahmavidyāyāṁ yogaśāstre śrīkṛṣṇārjunasaṁvāde
ज्ञानविज्ञानयोगो नाम सप्तमोऽध्यायः श्लोकः २९
jñānavijñānayogo nāma saptamo'dhyāyaḥ ślokaḥ 29

Om-Tat-Sat—Om (Braham) is the sole Reality. In the Yogic Scripture on the Science-of-Braham,
the Shrimada-Bhāgvada-Gītā Upanishad, we hereby conclude Shloka 29 of the Dialogue between
Shrī Krishna and Arjuna entitled Jnana-Vijnana-Yoga, Canto VII.

— ॐ श्रीकृष्णाय नमः ॐ —

O, Look at the Wise!

They dive not for pearls—But for "freedom from the Waves"—
Which waves are roiling up above—on the surface of existence.

They have seen Time's tides. Felt the salt of Decay.
So they dive to the most absolute Depths—
Swim to Krishna—that still bed beneath all sway & waves.

And in that silence, they get to know of Braham—
Not as some outer word heard—but as their very own breath,
For lo—these great depths have no waves—just only wavelessness.

Behold, for the Self shines so pristinely clear here!
Here actions, thoughts become like mere ripples. Nay, not even that.
This here is deep, deep currents—in stark arrant stillness!

Let he who seeks no return to **Dukhalyam**—this world of sorrows—
Find his refuge in this shoreless realm of non-dualness!

O come, let's escape this Tireless-Turning of the Wheel-of-Life.
It spins. And it spins again. Then spins yet again.

The wheel keeps turning. And we keep returning—
Through a creature's womb, In new name & form. With hopes renewed.

We step into the world always with new Hopes—
But always end up stepping into new Sorrows.
Hope-sorrow, birth-death, pain-delight—it's always a conjoined pair.

śrīmadbhagavadgītā – saptamo'dhyāyaḥ – jñānavijñānayogaḥ

ॐ गीता श्लोकः ७.३० – GĪTĀ VERSE 7.30

ॐ श्रीमद्भगवद्गीतासूपनिषत्सु ब्रह्मविद्यायां योगशास्त्रे श्रीकृष्णार्जुनसंवादे
om śrīmadbhagavadgītāsūpaniṣatsu brahmavidyāyāṁ yogaśāstre śrīkṛṣṇārjunasaṁvāde
ज्ञानविज्ञानयोगो नाम सप्तमोऽध्यायः श्लोकः ३०
jñānavijñānayogo nāma saptamo'dhyāyaḥ ślokaḥ 30

— ॐ —

साधिभूताधिदैवं मां साधियज्ञं च ये विदुः ।
sādhibhūtādhidaivaṁ māṁ sādhiyajñaṁ ca ye viduḥ

प्रयाणकालेऽपि च मां ते विदुर्युक्तचेतसः ॥७-३०॥
prayāṇakāle'pi ca māṁ te viduryuktacetasaḥ (7-30)

They who know My integral Being—comprising of *Adhibhūta* (the field of Matter), and *Adhidaiva* (the all-pervading Brahama), and *Adhiyajna* (the indwelling soul in all)—and who have fixed their mind firmly upon Me with that understanding, they directly realize My Being when the body falls away."

(7.30)

—: *Word-by-Word* :—

स-अधिभूतम् sa-adhibhūtam – with the governing principle of all beings; अधिदैवम् adhidaivam – and the governing principle of the divine; माम् mām – Me; स-अधियज्ञम् ca sa-adhiyajñaṁ – and with the governing principle of sacrifices; च ca – and; ये ye – those who; विदुः viduḥ – know; प्रयाणकाले prayāṇa-kāle – at the time of death; अपि api – even; च ca – and; माम् mām – Me; ते te – they; विदुः viduḥ – know; युक्तचेतसः yukta-cetasaḥ – with steadfast mind.

—: *Understanding The Verse* :—

— ॐ श्रीकृष्णाय नमः ॐ —

In this culminating verse of the seventh chapter, Bhagwān Shri Krishna describes the state of those rare and steadfast souls who attain full realization of His integral being—not merely as the abstract Braham, but as the all-encompassing Reality manifest through every plane of existence: Adhibhūta (matter), Adhidaiva (the cosmic principle), and Adhiyajña (the indwelling Divine who receives all sacrifice).

These knowers, with minds unwaveringly fixed on Him, remember Him throughout life, right up to the final moment—the hour of death—and thereby attain Him in actuality.

— ॐ श्रीरामाय नमः ॐ —

This verse is not only a summation of this Canto but also a transition to the next Canto, where the Lord expands on these threefold manifestations of His presence.

It completes the circle that began with the Lord's promise to explain His full nature (jñānaṁ vijñāna-sahitam), and affirms that such realization is not merely intellectual but salvific—it leads the soul to union with the Supreme.

—: Key Sanskrit Terms :—

— ॐ तत् सत् ॐ —

The chapter gathers into a sacred triad. Sanskrit lets अधिभूतम् अधिदैवम् अधियज्ञम् adhibhūtaṁ, adhidaivam, and adhiyajñam sound like three deep bells, each echoing within the same unseen hall. माम् mām – Me; ते te – they; विदुः Mām viduḥ glimmers with recognition, and प्रयाणकाले prayāṇa-kāle hovers like a final, silent threshold.

The verse does not end—it consecrates. Here Sanskrit becomes a final, radiant alignment, where all divisions of being are drawn into one luminous, attentive knowing.

Now let us examine the verse. We will place one term beside another, not as stones in a wall, but as notes in a melody—each meaningful on its own, but glowing differently when held in relation to the next.

— ॐ —

साधिभूताधिदैवं मां (sādhibhūtādhidaivaṁ mām):
"Knowing Me in relation to Adhibhūta and Adhidaiva."
अधिभूत Adhibhūta refers to the principle of the perishable elements — the entire field of material existence.
अधिदैव Adhidaiva signifies the cosmic intelligence, the presiding deities who govern the forces of nature. The Lord encompasses both the material and the celestial realms.

— ॐ —

साधियज्ञं च (sādhiyajñaṁ ca):
"And knowing Me as Adhiyajña."
अधियज्ञ Adhiyajña is the indwelling Supreme within all beings, the One who accepts and sustains all sacrificial offerings, the secret Witness of all acts of devotion and Dharma.

— ॐ —

ये विदुः (ye viduḥ):
"Those who know Me thus."

विदुः Viduh (they know) indicates not mere intellectual knowledge, but the direct, intuitive realization of the Lord's presence pervading all levels of existence.

— ॐ —

प्रयाणकाले अपि च (prayāṇakāle api ca):
"Even at the time of departure (death)."
प्रयाणकाल Prayāṇa-kāla — the final moment when the soul prepares to leave the body.
Even then, those of purified understanding remain fixed in their knowledge and remembrance of the Lord.

— ॐ —

ते विदुः युक्तचेतसः (te viduḥ yuktacetasaḥ):
They know Me, their minds harmonized and absorbed.
युक्तचेतसः Yukta-cetasaḥ describes those whose consciousness is steadfastly united with the Divine — unwavering even in the ultimate test, the hour of death.

—: In Brief :—

— ॐ श्रीकृष्णाय नमः ॐ —

This verse completes a majestic unfolding of Divine Reality.

The Lord, having previously declared that वासुदेवः सर्वमिति "Vāsudevaḥ sarvam iti" (7.19)—"All this is indeed Vāsudeva"—now articulates how the wise perceive that Reality through its three principal manifestations, corresponding to the field, the cosmic, and the sacrificial dimensions.

— ॐ रघुकुलोत्थमाय नमः ॐ —

अधिभूत Adhibhūta, the field of perishable matter, refers to the visible, changing world—Apara Prakṛti—composed of the five gross elements and subject to decay. Yet even this mutable realm is none other than an expression of the Lord's energy.

अधिदैव Adhidaiva, the cosmic principle, refers to the universal intelligence (Hiraṇyagarbha) that governs the subtler operations of the universe—the presiding deities, the cosmic forces, the celestial intelligences. It is the divine blueprint, the invisible regulator behind the visible cosmos.

अधियज्ञ Adhiyajña, the indwelling recipient of all sacrificial acts, is Bhagwān Himself residing in the heart of every being as the Antaryāmin—the Inner Controller and Witness. He is both the object and the enjoyer of all true sacrifice, and it is by knowing Him in this role that action is sanctified and spiritualized.

— ॐ पुण्योदयाय नमः ॐ —

The seeker who realizes the Lord in all these aspects—as the eternal substratum of nature, the universal divine order, and the indwelling Self—has come to know the Integral Supreme Absolute.

His चेतसः cetas (mind) is now विद्युयुक्तचेतसः yukta—concentrated, harmonized, unwavering.

What is striking is the Lord's affirmation: "even at the hour of death" (प्रयाणकालेऽपि prayāṇa-kāle 'pi).

The inclusion of api signifies that such realization is not limited to the moments of prolonged contemplation during life. Even if the vision dawns at the time of death—if the heart is purified and the mind is steadfast—the soul attains to the Supreme.

— ॐ त्रिलोकरक्षकाय नमः ॐ —

Death is the final test of consciousness.

For most, it is a moment of fear, confusion, and disintegration of awareness. But for the युक्तचेतसः yukta-cetasaḥ—those whose minds are absorbed in the Divine—**death becomes a passage**, not an end.

They do **not fall back into the cycle of birth and death**, but attain the परमं गतिः paramaṁ gatiḥ—the Supreme Goal.

— ॐ जितेन्द्रियाय नमः ॐ —

The verse affirms a non-dual vision: all categories—Brahammā, matter, gods, sacrifice—are not separate. They are differing facets of the One Undivided Reality, known in fullness only by the Lord's devotee.

To understand these as distinct concepts is **jñāna**;
to see them as One is **vijñāna**;
to realize that One as oneself and offer oneself into it with devotion—that is the ultimate: the **mokṣa**.

Thus, the seventh chapter concludes with the highest synthesis of devotion, knowledge, and liberation.

— ॐ संकर्षणाय नमः ॐ —

The Lord has revealed not only the glories of His cosmic manifestations, but also the inward path to attain Him. The path is reserved not just for the learned and elite, but for those with purified hearts, resolute minds, and unwavering faith.

In the next chapter, Bhagwān Shri Krishna will expound further on these threefold manifestations—Adhibhūta, Adhidaiva, and Adhiyajña—and guide the aspirant into the deeper mystery of how remembrance of the Lord at the time of death leads to final liberation.

— ॐ तत् सत ॐ —

Before moving on, let us once more bow in deep reverence before this sacred verse of the Bhagavad-Gītā, an eternal beacon of wisdom that ceaselessly illumines the path of seekers. Engage with its form—inscribe it with your own hand, let your heart dwell upon its meaning, and raise your voice in its chanting—for within these syllables echoes the undying proclamation delivered millennia ago on the battlefield of Kurukshetra. These words, transmitted unchanged across the unbroken chain of generations, form a living bridge, linking us to that sanctified era when Bhagwāna Shri Krishna Himself walked this earth and bestowed this divine teaching. Through the luminous vibration of these sacred Sanskrit sounds, we are drawn nearer to His timeless presence, touching the very heartbeat of the Eternal.

— ॐ —

साधिभूताधिदैवं मां साधियज्ञं च ये विदुः ।
sādhibhūtādhidaivaṁ māṁ sādhiyajñaṁ ca ye viduḥ
प्रयाणकालेऽपि च मां ते विदुर्युक्तचेतसः ॥७-३०॥
prayāṇakāle'pi ca māṁ te viduryuktacetasaḥ (7-30)

— ॐ —

साधिभूताधिदैवं मां साधियज्ञं च ये विदुः ।
sādhibhūtādhidaivaṁ māṁ sādhiyajñaṁ ca ye viduḥ
प्रयाणकालेऽपि च मां ते विदुर्युक्तचेतसः ॥७-३०॥
prayāṇakāle'pi ca māṁ te viduryuktacetasaḥ (7-30)

ॐ तत्सदिति श्रीमद्भगवद्गीतासूपनिषत्सु ब्रह्मविद्यायां योगशास्त्रे श्रीकृष्णार्जुनसंवादे
om tatsaditi śrīmadbhagavadgītāsūpaniṣatsu brahmavidyāyāṁ yogaśāstre śrīkṛṣṇārjunasaṁvāde
ज्ञानविज्ञानयोगो नाम सप्तमोऽध्यायः श्लोकः ३०
jñānavijñānayogo nāma saptamo'dhyāyaḥ ślokaḥ 30

Om-Tat-Sat—Om (Braham) is the sole Reality. In the Yogic Scripture on the Science-of-Braham, the Shrimada-Bhāgvada-Gītā Upanishad, we hereby conclude Shloka 30 of the Dialogue between Shri Krishna and Arjuna entitled Jnana-Vijnana-Yoga, Canto VII.

— ॐ श्रीकृष्णाय नमः ॐ —

God is All that Exists in Existence

O seeker, mark the Jnāni—who sees just the-One in every part—
In stones & suns. In breath, life, death.
In Self. In Nature's sacred art.

Adhibhūta, Adhidaiva, Adhiyajña—a threefold gate,
Through which the Lord, in endless ways, reveals His changeless stillness.

He is not just the boundless sky, nor just the within Flame—
But He's in all domains, in every layer of existence.
Krishna alone exists—and sings akin—in every form of life.

So watch out what ye eat—O fool.
All creatures have soul just like thee.
Eat only what the śāstras have ordained.

If it does not run away to save its life,
If it yields willingly—as fruits and grains—as decreed by God's Nature.
Ye may partake—but by first asking God and saying grace.

— ॐ श्रीकृष्णाय नमः ॐ —

All is Krishna—the manifest form of Braham
To know Him—not as parts but Whole—is Wisdom's final Key.

Dharma, Karma, Bhakti, Jnāna—are various paths to one who seeks,
But they all converge as **One**—unto the wise sage who truly sees.
The wise one directly perceives: सर्वं खल्विदं ब्रह्म sarvam-khalvidam-braham.
All this is satt-chitt-ānanda braham—sporting.

Aye, **He sports**. But it behooves ye, O human, to **stay wise**.
Especially: Stay **not** the Conditioned Pavlov Donk of this luckless age.
For that is **Not** sporting—but staying yoked to **Kali's Wheel of Hell**.

— ॐ श्रीकृष्णाय नमः ॐ —

<u>Behold Krishna—and Fall on Thy Knees, O Human</u>
The Cosmos itself docked to attention—beholding Krishna's Presence.
Galaxies took pause. Stars tilted their faces in awe.
<u>And humans of earth?</u>
—Blind sailors in a harbor of light—
Mistook the Infinite Vessel for a little decorative lantern.

Even now the universe smolders with Krishna's arrant stance:
"I am the Harbor of Truth. Ye species—come and go as tourists."

<u>Yet out of His infinite Divine mercy—</u>
His benign grace for us little creatures,
Krishna once walked the dusty roads of Āryāvarta with bare feet—
But we petty men mistook His simplicity for smallness! Alas!

Even the dust of earth recognized Him—
Stood still beneath His step.
But the humanity did not.

From the air, river, dust of earth—itself rises this accusation:
"We saw Krishna—He who is God—while ye men merely saw a story."

— ॐ तत् सत् ॐ —

Repent, O Humans

There still could be time for redemption,
Gather together—around the sacred fire of Krishna's Gitâ,

Let its flames consume the veils of human ignorance,
Burn away all bonds of illusions & sorrows.

Raise your voices in fearless remembrance.
Say: ॐ तत सत Om Tat Sat — That-One alone is Real.

Beyond illusion's trembling shadows,
See the Real standing right there—
He—Satt-chitt-ânanda braham—whose manifest form is Krishna.

Behold the Eternal—who neither rises nor falls.
See the One Eternal Presence in all.
Stand illumined in the glow of thy awakened Beingness.

Let no darkness extinguish this sacred flame of Wisdom.
Let ॐ तत सत Om Tat Sat resound through the very heart of existence.
Walk onward with steadfast vision & In embrace of Krishna's grace.

Let the fire of Gitâ's truths burn forever bright—
On the broad landscape of Sanâtana-Dharma life.

— ॐ श्रीकृष्णाय नमः ॐ —

O pilgrims, Arise.
Just like Arjuna—let thy tears turn into pearls of wisdom.
Let thy fears dissolve like mist before the morning Sun: Krishna.

O child of eternal breath, rest in the changeless truth:
ॐ तत सत Om Tat Sat—That-One, alone is Real—He Krishna.

May thy heart abide in the Infinite without trembling.
May thy mind awaken to the clarity of the Âtmâ & Param-Âtmâ.
Never forget what Krishna, in the Gitâ, has told us:

Neither birth nor death defines thee.
Neither joy nor sorrow confines thee.
Thou art the very luminous ground of Beingness. Thou art part of Me.

Stand fearless in this eternal knowing.
Peace be upon thee, O awakened soul.
Say ॐ तत सत ॐ Om Tat Sat Om.

— ॐ तत सत ॐ —

🕉 CHAPTER-SEVEN RECAP

— 🕉 तत सत 🕉 —

JÑĀNA-VIJÑĀNA YOGA: THE REVELATION OF THE SUPREME

In the sacred unfolding of the Bhagavad-Gītā, Chapter-Seven—Jñāna-Vijñāna Yoga—marked a shift in tone and depth.

Until now, the Lord had instructed us seekers in the ways of selfless action, renunciation, and meditation.

But here, a profound unveiling begins.

No longer does Krishna merely guide the path—He now reveals Himself as its very goal.

In this chapter, we were not merely instructed—we were drawn into the Divine mystery.

We learnt that true knowledge (jñāna) must culminate in realization (vijñāna)—a direct, living, inward knowing of the Lord who is both beyond and within all creation.

And this knowing is not gained by mere study or ritual, but by purity of heart, unwavering devotion, and the grace that flows when ego and desire fall away.

We were told that the Divine is not hidden by distance, but by delusion.

Though the Lord pervades all, He remains unseen to the one enmeshed in the dualities of desire and aversion.

But for the pure-hearted, who seek Him alone, the Lord reveals Himself—not as an abstract principle, but as the personal, all-sustaining Supreme.

Let us now retrace with reverence the terrain of this luminous chapter—guided not by verse-by-verse detail but by the broad themes of wisdom offered.

Verses 1–3:

The chapter began with an intimate invitation. The Lord urged Arjuna to listen with a heart devoted and mind absorbed, for He was about to reveal the supreme knowledge that leads to complete realization. Yet, He reminded us, such attainment is rare—even among thousands, few truly know Him as He is.

Verses 4–7:

Krishna then disclosed His twofold nature: the lower (aparā)—comprising the elements, the mind, intellect, and ego; and the higher (parā)—His conscious, sustaining presence within all beings. He declared Himself the origin and essence of the entire cosmos, saying, "There is nothing higher than Me; all is strung upon Me like pearls on a thread."

Verses 8–11:

We then learnt to recognize the Divine not as remote, but as the very taste in water, the light of the sun and moon, the sacred syllable Oṁ, the fragrance of the earth, the strength in the strong, and desire itself—when aligned with dharma. Thus, the Lord revealed Himself as the sacred essence dwelling silently in all forms.

Verses 12–15:

Although the Lord is the origin of the three guṇas—sattva, rajas, and tamas—He remains beyond them. Yet beings, deluded by His divine māyā, fail to recognize Him. Ensnared by false values and distorted understanding, the worldly turn away from the Supreme, seeing only the surface of things.

Verses 16–19:

We were then shown four kinds of devotees: the distressed, the seeker of knowledge, the seeker of worldly blessings, and the wise. All are dear to the Lord, but the wise—who seek Him alone, and not for gain—are most beloved. And rare indeed is the one who, after many births, comes to know: "Vāsudeva is all."

Verses 20–23:

We learnt that others, driven by desire, worship various deities according to their nature. The Lord, dwelling in their hearts, grants them faith and fulfillment—yet their attainments are limited and perishable. Only those who worship the Supreme attain the eternal.

Verses 24–26:

Deluded by form, many believe the Infinite to be finite. The Lord, veiled by His own yoga-māyā, remains unseen by those whose vision is clouded. Yet He knows all beings—past, present, and future— though they know Him not.

Verses 27–30:

We were reminded that all beings are born into delusion, overwhelmed by attraction and aversion. But those who perform meritorious acts and purify themselves through many lives come to seek refuge in Him, aspiring for liberation. Such seekers strive to know Him as the Supreme Being, the inner Self, and the ultimate foundation of sacrifice. And even at the hour of death, such a one, steadfast in devotion, knows the Lord and attains Him.

CLOSING REFLECTIONS

In this chapter, we learnt not only of the nature of true knowledge, but of the very nature of God. Shri Krishna unveiled Himself not merely as teacher, nor even only as the formless Braham—but as the all-pervading, all-sustaining, all-loving Bhagwān, immanent in creation and yet untouched by it.

We were taught that He dwells in all forms, in every element and experience; that He grants every prayer according to the faith of the devotee; and that He remains unseen, not due to distance, but due to the veil of delusion. To pierce that veil, one must abandon all lesser aims and turn with single-hearted love toward Him alone.

This chapter was not merely a teaching—it was a divine self-disclosure. It prepared us souls not only to seek the truth but to see the Divine, to recognize Him in the world and in oneself, and to enter into an abiding relationship with the Lord.

At the next threshold, Chapter-Eight, the inquiry will deepen further—into the mystery of the eternal at the time of death, the nature of the soul's final journey, and the remembrance of the Divine at life's most sacred transition. But here, in Chapter-Seven, we have received a rare gift: the Lord has spoken of Himself—not as remote Absolute, but as near, intimate, and ever-present—waiting to be known by the eyes of love and the stillness of wisdom.

ॐ तत्सदिति श्रीमद्भगवद्गीतासूपनिषत्सु ब्रह्मविद्यायां योगशास्त्रे श्रीकृष्णार्जुनसंवादे
om tatsaditi śrīmadbhagavadgītāsūpaniṣatsu brahmavidyāyāṁ yogaśāstre śrīkṛṣṇārjunasaṁvāde
ज्ञानविज्ञानयोगो नाम सप्तमोऽध्यायः ॥
jñānavijñānayogo nāma saptamo'dhyāyaḥ

Om-Tat-Sat—Om (Braham) is the sole Reality. In this Yogic Scripture on the Science of Brahama—the Shrimada-Bhāgvada-Gītā Upanishad—hereby ends the dialogue between Shri Krishna and Arjuna entitled: Jnana-Vijnana Yoga, Canto VII.

—::==::==::—

[O Seeker, we thank thee for reading thus far. This has been a brief commentary and lots still remains unsaid. Rāma-willing, our exhaustive commentary will become available beginning 2027. This is our init endeavor and surely it's full of many faults which we fully own—and we pray you will take it in thy heart to pardon us. We have endeavored to keep our commentary opinion-free. The poesy "fillers"—which come at end of chapters—might be construed to be opinionated though, and so too perhaps a para or two here and there; so sorry. Bhagavad-Gita is a celestial stream and any human touch, however well-meaning, only sullies it some. We hope to be forgiven by Bhagwana Shri Krishna for daring to torture this sublime text of His, which has no parallels anywhere—never will.]

ॐ गीतामाहात्म्यम् GĪTĀ-MĀHĀTMYAM

[Verses on the glory and import of the Bhagavad-Gītā]

— ॐ —

गीताशास्त्रमिदं पुण्यं यः पठेत्प्रयतः पुमान् ।
gītāśāstramidaṁ puṇyaṁ yaḥ paṭhetprayataḥ pumān ,

विष्णोः पदमवाप्नोति भयशोकादिवर्जितः ॥
viṣṇoḥ padamavāpnoti bhayaśokādivarjitaḥ .

One who diligently studies this Bhagavad-Gītā—the bestower of all virtues—with firm devotion and a regulated mind—verily attains Vaikuntha—the holy abode of Māhā-Vishnu—and he stands freed of all the fears and sorrows of this mundane world.

— ॐ —

गीताध्ययनशीलस्य प्राणायामपरस्य च ।
gītādhyayanaśīlasya prāṇāyāmaparasya ca ,

नैव सन्ति हि पापानि पूर्वजन्मकृतानि च ॥
naiva santi hi pāpāni pūrvajanmakṛtāni ca .

One who performs Prāṇāyāms and studies the Bhagavad-Gītā regularly and sincerely—all his sins melt away, even those from all prior lives.

— ॐ —

मलनिर्मोचनं पुंसां जलस्नानं दिने दिने ।
malanirmocanaṁ puṁsāṁ jalasnānaṁ dine dine ,

सकृद्गीताम्भसि स्नानं संसारमलनाशनम् ॥
sakṛdgītāmbhasi snānaṁ saṁsāramalanāśanam .

A daily bath removes external bodily taints, but a single bath in the sacred waters of Bhagavad-Gītā is enough to remove all the taints of this Saṁsāra—this polluting worldly existence of joys, sorrows, births, and deaths.

— ॐ —

गीता सुगीता कर्तव्या किमन्यैः शास्त्रविस्तरैः ।
gītā sugītā kartavyā kimanyaiḥ śāstravistaraiḥ ,

या स्वयं पद्मनाभस्य मुखपद्माद्विनिःसृता ॥
yā svayaṁ padmanābhasya mukhapadmādviniḥsṛtā .

Why go in for other elaborate scriptures, when you can chant the Gītā—the essence of all Vedic scriptures—which issued forth from the lotus mouth of Māhā-Vishnu Himself—on whose navel is the lotus of Creation.

— ॐ —

भारतामृतसर्वस्वं विष्णोर्वक्त्राद्विनिःसृतम् ।
bhāratāmṛtasarvasvaṁ viṣṇorvaktrādviniḥsṛtam ,

गीतागङ्गोदकं पीत्वा पुनर्जन्म न विद्यते ॥
gītāgaṅgodakaṁ pītvā punarjanma na vidyate .

There is no more rebirth for one who partakes of the sacred waters of the Gītā-Gangā—the holy stream which flowed out from the lotus lips of Shri Māhā-Vishnu—the nectar which is the quintessence of Māhā-Bhārata.

— ॐ —

एकं शास्त्रं देवकीपुत्रगीतमेको देवो देवकीपुत्र एव ।
ekaṁ śāstraṁ devakīputragītameko devo devakīputra eva ,

एको मन्त्रस्तस्य नामानि यानि कर्माप्येकं तस्य देवस्य सेवा ॥
eko mantrastasya nāmāni yāni karmāpyekaṁ tasya devasya sevā .

The holy Gītā of Krishna—son of Devakī—is the One Scripture; Krishna—son of Devakī—is the One God; the name Krishna—son of Devakī—is the One Mantra; service to Him (nurturing Sanātana-Dharma)—the One and only Duty.

— ॐ —

श्रीकृष्णचरणार्पणमस्तु
śrī kṛṣṇa caraṇaarpaṇamastu
(Hereby dedicated to the Lotus Feet of Bhagwān Shri Krishna)

कायेन वाचा मनसेंद्रियैर्वा । बुद्ध्यात्मना वा प्रकृतिस्वभावात् ।
kāyena vācā manasemdriyairvā , buddhyātmanā vā prakritisvabhāvāt ,

करोमि यद्यत् सकलं परस्मै । नारायणायेति समर्पयामि ॥
karomi yadyat sakalaṁ parasmai , nārāyaṇāyeti samarpayāmi .

Whatever it is I do—through body, mind, speech, or sense-organs, or with my intellect and soul, or with my innate natural tendencies—whatever it be—I offer it all unto Narayana (Bhagwān Shri Krishna / Bhagwān Shri Rāma).

— ॐ —

या गीता सनातनस्य धर्मस्यामृतरूपिणी । लोकानां मार्गदर्शिनी तस्याः मूलं प्रयच्छामि ॥
yā gītā sanātanasya dharmasyāmṛtarūpiṇī , lokānāṁ margadarśinī tasyāḥ mūlaṁ prayacchāmi .

That Gītā, which's the nectar-form of Sanātana Dharma—the guide of the worlds upon The-Path—towards Her sacred roots I now proceed to take refuge.

स्वयं प्रेरितो प्रेरय मित्रबान्धवम् । गीता-ज्ञानस्य दीपं सर्वहृदि दीपय ॥
svayaṁ prērito prēraya mitra-bāndhavam , gītā-jñānasya dīpaṁ sarva-hṛdi dīpaya .

Be inspired and inspire thy friends and companions. Light the Lamp of Gītā-Wisdom in all hearts.

Be Inspired and Inspire Others. Light a Lamp of Wisdom.
Start your own Gītā Classes with a Friend Today.

सनातनधर्मस्य संकल्प-व्रतः sanātana-dharmasya saṅkalpa-vrataḥ
"The Vow of Commitment to Sanātana-Dharma"
(A solemn declaration for those who align their life with the eternal path through inner fire)

(1) ॐ एकाक्षरं मे मन्त्रः । oṁ ekākṣaraṁ me mantraḥ
(2) सनातनधर्मो मे पन्थाः । sanātana-dharmo me panthāḥ
(3) श्रीकृष्णः मे दीपः । śrīkṛṣṇaḥ me dīpaḥ
(4) कृष्णः एव मे गुरुः । kṛṣṇaḥ eva me guruḥ
(5) भगवद्गीता मे शास्त्रं । bhagavad-gītā me śāstram
(6) आत्मैव मे सत्यं । ātmaiva me satyam
(7) अधर्मो पततु । adharmo patatu (8) धर्मोत्तिष्ठतु । dharmo-ttiṣṭhatu
(9) भास्वरं यज्ञवद् जीवनं मे भवतु । bhāsvaraṁ yajñavad jīvanaṁ me bhavatu
(10) एवं व्रमे । एवं चरामि । एवं भवामि । evaṁ vrame - evaṁ carāmi - evaṁ bhavāmi
(11) धर्मसंस्थापकं तं कृष्णं वन्दे जगद्गुरुम् । dharma-saṁsthāpakaṁ taṁ kṛṣṇaṁ vande jagad-gurum

(1) Om—the single syllable—is my mantra. (2) Sanātana-Dharma is my path.
(3) Krishna is my Light. (4) Krishna alone my Guru.
(5) The Bhagavad-Gītā is my scripture. (6) The Ātmā alone is my truth.
(7) Let Adharma perish. (8) Let Dharma prevail.
(9) Let my life be radiant like a sacred Yajña.
(10) Thus I vow. Thus I walk. Thus I become. (11) I bow to that Lord who establishes Dharma and guides all creation—He, Bhagwān Shri Krishna.

EXPLANATORY NOTE TO THE VOW-TAKER: ▪ This Sanskrit vow does not seek entry into a sect—but a return to who we are. ▪ It is a sacred declaration—not of conversion, but of remembrance. ▪ It is a divine resolve of finding our way back home to where we belong—in Sanātana-Dharma. ▪ It is a vow to live our life staying aligned with Dharma—the timeless current of awakened living -- in truth, through action, and by our entire beingness. ▪ It is not a mere utterance of affiliation, but a radiant declaration of independence. ▪ It is not a sectarian act but the awakening of the soul to his true nature—as identical with Braham. ▪ This vow aligns the soul back to living in Sanātana-Dharma. ▪ It renounces illusion and reclaims life as an oblation in the cosmic yajña of Braham—whose manifest form is Bhagwān Shri Krishna. ▪ Speak it not lightly, O pilgrim! Take it as one who stands before the Divine—before Time, Truth, Fire, and the Self.

EXPLANATORY NOTE TO THE VOW: ▪ Each line is a pillar affirming: the Bhagavad-Gītā as the crown scripture; Bhagavān Shri Krishna as the inner light and Guru; Aum as the sovereign mantra; and our within Self, the Ātmā as the ultimate Truth. ▪ By affirming the Gītā as śāstra, one embraces the distilled essence of all dharmic teaching. ▪ By naming Krishna as Guru and Aum as mantra, one enters directly into the fire of Divine instruction—not as a follower of outer forms, but as a walker of the eternal path. ▪ "Let Adharma perish" is a resolute vow to uproot fear, selfishness, and moral weakness—within ourselves and in the world. It refuses all submission to falsehood, injustice, and inner compromise, committing instead to their conscious defeat. ▪ "Let Dharma prevail" affirms a living commitment to truth, compassion, discipline, responsibility. It calls us to embody these principles in thought, word, and action, upholding Dharma as the guiding force of the Eternal Order. ▪ Together, they declare that life is not escape from struggle, but sacred participation in restoring harmony—within and without. ▪ Adharma cannot be ignored; it must be annihilated. ▪ Dharma must not merely survive; it must triumph.

<u>EXPLANATORY NOTE ON GURU AND MANTRA</u>: The vow affirms ॐ (Aum) as "my mantra" and Shri Krishna as "my Guru"—not as personal preferences but as eternal recognitions, not as personal innovations, but as the revealed truths of Sanātana-Dharma. ▪ The Ekākshara Mantra, Aum, is the primordial vibration—the seed of the Veda, the sound of origin, the breath of creation and the syllable explicitly declared by Krishna in the Gītā (10.25) as His own: "aksharānām akāro'smi"—Of syllables, I am A; and again in Gītā 8.13: "aum ity ekāksharam brahma... mām anusmaran —Uttering the one-syllable Brahman—Aum—while remembering Me..." ▪ To declare Aum as "my mantra" is to stand aligned with the very breath of Sanātana-Dharma—a mantra not sought elsewhere, but received already, from Krishna Himself. ▪ Aum is not apart from Krishna—it is His voice, and He has already breathed the Ekākshara Mantra into thy ear through the Gita, and He has further extolled it in chapter 17. ▪ As to the Guru, Krishna is not only Arjuna's Guru but the Jagad-Guru, the eternal Teacher of all. ▪ To declare Krishna as one's Guru is to take refuge in the supreme Teacher of the Gītā—not as an abstract concept, but as living surrender. ▪ Arjuna did not become His disciple by any rite or ritual—he simply surrendered; he fell at Krishna's feet, tears in his eyes, and cried out: **"śishyas te 'ham śādhi mām tvām prapannam"** (I am Your disciple; teach me; I surrender to You -- verse 2.7). ▪ Śāstric rituals are important, but not here—when the Guru is God Himself. ▪ Arjuna became a disciple from heart as he declared: 'I am Thy śishya'. In that very sacred moment, Krishna became his Guru. ▪ Likewise, for us: no formal ritual is needed, no formal rite required—only the turning of the heart and the utterance of the verse of utter surrender—Gītā 2.7. ▪ Remember that on the battlefield, Arjuna was surrounded by many elders, teachers, and respected guides. Yet, at the moment of deepest crisis, he set aside all human authority and chose Bhagwān Śrī Krishna as his sole guide. ▪ In this age of Kali, when many are shaped by systems rooted in materialism, competition, and moral confusion, it is wise to exercise discernment in choosing whom to follow. Not every teacher, of this malefic age, embodies true Dharma. ▪ This vow therefore chooses the direct refuge—of He, Bhagwān Shri Krishna, whose perfect guidance shines eternally through the Bhagavad-Gītā. ▪ The wait for Guru is now over; the Sanskrit Gītā is already by thy side. Cry out to Krishna; fall at His feet; invoke the word; invoke verse 2.7 with sincerity—and thou art Krishna's disciple. ▪ The fire is lit. His Word is already in thy hands. Now you just have to be a sincere śishya.

<u>CLOSING REFLECTION</u>: Do not start a sect. Do not join a sect. Sanātana-Dharma is an Ocean, let it remain like that. ▪ O pilgrim, this vow is not a borrowed creed, but a homecoming—a return to what has been thy home all along. ▪ Take this vow not in haste, but as an intelligent upright soul—one who can stand midst the flame, unshaken. ▪ Here there is no need of rituals. Just as Arjuna, standing on the battlefield of despair, became a disciple of Krishna without ceremony, so too may one surrender to Krishna and His Gītā. ▪ Fall at Krishna's feet, open the Bhagavad-Gītā, and walk henceforth in Gītā's light. ▪ This vow is not made to, or for, the world—but is made irrespective of the world. ▪ It is not for external show—but made unto the silent witness: the within Ātmā. ▪ It is not to impress others, but to ourselves awaken. ▪ It is not to become bound, but to become liberated. ▪ In the presence of the Gītā, in the light of Krishna, and before the altar of Time itself—this vow is uttered as one's Life lived as a Yajña unto Sanātana-Dharma. ▪ Remember to respect all life—since all creatures have soul just like us. ▪ Let the Bhagavad-Gītā stay illumining our life as fire eternal. ▪ Let it echo in the heart, deeper than sound. ▪ Let it live not just in recitation, but in soul.
▪ So be it; So it is; So it shall blaze. Jai Bhagwān Shri Krishna.